Chri

Merry Christmas Jack!
Love,
Doris Henry & J.H.

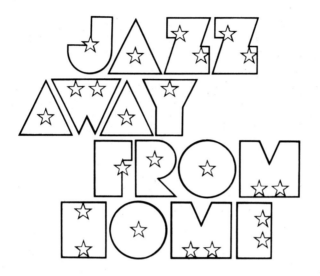

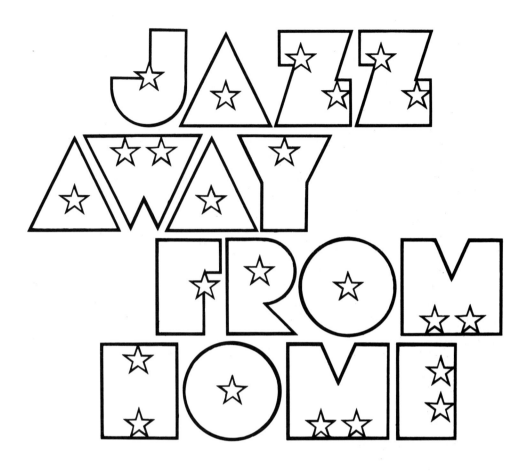

JAZZ AWAY FROM HOME

CHRIS GODDARD

PADDINGTON PRESS LTD

NEW YORK & LONDON

*This book is dedicated to all the people
who helped make it possible and in particular to
Leo Arnaud-Vauchant, a great man and
a great musician.*

Library of Congress Cataloging in Publication Data

Goddard, Chris.
  Jazz away from home.
  Includes index.
  1. Jazz music – Europe. I. Title.
ML3580.G6   785.4'2'094   79-10542
ISBN 0 448 22367 8 (U.S. and Canada only)
ISBN 0 7092 0279 2

Filmset in England by SX Composing Ltd., Rayleigh, Essex
Printed and bound in the United States
Designed by Sandra Shafee

In the United States
PADDINGTON PRESS
Distributed by
GROSSET & DUNLAP

In the United Kingdom
PADDINGTON PRESS

In Canada
Distributed by
RANDOM HOUSE OF CANADA LTD.

In Southern Africa
Distributed by
ERNEST STANTON (PUBLISHERS) (PTY.) LTD.

In Australia and New Zealand
Distributed by
A. H. & A. W. REED

CONTENTS

☆ ACKNOWLEDGMENTS

MY SINCERE THANKS go to the many people who helped me with this book and in particular to the following.

Without the assistance of Angela Doyle I could not have found, obtained or, eventually, returned many of the books I used in my research. Jocelyn "Frisco" Bingham gave me the enormous benefit of his personal insights into the night life of Paris in the 1920s and 1930s and also allowed me to reproduce many of his remarkable collection of original photographs. Mahfooza Hamid patiently deciphered my handwriting in order to type so much of the manuscript.

Henry Pleasants, Brian Rust, Karl Gert Zur Heide, Father A. M. Jones and John R.T. Davies, each agreed to read various sections of the manuscript and I am in debt to them all for their invaluable comments.

☆ PICTURE CREDITS

The author and publishers are grateful to the following individuals and agencies for their kind permission to reproduce the photographs in this book:

FRED ADISON 199 (both), 201; LEO ARNAUD-VACHANT 40–1, 42 (all), 202 (below), 205 (above); ARTHUR "FRISCO" BINGHAM 36 (above), 50–1, 205 (below), 206–7 (all), 208–9 (all), 210–11 (all), 212 (all), 213 (below), 214–15; IVAN BROWNING 93 (both), 94–5 (all), 96 (below), 198 (both), 203 (center left); PHILIPPE BRUN 34 (below), 142–3 (all), 144 (below), 144–5, 145 (below left), 147 (below left & right), 195 (top & center), 196 (both), 203 (bottom); JOHN BUBBLES 96 (above); ELLIOT CARPENTER 37 (both); NOEL CHABOUST 147 (above), 202 (above), 203 (top); ROGET CHAPUT 250 (above); CULVER PICTURE LIBRARY 33 (above), 98 (below), 99 (all), 101 (top); ART VAN DELDEN 100, 101 (center & bottom); FRANK DRIGGS 36 (below), 39 (above), 197 (above), 216 (right above & below); MME. EKYAN 44, 45 (above), 46–7 (all), 204, 215 (below), 255 (both); HERB FLEMMING 35, 98 (above); HORST 215 (above left & right); ALBERTA HUNTER 102 (both); ART LANIER 39 (below), 48 (both); GERARD LEVECQUE 249 (both), 252 (below), 253 (above), 256–7 (all), 259 (above & below right); BERT MARSHALL 34 (above); BOBBY MARTIN 43 (all), 49 (below left & right), 145 (below right), 216–17; NEW YORK PUBLIC LIBRARY 33 (below), 96–7; PIERRE NOURRY 250 (below); RAM RAMIREZ 38 (all); EMILE SAVITRY 45 (below), 197 (below), 203 (center right), 213 (above left & right), 251 (all), 252 (both); LESLIE THOMPSON 146 (all); RAY VENTURA 195 (bottom); LOUIS VOLA 49 (above), 248, 252 (above), 253 (below), 258, 259 (below left).

 FOREWORD

JAZZ AWAY FROM HOME looks at what is perhaps the most important development in music in this century. Until 1920, European musical supremacy was unchallenged. The appearance of jazz drastically altered that situation. This book examines how and when and in what form jazz reached Europe and a revolutionary Afro-American fusion came face to face with the musical establishment. I have been concerned throughout to examine the difficulties Europeans had in assimilating the new music but I have not attempted to write a comprehensive history of early jazz in Europe – such a task demands years of research involving sources which are often scattered and incomplete. It must wait for someone better qualified than I to undertake.

I have drawn mainly on the situations in Paris and London. I have not tried to give a complete record of events in either place, but rather to use the information to support a general thesis. I have even deliberately set out to examine certain things which purists may not consider to be jazz at all. This, I believe, helps to revise opinions which have remained unchallenged for too long. Accordingly, there are chapters dealing with the use of jazz-influenced music in the theater in the 1920s; on the social attitudes of the European high society which considered itself "jazz crazy"; and on the not very satisfactory attempts by European composers to adapt jazz to their own ends. The purpose of these chapters is to set the arrival of jazz in Europe in its cultural context, and so explain the many difficulties which educated Europeans and Americans had in accepting this revolutionary new sound.

The "Jazz Age" of the 1920s certainly witnessed a musical revolution of sorts. But more important even than this, it saw a revision of codes of behavior, and jazz played a part in this. In its early days, jazz provided an interesting diversion for the elite of European society, and glamorous night spots sprang up in Paris and London where jazz was a main attraction. Jazz was fashionable but it remained popular only so long as it *was* in fashion. At the same time, the players themselves went to Europe for social rather than musical reasons and this was particularly true of the black musicians who hoped to escape the racial prejudice back home in America. In this they were only partially successful. Although wealthy Europeans considered black musicians contributed to the exotic atmosphere of the night clubs, it was still predominantly the white players who got the opportunities to record.

The jazz craze declined after the Wall Street crash. As the Depression set in, few people could afford the extravagant life style which characterized the "Jazz Age" in Europe. Thereafter, the music waned in popularity and became a specialist interest for a tiny minority of diehard enthusiasts who were concerned to investigate its roots in the black, urban subculture of America. Unfortunately this serious interest was seldom taken seriously because of the narrow mindedness of the European intellectual establishment. Even in the diluted form in which most Europeans heard it before 1935, jazz was too vulgar, too shocking, to be admissible by their atrophying standards of intellectual refinement.

The European musical establishment has been particularly guilty of wearing cultural blinkers and there has always been a lamentable neglect of so-called "primitive" forms. The tragedy is that too great a concern with Art has meant that most Europeans, and, come to that, Americans, have only woken up to the artistic qualities of jazz when it is already too late.

The recollections of the 1977 Nice Jazz Festival, which end the books, suggest that although Europeans today genuinely enjoy black music, and in a way that would not have been possible fifty years ago, the jazz experience is as foreign to them now as it ever was.

JAZZ
REACHES
EUROPE

AZZ, WE WERE TOLD by historians, began in 1917 with the first recordings of the Original Dixieland Jazz Band. Later research showed that a richer and more developed form of jazz was being played by black musicians in New Orleans at least ten years before that, and that the various tributaries which combined to form this music can be traced back to the Civil War. Still, there is a sense in which the original premise is true. Records were of vital importance in the evolution of this music. Jazz might never have progressed from folk music to art without the invention of the phonograph. Recordings are a sterile means of communication: they do not engender creativity, and their value as a means of teaching musicians to play jazz is strictly limited. But they were an important kind of shorthand, a coded message which spread the news of what was happening. Records, and the radio stations which played them, told jazzmen in one part of America what those in another part were doing. Particularly among black people, this probably encouraged a desire not to copy but to compete, to surpass, to turn yesterday's improbabilities into tomorrow's achievements. It is this fiercely competitive spirit among jazz musicians which has carried the music from infancy to decline in little more than sixty years.

European jazz undoubtedly began in 1917. In April of that year the United States declared war on Germany. With no apparent sense of the implied irony, several hundred thousand poor, underprivileged black citizens were drafted and sent overseas to fight for a country which had treated them with a shameful disregard of its own much-vaunted Bill of Rights. The armies brought not only musicians, many of whom played something resembling jazz, but records as well.

In these days of mass communication, it is hard to imagine the effect of the sudden usurpation of an ancient tradition by a new continent and a new civilization. By 1917, Europe had experienced the cakewalk and was weathering a ragtime craze. But the arrival of jazz was an altogether more profound upheaval, an overturning of tradition of almost volcanic proportions. From that moment, the seeds of a cultural influence were

10

planted which has persisted to the point where, today, there is no field of popular entertainment which is free from American influence. In fact, the twentieth century is in many ways an Afro-American age. Records alone made this possible. Despite two thousand miles of Atlantic Ocean and wide cultural differences, the flood of recorded music from America restored some aspects of an oral tradition which Europe had forgotten for centuries.

☆ "WE FELL DOWN A WELL AND CAME UP WITH A ROAST DINNER."

The fact that the new influences were basically African, and incorporated elements which were quite incompatible with twentieth-century European music, is an astonishing testament to the power of recordings. All modern "pop" is directly inspired by the music of the American black. This is a fact which has affected not only music but all forms of social behavior. So, by a curious inversion of snobbery, some of the "jive" style of speech and attitude of the poorest black sections in Kansas City and Chicago in the thirties persists today at both smart Knightsbridge parties and Yorkshire working men's clubs. Any study of the cultural invasion of Europe by America will necessarily involve an examination of the influences of this new manner of behaviour, the problems Europeans experienced in "getting the message" and the extent to which the message was itself altered by the nature of the medium. But first who were the American musicians who came to be in Europe during the First World War, and what sort of music did they bring with them?

In 1917 the most famous black musician in New York was James Reese Europe who had become rich and famous as the leader of the city's leading black dance orchestra. It was a time when black bands regularly worked for the city's most fashionable families. The huge influx of blacks into the northern and industrial cities was only just beginning, and the more relaxed racial attitudes of that time still afforded good opportunities for black musicians. Europe founded the Tempo Club in April, 1914 in order to promote these activities even further. He was so successful that in 1915 alone his booking agency handled nearly one hundred thousand dollars worth of business. In fact, it was a golden age of black music.

In the early 1900s minstrelsy had reached a new level of sophistication with the theatrical shows of Williams and Walker and others whose lavish productions set new standards for black performers. Partly as a result of this, the cakewalk, and later ragtime, swept across America helping to launch a craze for dancing. The turkey trot, the grizzly bear, the buzzard lope and many others were all inspired in various ways by black dance styles which flagrantly violated the old European traditions of whalebone corsets and dancing masters.

This trend was to have an incalculable effect on the development of jazz. Suddenly, no restaurant could hope to succeed without a dance orchestra. The famous Reisenweber's in New York had no less than seven dance floors, each catering to a different taste. New fashions were created as quickly as the old ones disappeared. A young couple named Irene and Vernon Castle earned fabulous sums giving demonstrations of a new dance they had invented called the fox trot. Their youth, their elegant yet entirely contemporary style, and their good looks gave tremendous impetus to the mania for dancing which was sweeping the country. Their phenomenal success carried Jim Europe with it, establishing him as the most important black musician in New York.[1]

When war was declared, Europe enlisted in New York's black regiment. Its Colonel, William Haywood, in that competitive spirit which outbreaks of patriotism so often produce, decided to organize "the best damn brass band in the United States Army." No expense was spared in combing the country looking for the best musicians. A local businessman, Daniel C. Reid, backed the project with ten thousand dollars and the search went as far as Puerto Rico to find suitable clarinet players to complete the reed section. Naturally, Jim Europe was put in charge of the band's organization. He hired Jaçon Frank de Braithe, Chicago's leading cornet player, as soloist and appointed the Harlem dancer Bill "Bojangles" Robinson as drum major. The "best damn brass band," dubbed the Hellfighters, was ready for France.

The Hellfighters were not a jazz band in any sense we would understand today. Even so, it was much more than just a brass band. Europe seems to have organized it very much along the lines of a minstrel show. His models seem to have been the black concert bands run by men like W. C. Handy and Will Marion Cook. Handy and Cook prided themselves that their orchestras could play anything. Their repertoires included everything from cakewalks to the classics, taking in plantation melodies, special instrumental features, songs, sketches and comedy routines on the way. Jazz, which at that time was the name given to novelty music specializing in freak instrumental effects and "barnyard" imitations,

12

was also increasingly in demand. Accordingly, Jim Europe included men who could sing, dance, do comedy and other kinds of entertaining. So with Bojangles strutting out ahead, the Hellfighters were not only in a class by themselves as a marching unit, but the band "could break down into several dance orchestras, or into theater bands to accompany the versatile talents of its various entertainers."[2]

The band was an immediate sensation in Europe. Between February 12 and March 29, 1918, the Hellfighters traveled two thousand miles throughout France. Lt. Arthur Little, the band's executive officer, described the scene which greeted them in town after town. "When we arrived at the railroad station and the train rolled, or rather crept in, a guard of police and railroad attendants had to precede it to clear the tracks. . . ." Later, when the band left, "The crowd cheered without ceasing; women and children wept."[3]

Noble Sissle, who later replaced Bill Robinson as drum major, has given a detailed picture of what a Hellfighters' concert was like. In an article for the *St. Louis Post-Despatch* dated June 10, 1918, he wrote:

The program started with a French march, followed by favorite overtures and vocal selections from our male quartet, all of which were heartily applauded. The second part of our program opened with "The Stars and Stripes Forever," the great Sousa march, and before the last note was finished, the house was ringing with applause. Next followed an arrangement of plantation melodies, and then came the fireworks, "The Memphis Blues."

Lieutenant Europe, before raising his baton, twitched his shoulders, apparently to be sure that his tight-fitting military coat would stand the strain, a musician shifted his feet, the players of brass horns blew the saliva from their instruments, the drummers tightened their drum-heads, everyone settled back in their seats, half closed their eyes, and when the baton came crashing down with a swoop that brought forth a soul-rousing crash, both director and musicians seemed to forget their surroundings; they were lost in scenes and memories. Cornet and clarinet players began to manipulate notes in that typical rhythm (that rhythm which no artist has ever been able to put down on paper), as the drummers struck their stride, their shoulders started shaking in time to their syncopated raps.

Then it seemed the whole audience began to sway, dignified French officers began to pat their feet, along with the American general, who temporarily had lost his style and grace. Lt. Europe was no longer the Lt. Europe of a moment ago, but Jim Europe, who a few months ago rocked New York with his syncopated baton. His body swayed in willowy motions and his head was bobbing as it did in days when Terpsichorean festivities reigned supreme. He turned to the trombone players who sat impatiently waiting for their cue to have a jazz "spasm" and they drew their slides out to the extremity and jerked them back with that characteristic crack.

The audience could stand it no longer, the "jazz germ" hit them and it seemed to find the vital spot, loosening all muscles and causing what is known in America as an "eagle rocking it" . . .

All through France, the same thing happened. Troop trains carrying Allied soldiers from everywhere passed us en route, and every head came out of the window when we struck up a good old Dixie tune. Even German prisoners forgot they were prisoners, dropped their work to listen and pat their feet to the stirring American tunes.

But the thing that capped the climax happened up in northern France. We were playing our colonel's favorite ragtime, "The Army's Blues," in a little village where we were the first American troops there, and among the crowd listening to that band was an old woman about sixty years of age. To everyone's surprise, all of a sudden she started doing a dance that resembled "Walking the Dog." Then I was cured and satisfied that American music would one day be the world's music.

Other New York regiments, inspired by Europe's success, made determined attempts to match his achievements. Lt. Tim Brymn's 350th Artillery Band performed under the name the Seventy Black Devils. Brymn's music, which he described as "a military symphony engaged in a battle of jazz," created a sensation playing for President Wilson at the Peace Conference. Another band was led by Lt. Will Vodery, one of whose tenor horn players was a young man named Sam Wooding, who was to bring his own highly successful jazz orchestra to Europe in 1925. The newspapers described Vodery's band as "the jazziest, craziest, best tooting outfit in France."

The "jazz germ" was spreading. The very word "jazz" seemed to suggest a clash of cultures, something brazenly cocksure and contemporary. It was a word which soon became one of the things which most typically characterized the victorious Americans. Indeed, it was the word more than the music which attracted attention. Few people had heard jazz in 1918 and fewer still had any idea what to make of it. But almost everyone had heard of it. There was an immediate demand for jazz musicians in Paris.

The black drummer Louis Mitchell, a close friend of Jim Europe, was sent to New York to recruit a band for the Casino de Paris where he

14

had previously been working as a drum soloist. He returned with a seven-piece orchestra which he called the Jazz Kings and which included Cricket Smith on cornet, Frank Withers on trombone, James Shaw on saxophone, Joe Mayers on piano, Walter Kildare on banjo and Dan Parrish on bass. Jazz had entered one of the main citadels of European culture like some sort of Trojan Horse.

On October 14, 1918, Noble Sissle wrote to ragtime pianist and composer, Eubie Blake: "Well, on my way here, I passed through Paris. I saw Mitchell. He said you wrote to him. Well, old boy, hang on and we'll be able to knock them cold after the war. It will be over soon. Jim [Europe] and I have Paris by the balls in a bigger way than anyone you know. . . . Tell Stern that 'Camp Meeting Day' [written by Sgt. F. E. Mikels] is the big hit that runs through the Paris Follies of 1918 at the Marejin [Marigny] Theater."[4]

The music which Mitchell's band played was not really jazz. Stylistically, it was the same rough blend of brass band music and ragtime which Jim Europe had so successfully developed from years earlier as accompaniment to the Castles' famous new dance steps. Most of it was written out and only a few, if any, of the solos were improvised. But even so, the fiercely insistent, if rather heavy beat, the built-in syncopations and the way notes were deliberately and effectively pitched sharp or flat, were in dramatic contrast to the rather painstaking formalities of European dance music.

There is no doubt that such music, which so boldly flouted tradition, fitted the mood of the time exactly. Europeans who had so recently escaped Armageddon were ready for anything. From now on everything was going to be different and that went for music too. In fact, Europeans almost fell over themselves in their desire to invest jazz with novel and exotic qualities. There is a footnote in Jean Cocteau's *Le Coq et l'Harlequin*[5] which describes the scene at the Casino de Paris in 1918.

The American band accompanied [the dance] on banjos and thick nickel tubes. On the right of the little black-coated group, there was a barman of noises under a gilt pergola loaded with bells, triangles, boards and motor-cycle horns. With these he fabricated cocktails, adding from time to time a dash of cymbals, all the while rising from his seat, posturing and smiling vacuously.

Mr. Pilcer, in evening dress, thin and rouged, and Mademoiselle Gaby Deslys, like a ventriloquist's doll, with a china complexion, flaxen hair and a gown of ostrich feathers, danced to this hurricane of rhythm and beating of drums a sort of tame catastrophe which left them quite intoxicated and blinded under the glare of six anti-aircraft searchlights. The house was on its feet to applaud, roused from its inertia by this extraordinary turn, which, compared to the madness of Offenbach, is what a tank would be to an 1870 State Carriage.

This stream of hyperbole tells us very little about the music, except that its relationship to jazz was tenuous, but it says a lot about prevailing European attitudes at that time. The problem was less that the French did not understand jazz, but that they thought they did. Jazz was "rhythm" and "improvisation." So far so good. But it was the nature of rhythm and improvisation itself, traditions which Europeans had neglected for over 150 years, which were misunderstood. According to the pianist Jean Wiener: "People understood almost too well that jazz was improvisation – but they didn't understand how to do it. So you got jazz bands whose only purpose was to make as much noise as possible – bells, klaxons, drums, revolvers, etc. The music was absolutely foreign to the French at that time."

The trombonist and arranger Leo Vauchant[6] who, at the age of fourteen, was the drummer in the pit orchestra in the Marigny Theater when Louis Mitchell's Jazz Kings were part of the show, confirms this impression.

There were no good improvisers in those days . . . it started with that orchestra, the Mitchell one. It started with that and it was a long time before anyone else showed up. But right away, there were French orchestras going all over who didn't know what they were doing. They were just awful – but they played. When that thing started all the little theaters had to have a jazz band. The jazz band meant the drummer. "Who is the jazz band at the Olympia?" They didn't know that jazz band meant an orchestra. The Follies Bergères, all those theaters, were copying from each other. There was a guy playing C-melody sax reading from the piano copy, and there was no bass. There was a banjo, there was a violin and there was a drummer – that was it. It was atrocious.

In those early days jazz in Europe was more spectacle than music. As such, it was soon featured in the theaters. The jazz band would play at the bar during intermission and, more rarely, on stage during the finale when it would be accompanied by the pit orchestra. Leo Vauchant, who of all European musicians seems to have had the most natural talent for jazz, talked about playing drums in the show which featured Louis Mitchell's Jazz Kings. It was to be one of the most important experiences of his musical life.

16

I've lied to more people. I've said, "Oh, yes. I've listened to American records." I swear to God, I didn't even have a machine. I wouldn't spend the money to buy records. I got what I got from listening to this one band. Then I went my way . . . I loved those black guys. I used to stay up at night because I enjoyed their company, and playing with them. Frank Wither's wife Maisie was a pianist and she played trombone too. And we would write each other stuff you know, to play for three trombones. There was always a pianist and a drum set and so we played. Mitchell formed a Tempo Club above Joe Zelli's club and I was the only white guy in that outfit. I enjoyed cooking corned-beef hash and potatoes with an egg on top. They accepted me because I played their way, you know. They enjoyed that. It was a challenge – learning their way of playing. I found it novel. I liked the way they approached dance music. It was rhythmical, and the tempo never varied within the tune. Whereas, when the French would play, there was no sense of beat. They were playing things with rubato – there was no dance beat. It didn't swing. It didn't move. The blacks, on the other hand, seemed to be skilled musicians. They knew about chords. At least that trombone player did – Frank Withers. And Cricket Smith certainly did. If he didn't know the name of a chord, he certainly didn't miss any of the notes. When he improvised, it was right on the nose. It was a little out of tune. Most of those bands were out of tune. They never tuned. They just started to play. And those pianos were not too well tuned in those joints either.

Equipped with new insights into Afro-American music, it was not long before the fourteen-year-old Leo, with all the brash self-confidence of inexperience, was suggesting to the startled conductor ways of improving his show.

This was an American show that was brought to the Marigny Theater on the Avenue Marigny for the benefit of the American troops while they were in Paris. This would be around 1917/18. This began the train that the Casino de Paris began to have later – *Hello Boy* and shows that had American titles. And the fellow that introduces the thing comes forward and says something like, "*Hello ma chérie. Maintenant je t'emmène aux Pays des Oranges.*" And the band would play a lousy one-step that had nothing to do with oranges. But that's the way the shows were running in those days. They started to give an American twist to everything. . . . So I started to write stuff for that show. It wasn't difficult to do, you know. I knew the tunes – I knew the tricks they were doing. So I asked the conductor. I said, "You know we are not playing it the way they do. I told you about that down-beat." I said, "Would you allow me to fix it?" And I would fix all the trumpets and the glissandos on the trombones. But it had to be written out before the French guys could play the syncopations. But even if it was written out, it was still better than what they were doing before. So some of the stuff I would write out in quarter triplets across the beat. And I would start to do little things with the bass. Because they had a bass with that Mitchell band. It was the only band I heard that had a bass. Later on, they came in with those sousaphones. That was terrible.

In all this, young Vauchant showed himself to be exceptionally perceptive. His reference to "the down-beat" is particularly interesting. Most French light music of the time favored time signatures in 2/4 and 3/4. French marches, for example, were almost invariably written in 2/4, as opposed to their slower-paced British and American equivalents, which were usually in 4/4. The significance of a smaller rather than a larger number of rhythmic units to the bar is that it allows less room for what Gunther Schuller has called the "democratization" of the beat.[7] 2/4 and 3/4 time signatures unavoidably stress the first beat in the bar. Afro-American music prefers a larger number of beats to the bar and stresses them either equally or, frequently, with greater emphasis on the "weak" second and fourth beats. This creates a dynamic tension in the music which is the basis of swing. This was a concept which was quite foreign to European classical music at that time, although there were traces of it in some forms of folk music. In pointing out its importance, Vauchant had put his finger on the single biggest obstacle to the assimilation of African elements into European music.

Nevertheless, despite the difficulties, jazz was the indispensible thing in the early 1920s. The flirtation with all things American which began with the war grew into a fully fledged romance after the Armistice. The troops withdrew and were replaced by fresh armies of American tourists. This opened up new opportunities for musicians. Mabel Mercer was working as a singer at Bricktop's nightclub in the Rue Fontaine.

> Paris was a popular hang-out for the American musicians because of the tourists. The American tourists would come for the different seasons. In the spring they came for the dress season and the art season. Then there was the motor season later on in the summer – a lot of Americans came for that. Of course, they congregated in Montmartre and everywhere there was an American band. . . . Everybody was out to have a good time, and have a good time they did.

Back in New York, demobilized musicians spread stories of the fabulous salaries to be earned in a land where blacks were welcomed as

18

conquering heroes. It was all doubly attractive to men who found that local opportunities for work were shrinking. Racial attitudes were hardening as tens of thousands of southern blacks poured into northern cities in search of jobs in the new wartime industries. The days when Jim Europe had cornered the fashionable entertainment market were over. Black orchestras found themselves increasingly squeezed out of the better paid downtown jobs. Harlem soon found it had more musicians than it could support. Finally, on May 9, 1919, Jim Europe was dramatically murdered by a member of his own orchestra during the intermission of a concert in Boston. The man on whom the last hopes of a revival were centered was gone.

Meanwhile, opportunities for work continued to multiply in Paris, where, ironically, there was strong pro-black prejudice. The French, it seemed, were convinced that all blacks were automatically jazz musicians. Consequently, any black man who applied for a job was sure of success. The black boxer Gene Bullard was so impressed with the opportunities for work that he took up the drums in order to earn money between fights. "I think I was rotten," he wrote in his journal, "but it seemed every dancing place wanted a colored jazz drummer, and they had auditioned me before hiring me, so what could I lose?"[8] Indeed, it reached the point where it was soon hard to find work if you were not black. The piano player Alain Romans remembers working with a band led by Benny Peyton in the early twenties. A condition of employment was that he should "black up." "One day, the little daughter of the owner of the Casino de la Forêt [in Le Touquet] came over and touched my face. When she saw she had black on her fingers, she started to scream. Her father appeared, and when she told him what had happened, he got an ice-bucket and a napkin – this is the funny part – and wiped every face except mine. Then he spanked the little girl for telling a lie, and we played on." Romans played out the rest of the engagement with the piano pushed into as deep a corner as possible, his Caucasian features shaded by a potted palm.

It was no wonder that black musicians jumped at the chance of going to Europe. Early in 1920, the piano player Elliot Carpenter was approached by a Mr. Wickes, the president of New York's Clef Club, to find musicians for a new club which was opening in Paris. Carpenter's band, which had taken over some of the work previously done by Jim Europe before the war, was popular. Moreover, Carpenter had never been to France and he was sceptical of the stories he had heard.

Two of the boys, Opal Cooper and Sammy Richardson, had just come back from the war. So I went to them and said, "Do you guys want to go to France?" And they said, "My God, yes!" And they started to tell me about the beauties of Paris – what they did and didn't do. They raved, "Yeah, man. Let's go back there!" So I said, "Hey, wait a minute. I haven't said anything about money." And they said, "The hell with that! Let's just get back to Paris." They used to call me Eli – "Eli you don't know! Whatever you do, don't pass this up." So I went back to Mr. Wickes and I told him I thought I could get my boys to go, and I asked him about money. "Oh, you've got nothing to worry about," he said. "I'll tell you what I'll do. I'll get each of you fifty dollars a week." So I told him I'd go and talk to my boys and come back. And when I told them, they said, "Take it for ten – what the hell!" I tried to remonstrate with them. I said, "Now wait a minute fellers . . ." And they got mad. "Man, it's the opportunity of a lifetime and you're about to go and throw it through the window." So I go back and tell Mr. Wickes it's OK. My wife tells me I must be crazy. I said, "Listen, these boys want to go so bad! And from what they tell me, we're going to be millionaires twenty-four hours after we get there."

Incredibly, Carpenter found on arrival that the situation was almost as it had been described to him.

It was no more than two days before a boy who'd come over before the war came by to see me. We used to call him "Subway" Johnson, because he was always hanging around the subway looking for girls. Anyway, Subway was working in Paris as a singer and a drummer. So when I got through playing, he said, "How much money are you getting?" So I told him "Fifty dollars a week." He said, "Oh, for Christ's sake! Did you come all the way here for that? I'll tell you what. I'll give you a hundred dollars a week to come and work for me." I said, "I can't leave these boys – we're here now." He said, "150 dollars." I said, "Where d'you get that kind of money?" So he told me, "That's what you should be getting. You should be getting two hundred dollars a week each." So I asked Cricket Smith, who was working over at the Casino, and he told me he was getting 250 to 300 dollars a week! When I told him we came over for fifty he said, "Well, you came over for nothing."

Fortunately, relief was at hand. Two weeks later, an English agent heard the band and, spotting that they had no contract, signed them up for an engagement at Rector's in London for 350 dollars a week. In addition they were hired, under the name of Red Devils, for vaudeville at the Coliseum. "Within a few weeks we had six months of contracts in various music-halls. After that, we did more nightclub work and we were earning 750 dollars a week. So I said to Sammy Richardson, 'You know, we fell down a well and came up with a roast dinner.' "

☆ THE ORIGINAL DIXIELAND BAND

World War One, besides marking the transition to a new age of communication and mass production, blew what was left of the old world apart. By 1918 there were twenty million dead and wounded. For those who survived, the only way to face the future was to forget the past. "We'd suffered unimaginably – we had nothing left," recalls the French piano player Jean Wiener. "Suddenly it was all over. It was like the exit from hell. We couldn't believe it. We got up at seven in the morning and went to bed again at four o'clock the following morning. It was as if life had so much to offer we could never fit it all in the day."

The American way of life, corn-fed but confident, was positively refreshing to Europeans worn out by the agonizing perplexities of the recent past. Radiant with affluent optimism, it seemed to suggest a bright new future restored to peace and prosperity. Europe gave a great gasp of relief. It could never happen again – the world had finally come to its senses and to celebrate that fact people behaved with a special kind of madness. The "jazz age" had arrived.

Given this situation, some historians have suggested that if jazz had not appeared on the scene when it did, it would have been necessary to invent it. The joke ignores the fact that this is just what happened. The "jazz age" preceded any understanding of jazz by several years. The jazz which existed before 1920 was much less the product of New Orleans than the creation of that new concept of the age of mass communication: publicity. Jazz, or what people thought was jazz, was the answer to a press agent's prayer, and to that extent much of it was invented by men who had nothing to do with music at all.

The extraordinary rise to fame of the Original Dixieland Jazz Band is the most important example of this. A white band led by the enterprising Nick La Rocca, this group would never have enjoyed the success it did if the instruments for the dissemination, not only of their music, but of their publicity had not existed. Whether or not their music was good, it was good copy, and the fantasies of the press on the subject seemed inexhaustible. Reporters wrote of notes which "blat and collide," of violins which "snicker and shriek" and described the five-piece band as "a chorus of hunting hounds on the scent with an occasional explosion on the subway thrown in for good measure." The musicians themselves played up to all this by affecting a conscious snobbery of low-browism, boasting that "none of them knew music" and how "they did not know how many pianists they tried before they found one who could *not* read music."[9]

This kind of controversy is the stuff of which the greatest popular successes are made. "Livery Stable Blues," recorded by the band for Victor in 1917, sold over a million copies. In many respects they were the first modern pop group, recalling the fantastic success and acrimonious debate which surrounded the Beatles fifty years later. Like the Beatles, their success proves that what passes for novelty is, subconsciously, what many people have been expecting for a long time.

The Original Dixieland Jazz Band were "original" only in that they were the first jazz band to make records. The paper *Variety* noted, writing of New Orleans in 1917, that the city's "Negro bands . . . were the original jazz bands, and their expressions of 'jazzing it' and 'putting a little jazz on it' are still very popular at their picturesque balls." The Original Dixieland Jazz Band's claim to have invented the various barn-yard effects – the whinnying horse, the crowing rooster and the braying donkey – are also false. The New Orleans trombone player Preston Jackson relates that King Oliver used to take breaks "imitating a rooster and a baby . . . the La Rocca boys of the Dixieland Jazz Band used to hang around and got a lot of ideas from his gang."[10]

Nor were they the first to take the music out of New Orleans. As early as 1915 another white New Orleans band led by Tom Brown had caused quite a stir in Chicago. It was Brown who, unable to take the job himself, had recommended the Dixieland Band for the job at Reisenweber's in New York which finally launched them. Moreover, the Dixieland Band were not even the first to play in New York. On December 11, 1915, the *New York Clipper* reviewed a vaudeville act appearing at the Columbia Theater. It turned out to be a New Orleans jazz band led by the great black trumpet player Freddie Keppard.

> That Creole band of six pieces – cornet, trombone, guitar, clarinet, fiddle and bass violin – played a rather ragged selection for a starter, the clarinet being particularly strong for the comedy effect.
>
> The old darkey whom they were serenading responded by singing "Old Black Joe" and the band chimed in with fine harmony both instrumentally and vocally. The playing of such ragtime melodies worked the

old darkey to dancing pitch, and he did pound those boards until the kinks in his knees reminded him of his age. Lots of bows, an encore, more bows and another encore stamped this offering as OK.

In short, the significance of the Original Dixieland Jazz Band was not that they were new but that they were timely. They were the first band to make records. It is no coincidence that they were discovered in New York, the center of the recording industry and all its attendant publicity, rather than in Chicago where much better jazz was being played. True, Freddie Keppard's band had played New York at the same time, but they, unfortunately, were black. The review in the *Clipper* suggests that the Negro band was using the same kind of novelty effects which later were to make such a name for the Original Dixieland Jazz Band. Other black bands, notably Wilbur Sweatman's, Ford Dabney's and even Jim Europe's had already recorded music which might mistakenly have been thought of as jazz, and some of it even used freak effects. Even so, no Negro band could expect to make the same kind of impression on a press and recording industry which were dominated by whites.

By 1918, La Rocca's band had already waxed a large number of titles. Within a few weeks of the release of "Livery Stable Blues" the market was flooded with dozens of imitations, some of which, like "Yelping Hound Blues" by Alcide "Yellow" Nunez and his Louisiana Five, were almost as successful. Other bands who cleverly copied the Original Dixieland Jazz Band were Jimmy Durante's New Orleans Jazz Band and Earl Fuller's Famous Jazz Band.

The Dixieland Band also occupied an important position in the history of jazz in Europe. At the height of their popularity, in April, 1919, they made the seemingly extraordinary decision to come to England. Their first engagement was in a show at the London Hippodrome called *Joy Bells*, starring George Robey. Robey, who as star of the show was jealous of the group's success, insisted that they should be fired. Their next job was at Rector's nightclub, where their fame began to grow. When London's new Palais de Dance opened in Hammersmith they were a natural choice as a flamboyant source of publicity with which to establish the new dance hall's reputation. Indeed they were an overnight sensation. 5,800 people paid to hear them on the opening night alone.

"It was an entirely new sound," recalls trombonist Lew Davis. "We'd heard nothing like it in England before. . . . Listening to Emile Christian's trombone was what first inspired me to take up music. I'd be down at the

Palais night after night to hear him. . . . The band had no bass player but the drummer, Sbarbaro, used a cymbal and all kinds of cowbells and wood blocks, and played them in a very modern way."

The band's brief European interlude was an important indication of the factors governing the evolution of jazz at the time. They arrived in April, 1919, and departed in July of the following year. Their stay coincided almost exactly with Louis Mitchell's success in Paris. Significantly, whereas the Original Dixieland Band recorded seventeen titles in England, Mitchell's Jazz Kings had to wait until 1922, by which time they were just one more jazz band among many. Admittedly La Rocca's band was producing music which, by any standards, was more frantic and lively than anything else at that time. Its sheer physical momentum and apparently uncontrolled polyphony was a radically new departure, even by comparison with the Jazz Kings, whose music concentrated on simple melodies, played straight, and even simpler accompaniments. But it is doubtful if even these differences can explain the far greater commercial success of the Original Dixieland Jazz Band.

The conclusion must be that La Rocca's band was simply more marketable. In the first place his musicians were white, and therefore claimed the attention of the press to a far greater extent. La Rocca in particular had a genius for publicity which was never burdened with too much regard for the truth. However good his cornet playing, his starring role with the band was more as an unscrupulous liar who gave interviews not merely ignoring, but explicitly denying the black contribution to jazz. On April 10, 1919, the reporter for the *Performer* was assured that "there were only two . . . jazz bands in America . . . [and] the Dixieland lot are the original." La Rocca and his colleagues also never stopped bragging about the band's musical illiteracy. They shrewdly recognized that their refusal to compromise with the musical standards of the day was their most commercial asset, and skilfully used every means of publicity to promote the fact.

The Original Dixieland Jazz Band had reduced the subtleties of black music to a sure-fire formula. The shock tactics of dynamic rhythmic momentum and sheer energy were all compressed into a rigid format which had instant mass appeal. To be fair, the band was as good as its built-in limitations allowed. Their frenetic drive and their ability to take numbers at very fast tempos left all rivals standing. This and the publicity machine which attended them unleashed a flood of imitators, many of whom were far more guilty of the tasteless use of slapstick effects for which the Original Dixieland Jazz Band is usually held responsible. To this extent they fell victim to their own publicity. But there is no doubt that they changed the course of popular music. Jazz, which had previously been little more than novelty music rather reluctantly included by band leaders like W. C. Handy to keep southern audiences happy and to bolster the comedy routines of their shows, became a saleable commodity in its own right.

The fact that the Dixieland Band were as good as they were, and were also white, sheds fascinating light on the history and development of jazz. It seems that this ability of white men to play black music was determined by very complicated cultural factors. The surprising fact revealed by contemporary recordings is that black musicians who had been "schooled" in the white musical traditions had as much of a problem as anyone else in learning to play jazz. Many of the black inhabitants of cities like Washington and New York in 1917 had been resident in the North for a generation or more. Accordingly, there had developed a sizeable black middle class who were often as determined as whites to ensure a good education for their children. Musical instruction was inevitably affected by this and men like Louis Mitchell and others who were members of Jim Europe's famous Tempo Club were all musicians whose training was too academic to encourage the kind of liberties that must be taken if music is to swing. New Orleans, on the other hand, for complicated reasons which will be discussed later, was developing music which reflected the more natural rhythms and intonations of Negro folk song and dance rather than the academic niceties of the European tradition. Consciously or not, Nick La Rocca and his trombone player Eddie Edwards were making an important point when they boasted of their musical illiteracy. Certainly the fact that they were from New Orleans, where they had heard most of the great black pioneers like Freddie Keppard, accounts for the fact that in some important respects they played better jazz than Louis Mitchell's Jazz Kings. Despite many interesting musical qualities, the Jazz Kings lacked the drive of the Original Dixieland Jazz Band and showed hardly any aptitude for the intricate polyphonic skills which are the essence of good New Orleans jazz.

Some black musicians have described the almost painful efforts they made to acquire the new style of playing. Drummer Bert Marshall for example, who was working E. E. Thompson's band at the Abbaye Thélème in Paris in 1926, recalls:

> I wanted to get the swing of jazz on the drums, but although I could feel it, I couldn't play it. So after we left the Abbaye Thélème, there was a white band which came to Paris – I can't remember their name. They used to go

to a cafe after playing. And this boy used to get on the drums [most probably Dave Tough]. So I used to watch this guy doing this, and slowly I began to get it. I was also learning from records. We used to buy Red Nichols' records and take things off them.

It is not surprising, therefore, that the standard of many of the early jazz bands, black as well as white, was very low. Bert Marshall remembers joining E. E. Thompson's band in 1926.

> I'd always kept in touch with the drummer Billy Taylor. He stopped playing drums when he joined Thompson and took up saxophone. Through him I got the offer to join them. I thought the band was pretty lousy, but I couldn't just walk out after they had sent for me. I had to stick it. . . . They held the job at the Abbaye because there was a lot of pro-black prejudice in Paris. If you were black, they thought you were great even if you were terrible. Anyway, through Thompson's agent, who was a man called Smet, we got a job at the Folies Bergères with Josephine Baker. You know, the band was so lousy that when we went on stage we had to pretend to play while the pit orchestra played for us and we just mimed to it.

Returning to the Original Dixieland Jazz Band, it is interesting to compare their version of "Ostrich Walk" with a recording of "Indianola" by Wilbur Sweatman, which bears a curious resemblance to it. Sweatman's band worked in vaudeville, but it had already acquired a big reputation among other Negro bands for playing jazz. The dancer Ulysses S. Thompson relates that when, in 1916, his group the Tennessee Ten decided to incorporate a jazz band into their act, it was Sweatman to whom they turned for advice and instruction. This is confirmed by piano player Ike Hatch, who worked for Sweatman around 1920. "I used to work his Sunday concerts at the Eltinge Theater. . . . Wilbur was a wonderful hot man, but he made his reputation as a stunt player. He would play three or even four clarinets at a time, fingering them for chord passages. This brought the house down."[11]

Listening to Sweatman's records, this reputation as a hot player seems hardly justified by comparison with the Original Dixieland Jazz Band. The white musicians play significantly better, their individual voices displaying more imagination while at the same time making more collective sense. "Indianola" is a complicated assembly of ragtime strains, each sixteen bars long, beginning in G-minor. This modulates to the relative major B-flat, before passing back through G-minor to E-flat, to G-minor, to G and finally back to E-flat. If these players had

26

listened to black bands from New Orleans, there is no audible sign of it. The piece is arranged from start to finish. The clarinet leads throughout, usually in unison with either trombone or cornet, except on the G strain, where the latter, disastrously, takes the lead. The trombone seems quite unable to cope with the cornet's phrasing of a simple riff figure on the fourth beat of the bar. There is very little improvisation, and even Sweatman seems to have worked out his part beforehand. The instrumental breaks, which occur regularly throughout, are also arranged, in contrast to New Orleans bands who prided themselves on their skill in this respect.

Sweatman's band was both successful and well known. The fact that the group made such a poor showing at playing jazz is revealing. It suggests that most black musicians, particularly those not from New Orleans, were not playing jazz before 1920. Relatively few black musicians were recorded at this time, and those that were were usually players who worked New York and other eastern seaboard cities near the centers of the recording industry. The fact that such men had almost as much difficulty as whites in acquiring the new jazz skills is a powerful indication of the importance of New Orleans as the source of the music.

The Original Dixieland Jazz Band, on the other hand, was from New Orleans. Whether they denied it or not, La Rocca, Edwards and the rest had almost certainly heard black musicians like Freddie Keppard, Buddy Petit and others of the best New Orleans jazzmen. Even though there was far less improvisation in their music than La Rocca boasted, and although the absence of a bass player made it hard for the band to swing, they played uncompromisingly hot music which impressed some of the best musicians and critics. Bix Beiderbecke was inspired by hearing their records, and Robert Goffin, who could never be accused of racial prejudice, wrote of them, "I do not believe any band has ever topped the Original Dixieland Band. . . ." The greatest recordings of New Orleans jazz were not made until 1923, the year when King Oliver, Jelly Roll Morton, Sidney Bechet and Louis Armstrong were all first put on record. But, at least in 1918, the Original Dixieland Jazz Band achieved an emotional intensity and a coherent ensemble sound which was unique.

The influence exerted on the history of jazz by the Original Dixieland Band seems to have been crucial if confusing. Their records show unmistakably that they were inspired by authentic New Orleans jazz, so that their explicit denials of any black influences did a great deal to mislead people about the true origins of the music. This was particularly true in Europe, where it was ten years before the seminal role of the black musician in jazz was understood. The lies the Dixielanders told about their "originality" combined with their huge success to delay the evolution of the music by confusing it in people's minds with a number of corny, slapstick effects.

This mattered much less in America than in Europe. Right from the start of its history, jazz in Europe suffered from problems which have beset it ever since – problems which not even the age of radio and television has resolved. In the United States, the unending search for new forms of entertainment and the extraordinary strength and vitality of America's black music were bound to combine sooner or later. Europe, on the other hand, had to do this at second hand, relying only on a relatively small number of imported phonograph records for news of how things were developing in the States. If Europe first experienced jazz as a tidal wave, the effect was even more true of the aftermath than of the initial impact. As the initial popularity of jazz waned, the early pioneers found themselves stranded high and dry in an alien musical environment, cut off from the mainstream of development which was rapidly taking jazz in quite new directions in America. This was a serious situation for an evolving hybrid like jazz which even in America could have died at almost any stage of its history for lack of the necessary cross-fertilizations.

When trumpeter Doc Cheatham arrived with Sam Wooding's band in the second half of the twenties, most of the music he heard sounded hopelessly stiff and dated. "Musicians that I met who had gone over to Europe before I arrived with Sam seemed to me to be so behind in their playing. It was old-fashioned. That's why I wanted to come back after three years. They were playing what we call corny type of jazz. . . . So when I heard guys in Leon Abbey's band or Benny Peyton's Band, they sounded terrible. They sounded worse than anything I ever heard in my life."[12]

☆ BACKGROUND TO THE BLUES

The reigning obsession of the "jazz age" was not jazz but dancing. The passion for the fox trot introduced by Irene and Vernon Castle in 1914 was, in its way, a major instrument of social and musical change. Again, these were changes which would have been impossible without records and the radio. Before 1914 dance halls were not considered to be respectable places. Dancing was an upper-class activity confined to the safety of the homes of the wealthy. Then in 1914 Irene Castle published her best-selling book, *Modern Dancing*. It was a brilliant reconciliation of different social attitudes and was, in its way, revolutionary. Middle-class suspicions were lulled by her condemnation of the more obviously black-inspired dances, such as the monkey glide, the fish walk and the buzzard lope, as not merely inelegant but unfashionable. Instead, she preferred the more refined fox trot. At the same time, her book subtly but unmistakably suggested a new era of freedom from outworn social attitudes. It extolled a more relaxed, flexible approach to life, an absence of restraint, which was reflected even in the clothes you wore. "Don't fasten your blouse down too tightly, and be sure, in selecting one of those transparent, filmy little affairs now so much in vogue for dancing, that you can stretch your arms above your head without difficulty . . . ," she wrote.

"In speaking of hose, it may not come amiss to say that the new styles of stockings, with the elastic tops that hold them up snugly with the aid of only a round garter, are much better to dance in than the looser hose that require garters suspended from a corset."

Irene Castle completed her extraordinary appeal by bobbing her hair, smoking cigarettes, and refusing to wear corsets, so doing a great deal to set the style that was to be developed in the twenties.

The craze for dancing which had been started by the Castles was of vital importance to the rise of jazz. By 1920, there were five hundred dance halls in New York alone, and by 1925 the number had risen to eight hundred. All the major hotels soon featured ballrooms and dance bands, many of which made regular radio broadcasts, allowing people to exercise their obsession for dancing in their own homes. This continued throughout the Depression during the early thirties when the search for enjoyment changed into a means of escape, so enabling a surprising number of bands to survive at a time when many Americans were close to starvation. At this time, the general public saw little or no distinction between jazz and what later came to be called dance music, and jazz musicians benefited accordingly. Apart from those who worked regularly with large commercial bands, there were innumerable small groups run by musicians like the Dorsey brothers, Red Nichols, Bix Beiderbecke, Joe Venuti, Adrian Rollini, Phil Napoleon and Frankie Trumbauer, whose much more jazzy material was acceptable because it was danceable.

This, in the long term, was the real significance of the Original Dixieland Jazz Band. It seemed that the Dixielanders inspired unrivaled feats of endurance among the dancers who patronized Reisenweber's. *Variety* of March 19, 1917, had reported:

> Gingery, swinging music is what the dancers want, and it is even looked for by those who do not dance. . . . Late in the morning, the jazzers go to work and the dancers hit the floor, to remain there till they topple over, if the band keeps playing. It leaves no question but that they like to dance to that kind of music and it is a "kind." If the dancers see someone they know at the tables, it's common to hear, "Oh, Boy!" as they roll their eyes while floating past, and the "Oh, Boy!" expression probably describes the Jazz Band better than anything else could.

It was therefore no coincidence that the *Victor Record Review* dated March 7, 1917, promoted the new music they had just recorded with the same enthusiasm: "The Jazz Band is the very latest thing in the development of music. It has sufficient power and penetration to inject life into a mummy, and will keep ordinary dancers on their feet until breakfast time. . . ." The band's greatest successes in England were at dance halls, first at the Marten Club, and later at the Hammersmith Palais.

Meanwhile, the statements of Nick La Rocca turned the very existence of the group into a burning issue. One such remark, quoted in *The Palais Dancing News* in April, 1920 was: "Jazz is the assassination, the murdering, the slaying of syncopation. . . . I even go as far as to confess that we are musical anarchists. . . ." The *Star* of April 19 had commented wryly: "It is an interesting study to watch the faces of the dancers at the Palladium when the Original Dixieland Jazz Band is trying to murder music. Most are obviously bewildered by the weird discords, but some, to judge by their cynical smiles, evidently think that it is a musical joke that is hardly worth attempting. Perhaps they are right." Nevertheless, despite constant attacks in the British press, the public voted with their feet, turning out in their thousands nightly to dance the one-step and the fox trot to this strange discordant music.

While all this was going on, another band slipped almost unnoticed into England. Will Marion Cook's Southern Syncopated Orchestra arrived in June, 1919 to play an engagement at the Philharmonic Hall. Subsequently, they gave concerts at the Kingsway Hall, and a command performance at Buckingham Palace before King George V, who apparently greatly enjoyed a piece called "Characteristic Blues" played by a black clarinet player by the name of Sidney Bechet. However, the Southern Syncopated Orchestra was not a dance band in any sense, and therefore attracted that much less attention. From the reviews they appear to be just the kind of outfit the Dixielanders were out to "murder." *The Times* for December 9, 1919 wrote, with obvious relief:

> It is an entertainment which all would feel better for seeing and hearing. . . . One has grown used to associating syncopation with musical fireworks and jazz drummers who hurl themselves at a dozen instruments in their efforts to extract noise from anything and everything. The Southern Syncopated Orchestra can provide this kind of entertainment when required. It has a drummer who fascinated yesterday's audience – and more important still, the Coliseum's drum expert – by his lightning dexterity and his knack of juggling drum sticks. But the great point in their favor is that at a bound they can bring us back to the darkies' folk songs and melodies that will live long after jazz and ragtime numbers have enjoyed their spell of popularity. The harmony of some of their concerted numbers is a joy.

Clearly this was an orchestra with different ends in view. In the first place, no black band in 1920 was going to make the kind of aggressive statements about their music which had earned the Dixielanders so much notoriety. It is also clear from contemporary accounts that their music was presented with just the kind of subtlety which La Rocca was dedicated to destroying. The review in the *Sound Wave* for October, 1920 reads: ". . . Beneath the dash and fire of their ragtime performances, however, is the instinctive faculty of true art. No assemblage of instrumentalists ever played with a greater sense of orchestral balance. The wildest orgy of jazz effects never reveals for an instant any real discord, for each artist plays with the harmonious object of the complete performance uppermost in his mind." Whatever this reviewer may have thought, Cook's orchestra did not play jazz, although it incorporated almost all the elements which were soon to combine to create it.

In 1920 it was the Original Dixieland Jazz Band which made headlines, partly because they loudly discounted any black influences. Ironically, however, Dixieland music might well have suffered the fate of all gimmicks but for the civilizing influences of the Negro music they scorned. The freak effects adopted by the first white jazz musicians, which initially sounded so startling but which soon sounded so irretrievably corny, were only a rough parody of the black musician's more vocal approach to playing. By 1920 there were already examples of Negro musicians whose playing displayed these characteristics in a way which was wonderfully tasteful and musical. Even though the process by which black musicians came to accept their own musical heritage was slow, it was well under way by 1920. One of the most interesting examples of this was that of Will Marion Cook's orchestra

31

which arrived in Europe while the Original Dixieland Jazz Band was still there. Although Cook's orchestra was not a jazz outfit, he proved that it was possible to combine some jazz elements and, even more surprisingly, the blues, with a musical policy which was in perfect taste.

In order to understand the significance of this important cross-fertilization, it is necessary to take a brief look at the period of black musical history which immediately preceded the appearance of jazz in America. Will Marion Cook's Southern Syncopated Orchestra provides the perfect example, particularly as many of his musicians stayed on in Europe and made important contributions to the beginnings of European jazz.

Cook came from a middle-class black background. His childhood was spent in Washington, D.C., and it was there that he began studying the violin. He seems to have made remarkable progress and in 1892 he went to study at the Conservatoire in Berlin where his teacher was no less a master than Antonin Dvořák. Back in the States, he joined the Boston Symphony Orchestra and eventually was in line for the job of first violin. According to Arthur Briggs, who was first trumpet player with the Southern Syncopated Orchestra in 1919, Cook wasn't given the position because of his color. He left the orchestra forthwith. Briggs relates:

> From then on his attitude was: "If I can't get fame, I'd like to make money." So he started his Southern Syncopated Orchestra. . . . We played the classics – Brahms, Grieg and so on – and also quite a few of Cook's own compositions. Also, we played what we called "Plantation Melodies." We didn't play jazz, we played ragtime – numbers like "Russian Rag." The majority of the music was written down and arranged by Will Marion Cook, and he would write lip smears and glissandi into the arrangements to give them that Negro feeling. The truth is that the only improvising that was done was by Sidney Bechet, although we had a good fiddle player by the name of Shrimp Jones, and he improvised too – rather like Eddie South later.

Cook's policy seems to have been a curious mixture of musical intentions. He certainly disapproved of the highly commercial approach of Jim Europe's Tempo Club. Albert McCarthy has suggested in *Big Band Jazz* that Cook's repertoire was designed to prove that black Americans could achieve high technical standards rather than to make converts to ethnic music. At the same time, Elliot Carpenter, who worked as a pianist with Cook around 1916, recalls that although the band played the classics, they were often used as a basis for improvisation.

32

Black American troops
return home from
France, 1918.

James Reese Europe
with his band. He died
in 1919 soon after this
picture was taken.

LEFT Stungo's Jazzmaniacs at the Esplanade Assembly
Rooms in Southsea, England, 1925. Bert Marshall
is second from left.

BELOW LEFT Philippe Brun, playing cornet, with a
group of musicians which includes Danny Polo on
alto-saxophone, *c.* 1929.

BELOW Herb Flemming's band in Buenos Aires,
c. 1928. Herb Flemming is in the center front,
Cricket Smith (cornet) is behind him and Roy Butler
is in the back row, at extreme right.

RIGHT Gene Bullard (left) with Frisco Bingham the night club owner in the early 1930s.

BELOW Benny Peyton's band, *c.* 1925.

ABOVE & LEFT The Red Devils, *c.* 1924 – Elliot Carpenter, piano; Sammy Richardson, soprano-saxaphone; Opal Cooper, banjo; Roskoe Burnet, alto-saxaphone; and Creighton Thompson, drums.

Ram Ramirez in Europe
in the mid-1930s.

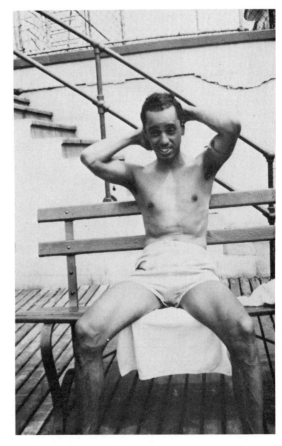

The Leon Abbey Band
– Leon Abbey (top
center), Art Lanier
(bottom right) – in the
early 1930s and BELOW
the band relaxing in
Venice.

Leo Vauchant clowning on a soprano-saxophone (extreme left) with friends in Paris, 1921.

Leo Vauchant: RIGHT at age sixteen; FAR RIGHT soon after he arrived in the United States; and BELOW as a Hollywood arranger in 1937.

Bobby Martin in Paris
in the mid-1930s:
BELOW LEFT with Louis
de Vries (left) and
LEFT at the Longchamps
races with his wife,
Thelma, Kaiser
Marshall (right) and an
unknown friend.

BELOW 1935 on the
beach at Cannes –
Benny Carter and
friends. Alex Combelle
is second from left.

A 1930s publicity shot of Pierre Allier.

ABOVE André Ekyan
(right) and his orchestra.

LEFT Unknown
saxophonist by the
celebrated French
photographer, Emile
Savitry.

André Ekyan (seated second from left) with unknown French musicians, 1928.

The White Rose's Five *c.* 1931 – André Ekyan is in the center.

The André Ekyan Band in the late 1930s.

BELOW Art Lanier in
Paris and ABOVE with
friends from the Leon
Abbey Band.

ABOVE (left to right) Noel Chiboust, Alex Combelle, Andy Lou Foster and Louis Vola.

LEFT Garnet Clarke, 1937.

LEFT Bob MacRae in Paris, 1937.

Many of the major black musicians in Paris during the early 1920s came together for this photograph – Big Boy Goudie (sixth from right), Sidney Bechet (seventh from right), Sammy Richardson (ninth from right) and Arthur Briggs (seated third from left).

"We'd take a classic—something from an opera, say—and we'd improvise around it. We didn't call it jazz then. We'd play around it, and then old man Cook would say, 'Take it!' and we'd cut loose." Even more significant was the fact that Cook also seems to have been one of the first of the older generation of "schooled" black musicians to have had a feeling for the blues. Leonard Kunstadt and Sam Charters, in their book *Jazz: A History of the New York Scene*, relate that he was one of the few "dicty" black musicians to encourage Perry Bradford in his early attempts to write and record blues songs.

There is probably a clue here to understanding the most extraordinary fact of all about Will Marion Cook's Southern Syncopated Orchestra—the inclusion in it of Sidney Bechet. On February 12, 1919, Cook's band appeared at the Orchestra Hall in Chicago. While there, he heard Bechet playing at the nearby Pekin Restaurant, and persuaded him to join him. The association lasted until June, when Bechet suddenly left to join Tim Brymn's Black Devils, who were playing at the Shelburn Hotel, Coney Island. Meanwhile, Cook had reorganized his orchestra for a grand European tour, and clearly wanted Bechet with him. According to Jean-Christophe Averti, writing in *Jazz Hot*, in May, 1969, Cook and some associates jumped Bechet on the steps of the Shelburn Hotel and virtually hijacked him aboard the ship which was to take them to England.

By the impeccably trained standards of Will Marion Cook, Bechet was musically illiterate. It was an extraordinary move to include him in an orchestra which played entirely from written scores, especially when one considers that six years later Sam Wooding rejected Bechet precisely because he could not read music.

Admittedly, it was already a well-established tradition to include a hot man in large orchestras — Johnny Dunn worked in a similar capacity for W. C. Handy, supplying wah-wah and other novelty effects when required — but Bechet was close to being a genius. He was from New Orleans, where he had been one of the stars of that supremely musical city. As Gunther Schuller has written in *Early Jazz*, Bechet could be regarded as the first really great jazz soloist:

Bechet is one of the supreme melodists in jazz. He had a natural gift for creating long melodies, developed unquestionably out of the blues in a conception much more vocal than that of any other reed player, except . . . perhaps Hodges. He dramatized the melodic content with subsidiary decorations, almost in the manner of seventeenth- and eighteenth-century techniques. But unlike many players with a bent for the decorative,

Bechet's melodic lines had an inevitability that marks the master . . . he had *in essence* a soloist's conception even before Armstrong did, at a time when the New Orleans musicians of Bechet's generation were still trying, with varying success, to preserve the New Orleans ensemble tradition.

Although several other Southern Syncopated musicians had, or were to have, jazz connections, Will Marion Cook's most important contribution to jazz history was to bring Bechet to Europe. Sidney was to spend ten of the next thirteen years away from home, a fact which kept him relatively unknown in the United States, but which laid the foundations for his triumphant return to France after the war, where he remained until he died, a rich man, in 1959.

Bands like the Southern Syncopated Orchestra seem to have been organized to attract the widest possible musical tastes. Even though Will Marion Cook had shown exceptional discernment in his choice of Sidney Bechet for his jazz soloist, jazz was just one such taste to be catered for. This kind of eclecticism was probably forced on band leaders by economic circumstances – they had to please everybody just to stay alive – but men like Cook and W. C. Handy appear to have prided themselves on their versatility. On April 13, 1919, an advertisement for Handy's band proposed a positive galaxy of talent:

> Special soloists who will appear will include . . . Will Parquette, singing "Goofer Dust" and "Death Where Is Thy Sting?"; Cricket Smith, star cornetist; Clarence Bush, with a new series of comic songs; Fred Simpson, trombone virtuoso; the Dixie Quartet, in southern folksongs and spirituals; George Hines, the comic trap drummer; Will Parick, the Alabama songster and banjo soloist; Charles Waters, singing "Mammy O' Mine" and other popular airs; William Riley, cello soloist. . . .[13]

This is further evidence that, even as late as 1920, the majority of black musicians were not jazz players. Ironically, it is what the early pioneers do *not* say when interviewed about their contributions to jazz history which provides the important clues. When W. C. Handy was interviewed by Leonard Feather, he seemed genuinely confused when pressed by Feather to define jazz: "I've played with many novelty musicians. Even in the minstrel days, we played music similar to jazz, but we didn't call it jazz."[14] Handy also claimed he "couldn't get a good clarinet player" – this at a time when Lorenzo Tio Jr., Achille Bacquet, Jimmy Noone and Sidney Bechet were all playing well.

The recollections of less well-known musicians are strikingly similar. Often these were men whose relative obscurity was the result of not being recorded rather than of lack of talent. Because they had not achieved fame they tended to work only within a limited area and their recollections therefore provide fascinating insights into the musical habits of different regions. The pattern which emerges is one of a multiplicity of local musical styles and tastes, hardly any of which were authentic jazz, but most of which had elements of something which later came to be called that. For instance, Garvin Bushell, a clarinet player who toured Europe with Sam Wooding in 1925, recalls, "There wasn't an eastern performer who could really play the blues. We later absorbed how from the New Orleans musicians we heard, but it wasn't original with us. We didn't put that quarter tone in the music the way the southern musicians did. Up north we leaned to the ragtime conception. . . ."[15] Arthur Briggs, who arrived in Europe as Will Marion Cook's first trumpet player in 1919, points out that a career as a jazz musician was unthought of in New York at that time. "Most of the guys were aiming at a straight musical career. The work was in the dance schools, where you had to read your part, so although we mostly had the feeling, it wasn't necessary to improvise. The leaders of the dance-school bands were usually fiddle players and they took choruses, but the rest of us didn't. We *never* played the blues. The dance schools were organized by the churches and they didn't like that sort of thing."

According to Gunther Schuller, the limitations imposed on violinist George Morrison were even more severe:

> Between about 1901 and 1911, when he was playing in a five-piece band formed with his brother-in-law, his repertory consisted of waltzes like "After the Ball," sentimental ballads like "Darling, I'm Growing Old" and marches like the famous "Double Eagle." Furthermore, according to Morrison, they played these "just straight" – "we couldn't improvise. We were lucky to play them straight!" When he was old enough to play in the red-light district of Denver [Colorado], the situation was more or less the same, for the finer houses did not tolerate any rough or vulgar music. Gentility was the key word, and accordingly, Dvořák's "Humoresque" or two choruses of a popular tune played on the violin, doubled on the cornet and accompanied by sentimental piano arpeggios was the typical fare.[16]

Only later, when jazz was more in demand, did Morrison enlarge his group to an eleven-piece band modeled on white bands like Art Hickman's. The repertoire by now contained jazz standards like "Ja-Da," "Royal Garden Blues" and "Dardanella," but these too were

54

played more or less straight with only Morrison improvising choruses on the violin.

Taken together, these comments suggest that, in 1920, jazz was still evolving in America as it was in Europe. This was partly because the music everywhere reflected the social and economic circumstances in which it found itself. Tastes varied from one locality to another, and the nature of the music which catered for those tastes was regulated by its precise social function. To that extent the music which formed the roots of jazz was genuinely popular music in that it reflected public taste rather than shaped it. Much of this music contained elements found in jazz, but hardly any of it could accurately be described as such. It was undoubtedly the radio and recordings which brought together these various musical elements in the kind of cultural cross-fertilization necessary for the rapid evolution of the music.

One of the first and most important of those musical elements was the blues. The blues tapped richer emotional sources than the tricky, slapstick music which at that time passed for jazz. The resulting trans-fusion did more than anything else to rescue jazz from its fate as novelty music, and to transform it into something capable of the highest emo-tional and artistic expression. The blues craze, which followed so closely on the heels of the jazz craze, almost eclipsed it in popularity. "Crazy Blues," recorded by Mamie Smith and Perry Bradford for Okey in November, 1920, sold seventy-five thousand copies in a month. Soon the market was flooded with literally hundreds of blues songs, many of them by such talented artists as Bessie Smith, Ma Rainey, Ethel Waters and Bertha "Chippie" Hill. The significance of this lay in the fact that this was black music in origin, conception and execution. The blues gave jazz depth, anchoring it to new roots which lay more in feeling than in musical technique. Here at last was something white people could not parody. From now on, the black qualities of jazz, however latent, were assured.

Just what were those black qualities and what made them so essential? The answer seems to lie in the realms of the emotions rather than in strict musicianship. The interviews already quoted provide conclusive evidence that the older generations of black musicians were "schooled" players, trained to reproduce ragtime or European music in the orthodox manner. While there is a popular idea that the early jazz players were primitives, the reverse seems to have been the case. The first twenty years of this century saw a marked deterioration in the social conditions of blacks in America, as migration to the industrial cities increased, and "Jim Crow" policies were correspondingly tightened. Standards of education declined fast and the numbers of the black middle classes decreased. This fact seems to be intimately connected to the development of jazz since the trained musicians were ragtime players, whereas the jazz and blues derived from the younger unschooled element. As early as 1910 a rift was developing in New Orleans between "Uptown" (where the poorest black sections were located) and "Downtown" music. Clarinet player Louis "Big Eye" Nelson, one of Sidney Bechet's mentors, made it clear in an interview with Alan Lomax that the crucial factor which distinguished jazz from "Downtown" music was its emotional content. "You've got to play with the heart. Picou[17] . . . he's a good enough musician, but they [the note-reading "Downtown" players] . . . don't play with the *heart*."[18]

Records and interviews suggest that although "Downtown" players like Picou and Lorenzo Tio played a kind of jazz, their music was not only technically but emotionally controlled – it was not hot. On the other hand, younger players who had not had the "benefit" of a musical education, felt free to invest their jazz with unabashed emotional zest and were less inhibited in incorporating all kinds of vocal mannerisms which would have been unthinkable for a trained musician. This theory is corroborated by Tom Bethell, who has interviewed many surviving New Orleans pioneers over the last sixteen years. He concludes, "Almost to a man, the early jazzmen received musical training and were 'note readers.' This has been definitely established in the case of Buddy Bolden, for example, who is reputed, probably correctly, to have been the leader of the first jazz band. The 'jazz' came, then, not in the liberation from slavery, but in the liberation from the European approach to music – that is, playing from a score."[19]

The blues were the purest expression of this. It was music which sprang from the poorest ranks of the black working class and was accordingly despised by middle-class, "dicty" black people. However, as tens of thousands of southern blacks poured into already overcrowded ghettoes a new proletariat was created which demanded its own folk culture. The existence of radio and records not only met that need, but broadcast the results to the nation. The result was an inevitable, but slow and, occasionally, painful process of assimilation. Nevertheless, the 1920s was the time when jazz began to grow up, and it did so to the extent that it absorbed the feeling and techniques of the blues.

Resistance was strong at the beginning. The scene, particularly in New York, was dominated by musicians with just the kind of middle-class education described above. Their backgrounds and aspirations,

56

even if they did not actively prejudice them against the blues, certainly encouraged them to ignore them. Even musicians like Fletcher Henderson, Duke Ellington and Don Redman, who were to play a crucial role in the development of jazz, had certain initial difficulties in this respect. Henderson and Redman had university degrees and Ellington's family background was equally middle class. Early recordings, particularly by Fletcher Henderson, showed little appreciation of the blues. Indeed, when Henderson's parents heard that he was to accompany Ethel Waters, they were so horrified by their son's association with a "low-down" blues singer that they insisted on screening the whole enterprise before allowing him to go on tour. Gunther Schuller relates that after they had done so, Ethel was so infuriated by Henderson's inability to accompany her properly that she insisted he listen to J. P. Johnson piano rolls until he improved.

With attitudes like these, it is easy to understand why early jazz resisted its African heritage for so long. As Garvin Bushell pointed out, the blues was an idiom which was quite alien to most northern and eastern players. It was no coincidence that the new impetus came from mid-western and south-western bands where migration had established strong links with the South. In fact, as late as 1929, a Fletcher Henderson tour of the South-West was a failure because the band's material was not sufficiently influenced by the blues. This must have been what Louis Armstrong was getting at when he wrote in his autobiography *Swing That Music*: "I think it turned out for the best that I did not go east at that time [1918]. I still had a lot to learn about jazz playing and there, in New Orleans, and on the riverboats and on Chicago's South Side, I was living and working all the time around men who could teach me what I needed."

If musicians in New York lacked the right jazz influences, the situation in Europe was correspondingly worse. Jazz has always been a rapidly evolving tradition, and the fact that there was no one to "teach" Louis Mitchell and his immediate successors explains why their music passed from novelty to anachronism without ever developing a life of its own. Almost all musicians who stayed on in Europe, or returned soon after the war, were easterners, many of them older generation players with a good deal of musical training. It was probably this, together with their middle-class backgrounds, that got them the offer of jobs in Europe in the first place. Certainly their "legitimate," often classical training, and their relatively sophisticated upbringing, was an important element in their success once they got there. According to saxophone player Joe Garland, this was what enabled Leon Abbey to fit his music to

European tastes so easily. "I would never classify him as a virtuoso on the fiddle, but Leon was a good director, he had a terrific memory, and he could play a pleasing melody. He did what he had to do to perfection, and he was a gentleman to go with it. The people over there were crazy about him because he was so soft-spoken and neat in his appearance."[20] Even though Abbey was from Chicago, all his early experience had been with J. Rosamund Johnson, a classically trained musician who would have abhorred jazz and blues as crude and vulgar.

For all these reasons the attempts to play jazz by Louis Mitchell and, to a slightly lesser extent, Sam Wooding and Noble Sissle who followed him, were more influenced by ragtime than the blues. Of the fifty-odd sides recorded by Louis Mitchell between February, 1922 and December, 1923, only a handful have blues titles. The few that are actually in the twelve-bar form sound much closer to the cakewalk style of Jim Europe's "Memphis Blues" than anything recorded by Ma Rainey or Mamie Smith. Mitchell's band was the best known and most respected in France at that time, and we must therefore assume that his relatively large output was an accurate reflection of contemporary musical styles. Considering that the journey to Europe not only cut the Jazz Kings off from new developments in the States, but from their own musical roots as well, it is remarkable that these recordings sound as good as they do.

All this brings us back to Will Marion Cook's Southern Syncopated Orchestra. Cook had arrived in England in July, 1919, just as the Original Dixieland Jazz Band were beginning to achieve their astonishing success. While the British press clamorously debated the rival interpretations of jazz, and spread tales of La Rocca's private and professional excesses, an extraordinarily perceptive review appeared in the *Revue Romande* by a young classical conductor and composer named Ernest Ansermet. He wrote, "The first thing which strikes one about the Southern Syncopated Orchestra is the astonishing perfection, the superb taste and fervor of its playing." He goes on to make almost every important point which characterizes black, as distinct from European music, pointing out that performance rather than original conception is the determining factor, and stressing the broad sonorities and individual tone which each musician cultivated. He concludes that this kind of originality flourishes only in aural, non-literate cultures, and in saying so he anticipated Marshall McLuhan by fifty years. He clearly understood the full extent of the Afro-American revolution which was about to take place. An even more remarkable fact was his grasp of the importance of the blues, at a time when even most black Americans were unaware of it. After declaring, "I am under the impression that the strongest expression of the Negro is in the blues," he ends with a glowing tribute to Sidney Bechet: "There is in the Southern Syncopated Orchestra an extraordinary clarinet virtuoso, who is, so it seems, the first of his race to have composed perfectly formed blues on the clarinet. . . . I wish to set down the name of this artist of genius, as for myself, I shall never forget it – it is Sidney Bechet."

These comments prove that Ansermet possessed a real understanding of Afro-American music, compared to which the jazz flirtations of his colleagues, Ravel, Milhaud, and Stravinsky, were merely a fashionable dilettantism. He seems to have realized that even if this music was not jazz, Will Marion Cook's orchestra demonstrated most of the contributory sources of which it is made up. They also demonstrated the extent to which the Southern Syncopated Orchestra provided elements which jazz badly needed if it was to grow. The Original Dixieland Jazz Band made a much better showing at playing jazz than any of their white contemporaries, but it had already been proved that their music lacked the rhythmic subtlety, the emotional intensity, the taste and sensitivity and, above all, the poignantly affecting statements of the blues which Will Marion Cook's orchestra provided.

☆ THE FIRST BANDS

The extent to which Will Marion Cook's music directly affected attitudes to jazz in Europe is hard to determine. But in the long run it seems that their influence, though more subtle than the Original Dixieland Jazz Band, was more lasting. The latter's music was good to the extent that it reflected the style of black bands in New Orleans. However, by the time other white jazz musicians were ready to absorb the same lessons, there were numerous recordings of black bands from which to learn, and the Original Dixieland Jazz Band had already passed into history. There was even a considerable reaction against the supposed anarchy of their music. Band leaders' attempts to reconcile jazz with the public taste for dancing ended in a compromise called "symphonic jazz." In the end, however, it was the rhythmically dynamic music of the black bands whose earthy, blues-influenced style undermined the symphonic pretensions of Paul Whiteman and others who claimed to play jazz, and created a distinction between jazz and dance music which had hardly existed at the beginning of the decade.

Accordingly, the influence of the Southern Syncopated Orchestra on the contemporary scene must be judged by its use of jazz elements rather than symphonic ones.

The most immediate and practical effect on the development of jazz came from the presence in the orchestra of musicians who would later spread what they learned all over Europe.[21] Apart from the many European musicians who heard them play, there were even some who worked with them. One of these was the trombone player Ted Heath, who himself was to play an important part in British jazz twenty-five years later. Heath acknowledges the debt he owes to Cook's musicians for teaching him many things he would have taken much longer to discover for himself:

> . . . Jenkins, the colored saxophonist who led the Roof Garden's band, introduced me to the manager of an all-colored American jazz band that was shortly to leave London for an engagement in Vienna. The Southern Syncopated Orchestra was short of both a trombonist and a trumpet player, so, in turn, I introduced my boyhood chum – Tommy Smith – to the orchestra.
>
> I don't think that the Negro band, of which we were the only two white members, would have been particularly bothered that neither Tommy nor I had much experience of jazz playing. The band was almost due to leave for Austria and musicians were not easy to find. In any case, there was no time for any kind of rehearsal, so our shortcomings were not so apparent.
>
> On the whole, they were a pretty rough crowd in that band, but I gained from the experience of working with it, even for so short a time. Until we said that we wanted to go home, the musicians were very helpful. In particular, Buddy Gilmore, the drummer, went out of his way to teach us something about the different approach and technique necessary for jazz. I came back to London with the know-how that I lacked before, and with an increase in confidence that knowledge brings.[22]

Opportunities for this kind of contact even increased as financial pressures forced the Southern Syncopated Orchestra to break up and parties of musicians went their various ways in small dance bands. By December 6, 1919, the original engagement at the Philharmonic Hall had ended, and Cook, beset by money problems, had returned to the States. In January 1920, *The Times* reported that George Latimore, the business manager, was suing a member of the Southern Syncopated Orchestra by the name of de Courville for trying to persuade other musicians to break their contracts. It appears to have already been too late. Benny Peyton's Jazz Kings, the most famous of the splinter groups from the Southern Syncopated Orchestra, had already been playing at the Embassy Club in Bond Street for a month. The group included Henry Sapiro (banjo), George Smith (violin), Pierre de Caillaux (piano), Fred Coxita (alto-sax), Sidney Bechet (soprano sax), and was led by Benny Peyton (drums).

Several others of Cook's musicians worked with British bands. Edward S. Walker, writing in *Storyville* for August–September 1972, traced the careers of some of them. His research revealed that trombone player Ellis Jackson was working with Victor Vorzanger's Broadway Band at the East Ham Palais between 1922 and 1923. He later played with Noble Sissle in Paris and London, and was with Billy Cotton from 1930 onwards. Billy Southward and Joe Caulk played drums and banjo respectively with a group called the Paramount Six at the Birmingham Palais in 1922. George Blake's brother Cyril was the trumpet player with the Happy Six at the Hammersmith Palais in 1921. Later in the same year, he led a group called the Syncopators at the Casino de Danse in Finchley Road, Hampstead. By 1933, he was playing in Dunbar's All-Colored Band at the Cossack Restaurant. Pierre de Caillaux was playing piano at the Quadrant Club in 1924. In the same year, he recorded two solos for Imperial – "Chinese Memories" and "Gigolette." The singer Bert Marshall, after joining a band in Edinburgh on drums, was found leading a group at the Esplanade Assembly Rooms in Southsea in 1925. Later on, he worked extensively in France, often as a vocalist with Django Reinhardt and Stephane Grappelly, with whom he recorded "I Saw Stars" and "I'm Confessin'" in 1934. Unfortunately, these titles, which were recorded for French Odeon, were never issued.

The list of ex-Cook personnel working on the Continent is equally impressive. The Belgian critic Robert Goffin recalls hearing Frank Withers playing with Louis Mitchell's Jazz Kings in a review at the Alhambra in Brussels in 1919. This was a group which Sidney Bechet also played with, an experience which he recalls in an interview with Charles Delaunay.

At that time, I made a little trip to Brussels because I had this holiday. And when I arrived . . . I ran into some friends who had a band. The leader was called Louis Mitchell. He was working at the Alhambra Theater with a revue. It was a revue which had Mistinguett in it, whom I like very much. At the interval, I went up and saw my friend, who said: "Sidney, do you want to sit in with us? What would you like to play?"

I said, "Yes, I'd like to play that number Mistinguett sang when they did that sort of dance which was so bad." So he told me, "That number's called 'My Man.' "[23]

This show appears to have been called *Laissez-les Tomber* and to have starred Maurice Chevalier, Rose Amy and Mistinguett.

Goffin also recalls hearing an orchestra at the Gaieté Theater in Brussels around 1921–2 which included "none other than that wonderful trumpet player Bobby Jones, who had Frank Withers with him on trombone." Goffin rated the band "superior to Mitchell's group." He remembers that they played several new numbers, including "You'll Be Surprised," "Margie," "Avalon," "Dardanella," "Chérie" and "Alice Blue Gown."[24]

Tragedy befell at least one member of the Southern Syncopated Orchestra. Jacob Patrick had joined a band formed by the Chicago drummer Hugh Pollard as trombone player. "We called him Trombonesky," recalls Arthur Briggs, who, on his return from a tour of Scandinavia in 1922, had also been asked to join the group.

> Trombonesky was a very strong boy who had been in the 368th Infantry band with Tim Brymn. We'd originally been playing for one of Mistinguette's reviews at the Alhambra. After that we moved on to Ostende. But things were not so good. The place closed. But anyway, we stayed on and finished the season on vacation. And during that time, Trombonesky went to a cabaret one evening and fell on a bunch of thugs. He asked some girl to have a drink with him – she was what you'd call a hostess. And he had some champagne and she ran up five or six bottles. In the end, he said he wouldn't pay for that number of bottles because he only ordered one. And the manager of the place happened to be the protector of that girl. And he had what you call a knuckleduster, and he almost killed the boy. Patrick was a strong man, but he almost killed him. And worse than that they then called the police, and without knowing anything about what happened, they finished him off. They whipped him on the shoulders, and when I saw him – I was called to the police station to see him – he was almost dead. He died about six months later.

Significantly, in view of his Chicago origins, Pollard seems to have been a fine drummer with a remarkably modern conception for the times. Goffin describes him as having "a subtle, unobtrusive swing and was the only one at that time to give a four to the bar beat on the bass drum." In fact, Goffin compares him favorably to the more famous Buddy Gilmore, who was leading a mixed black and white group at the same time and whom he describes as "a celebrated showman drummer, who had a big reputation, but did not match up to the driving power of Hugh Pollard."

So much for the whereabouts of some of those who had come to Europe with Will Marion Cook. But what did the bands they formed actually sound like? Unfortunately, apart from the sides recorded by Louis Mitchell for Pathé in 1922 and 1923, little recorded evidence exists. Benny Peyton's band had recorded "Tiger Rag" and "High Society" for Columbia in London in February, 1920, but even though the group included Sidney Bechet, these were not considered suitable for release and the masters have never come to light. In place of records, we are therefore forced to rely on brief and occasional eye-witness accounts. Apart from the fact that these may well have described performances which, for one reason or another, were untypical, the few who bothered to write down their impressions did so from a European point of view which did not distinguish jazz from the rest of Western music. Probably it was the very strangeness of what they heard which prompted men like Robert Goffin to report on it. But the mixture of shock and amazement with which they received these experiences is not necessarily the best basis for illuminating criticism.

In 1920, Goffin published the first critical article ever written about jazz. It appeared in *Disque Vert*, and described Louis Mitchell's Jazz Kings. "Mitchell, his handsome Creole face mobile smiling, always meticulously dressed in the latest style, as are all Negroes in Europe, a marvelous jazz drummer with a world of imagination, irradiating nervous tics which he delicately transmitted to his instruments to the amazement of the women who adored him; after Mitchell, the one who conducted the orchestra, always on his feet, exhaling nostalgia into a short cornet, old man Cricket, with his appearance of sturdy *bamboula* and an embouchure of steel, with the fine eyes of the good Negro, expressive and warm; then there was Joe (Meyers), an extraordinary banjoist whose hands fluttered without a pick over the taut strings of his instrument; a melodious saxophone player who moved his reed from side to side of his puffed-up mouth while playing (I was alluding here to Sidney Bechet, whose name I did not yet know); Parrish, an enormous pianist, who partially dismantled his piano to make it louder; a bass fiddle; and finally, Frank Withers, called the king of the trombone. . . . Oh, the first cocktail hours I spent, tucked neatly into a little corner of the bar religiously taking in the cadenced scrollwork of the Mitchells; the illumination behind me, the difficulty of setting the hiccups, the breaks and the counterpoint in order, so that a diffuse and intangible melody could seep through. . . ."[25]

The evidence of how Benny Peyton's Band sounded is even more sketchy. In October, 1920, *Dancing World* sent a reporter to interview Peyton, whose Jazz Kings were shortly to open at the Hammersmith Palais. His remarks were obviously edited and refined for the readers of *Dancing World*, but they clearly imply that his music had more to do with ragtime and novelty music than jazz: "They [the musicians], are chosen not only for ability on a certain instrument, but for versatility, which is the dominant feature of the band. . . . The Jazz Kings can entertain with tricks, stunts and so on." Evidently the style of the band dated from the pre-jazz era of James Reese Europe and Irene and Vernon Castle. At least two of Peyton's musicians worked with Europe. "Fred Coxita, our saxophone player was . . . at one time a leading member of James Reese Europe's band, probably the finest combination of jazz musicians of its time. The same applies to Mr. George Smith, our violinist, who was for some time first violinist in Europe's band. . . . He was always a great favorite with the late lamented Vernon Castle whom he accompanied on tour."

The obvious exception to this rule was Sidney Bechet. Although only twenty-three at the time, Bechet was already in a class by himself. Elliot Carpenter's Red Devils worked opposite Peyton's band at Rector's nightclub throughout most of 1920.

> Benny played for dancing, and we were the "entertaining" band. Opal Cooper, the banjo player, and Creighton Thompson, the drummer, both had wonderful singing voices. Sidney used to work with us as well as with Peyton. He used to play behind the vocals. He had the best ears of anybody I ever knew – *extra* good ears! He never needed to rehearse. His music was free. It was pure music. . . . His intellect never got in the way. . . . And Sidney had that blues influence too. It was typical of the way the boys from down south played – only better.

Bertin Salnave, who played flute with Will Marion Cook's orchestra, added another interesting testament to Bechet's genius in an interview published in *Storyville* in August, 1978:

> One day when the group was appearing at London's Kingsway Hall, Will Marion Cook's wife, Abby Mitchell, who sang with the orchestra, began performing Puccini's *Madame Butterfly*. Without saying anything to anyone, Sidney Bechet left his place and came to the front of the stage to play an obbligato on his clarinet. When the number ended, he started to return to his place to the acclaim of the audience. He knew he would have to face director's anger but Abby Mitchell rushed towards him, threw her

arms around him, and embraced him crying, "Ah, Sidney, only you could have done it like that!" Somewhat mollified, Will Marion Cook asked him, "But Sidney, why didn't you ask me?" "If I had warned you," replied Sidney, "you would never have allowed it."

In fact, it is clear that Benny Peyton did not exaggerate the general view when he concluded in his interview for *Dancing World*: "Bechet is regarded by many who are competent to judge as the most original, and possibly the greatest of known clarinet players (at least for dance music) in the world."

Robert Goffin does not seem to have heard the Benny Peyton band, but he makes some interesting comments about the orchestra led by Hugh Pollard, Bobby and Buddy Gilmore. He describes Pollard as the best drummer at that time. In addition, he notes that Arthur Briggs was the first black American he heard play the trumpet, rather than the more popular cornet. "He represented the very best of trans-atlantic jazz; he was gifted with a dazzling technique, he had great powers of expression when he improvised, and his authority gave the orchestra its typical swing long before the word existed. Briggs was one of the most notable American pioneers who taught jazz to the old world." He also records that the repertoire included numbers like "Stumbling," "Sweetheart," "Young Man's Fancy," "Montmartre Rose," "Red Head Gal," "Dapper Dan" and "Sunny Jack."

Buddy Gilmore's band does not seem to have impressed him much, and he rates Pollard a far superior drummer. But he is full of praise for Bobby Jones's band, which included Frank Mitchell on trombone before he joined Louis Mitchell. He wrote in *Aux Frontières du Jazz*:

> I can clearly remember the cellar of the Gaieté where the group played. Bobby Jones sometimes sang accompanied by a banjo player with a coal black face whose specialty was to launch into scat singing while agitating his adam's apple with his left hand, to the great delight of the audience. This unusual practice gave his voice a strange vibrato. As for Bobby Jones, he was an improviser who expressed himself equally well on cornet or alto saxophone at a period when the tenor had not yet become fashionable. . . . The curious thing is that this remarkable man, who would certainly have been recognized as a great musician in America, elected to remain in Europe from the time of his arrival there.

Twenty-five years later, in his *Histoire du Jazz*, Goffin attempted to give a rather more analytical appraisal of Louis Mitchell's band.

To get a vague idea of it, perhaps it is necessary to go back to the recordings of the Original Dixieland Jazz Band, although Mitchell's technique was less strident and more swinging. The ensembles showed a greater intermingling of the different instruments which recall the first records which King Oliver made for Gennett. Naturally, though, the drums played two beats to the bar, while Mitchell's two hands lost themselves in a sorcery of percussion. The banjo followed the melody rather than the rhythm. Sidney Bechet was already improvising solos which broke free of the jerkiness of the orchestra. Frank Withers who, if I am not mistaken, followed Bechet, was a great musician who played his trombone rather like George Brunis.

Listening to the band's Pathé recordings, it is difficult to agree with the comparison with King Oliver. Nevertheless, one can get some idea of what he was driving at. The Jazz Kings certainly had none of the strident quality of the Original Dixieland Jazz Band, and very seldom played at the same ferocious tempos. The rhythm is not exclusively binary, but varies between two and four beats to the bar according to the number played. The banjo player, Walter Kildare, obviously dates from the days of the Tempo Club, when the banjo was a lead rather than a rhythm instrument, and his tendency to trill against the melody sacrifices a lot of the group's momentum. Mitchell's version of "Now and Then," recorded in February, 1922, has the sad sweetness of ragtime, whose lovely but slightly ailing quality reminds one of a consumptive child who, though beautiful today, will die tomorrow. It is easy to see what Goffin means when he talks about Cricket Smith "exhaling nostalgia through his short cornet." The tune is in thirty-two bar form, and Smith leads throughout. There is none of the kind of exciting polyphony for which the King Oliver band was famous. Instead, the opening chorus has more of the feeling of a Bavarian village band. This impression is strengthened by the disastrous presence of James Shaw on tenor saxophone whose doubling of the trombone part almost completely obscures it and gives the music a cloying sweetness. When Cricket Smith tries to cut loose in the last chorus, his efforts resemble those of a fly trying to take off from a sea of treacle.

Even so, there are some fine moments. Frank Withers is a good trombone player whose nicely judged three against four figures in the second chorus provide a few seconds of genuine excitement, and Cricket Smith's last sixteen bars are a brave attempt to give some spice to the saccharine confections of James Shaw. Since Goffin evidently heard the band with Sidney Bechet in place of Shaw, it is obvious that their music must have sounded much better.

Turning to King Oliver's recordings of "Froggie More,"[26] is like passing from twilight into a bright new dawn. From the start the ascending parallel sevenths with which the piece opens have a radiant, vigorous quality which characterizes the whole number. This music is too exciting to sound nostalgic. The four voices (one more than Mitchell) of clarinet, two cornets and trombone weave intricate patterns which miraculously never clash. Oliver and Louis Armstrong maintain a lead of blistering heat, while Johnny Dodds, the mighty flea of the clarinet, dances indefatigably around them, and Honory Dutry smoothly lays down the harmonic basis for the melody. The way they manage the key change from B♭ to E♭ which introduces Armstrong's solo is masterly.

The meter is solidly four to the bar throughout, each beat snugly cushioned against the next, and the band swings accordingly. When the musicians cut loose on the first test of the Richmond session, the sound was so powerful it threatened to smash the equipment. Recording could only continue when Armstrong and Oliver backed off twenty feet from the recording horn. Even so, their warmth and intensity far exceeds anything previously recorded. Unlike the white trumpet players of the day, even the best of whom had a slightly quavering sound, Oliver's and Armstrong's vibrato seem to inhabit the music, giving each note a living, breathing quality which is infinitely expressive. Clarinetist Fess Williams remembers going to Richmond to hear Oliver make those first recordings: "I distinctly remember him telling me: 'Williams, I ain't going to give these white boys my best stuff – you'd better believe it!' "[27] One wonders what it would have been like if he had!

THE SENSATIONAL SUCCESS of the Original Dixieland Jazz Band in England between April, 1919 and July, 1920 created opportunities for other white Dixieland musicians, many of whom made an important contribution to the spread of jazz abroad. Among the first to arrive were Art Hickman's band, who recorded several numbers around that time for HMV. They were followed in 1921 by the Southern Rag-a-Jazz Band, a college group from South Carolina. Later still, a band called the Original Capitol Orchestra arrived and recorded for Zonophone, a subsidiary of HMV. We also know from Robert Goffin that an orchestra called the Georgians, led by Paul Specht's trumpet player, Frank Guarante, played at Lyons Corner House in London and later at Claridges in Paris in 1923. He also refers flatteringly to The Lido-Venice Band led by drummer Harold Smith.

As we've already seen, white bands like the Original Dixieland Jazz

67

Band initially found it easier to record in Europe than black players. This fact is best illustrated by the career of the great New Orleans clarinet player, Sidney Bechet. Perhaps Bechet could never have been the powerful influence which his great gifts warranted. His style was too personal, too emotionally intense, to be popular even in America, let alone in Europe where such outpourings of what is now called "soul" were not merely misunderstood but suspect. Nevertheless, he was undoubtedly the greatest jazz musician to work in Europe until the arrival of Louis Armstrong in 1932. Despite this, he left almost no trace of his ten-year stay there. His only recordings were two unissued takes with Benny Peyton on Columbia in 1920, and no white musician of the time seems to have heard him. Indeed, many only heard him years later when his rediscovery was part of the general revival movement of the late thirties. This neglect says something about the low level of understanding and appreciation of jazz in Europe at this time, and is a striking example of the extent to which white musicians were given opportunities to record before black ones.

It is worth paying some attention to Bechet's improvisational style before moving on to study the records made at the same time by white players. We can tell from comments made by such perceptive observers as Ernest Ansermet, by other black musicians who worked with him, and from listening to a remarkable set of recordings made with Clarence Williams in New York in 1923 and 1924, that Bechet's style was more or less formed by the early 1920s. Certainly there can have been no new formative influences after his arrival in London with Will Marion Cook.

The faultless assurance with which Bechet states his ideas in the Clarence Williams recordings indicates a man who knows his own musical mind to perfection. Out of sixteen sides, six are made with Thomas Morris on cornet, and the remainder are with Louis Armstrong. In many ways, the first six sides made with Morris are the most interesting. It is as if the extremely simple, almost uninspiring lead which the cornet gives leaves Sidney with the kind of room for maneuver he likes. He completely dominates these performances, and, in some instances, he lays a soprano saxophone statement of melody on top of Morris' cornet which is so strong as to drown him altogether. With Louis Armstrong, whose musical personality was at least equal to Bechet's, and who was starting to do many of the same things on the cornet his colleague was doing on the clarinet, this would have been disastrous. It is therefore no coincidence that when he is playing with Armstrong, Bechet tends to phrase much more on the beat and to restrict himself to a more supporting role.

68

Of the six records made with Thomas Morris, the two most interesting are "New Orleans Hop Scop Blues" and a rather sentimental tune written by James P. Johnson called "Old-Fashioned Love." In the first of these two, Morris states a simple theme and adheres to it throughout, except in his solo, where he attempts, rather unsuccessfully, to copy Bechet. Meanwhile, Sidney swoops and slurs above him, heavily emphasizing the flattened third of the scale and playing around the fact that this note is interchangeable with the seventh of the subdominant chord. It is a classic statement of the blues which, in the last chorus, surpasses itself and becomes a pointer towards the future. While the cornet and trombone lay down a simple riff based on the key note of B♭, Bechet uses the same harmonic idea he has developed throughout the number but in a way which completely breaks up the beat without ever losing the time.

This example has been taken from Gunther Schuller's excellent book *Early Jazz*. It is a brave attempt to notate what Bechet is doing, but one which is only an approximation of the extraordinary freedom of his timing. Listening to the record, it is quite clear that in some obscurely atavistic way he is doing for a few moments exactly what an African master drummer does when he sets up a certain rhythmic pattern and then departs as far from it as possible without ever losing the original idea. As jazz evolved, it gradually adopted this concept, consciously or not, and developed it. To this extent, Sidney Bechet was already anticipating in 1922 something which Charlie Parker elaborated to such an extraordinary degree twenty years later.

The same facility appears in "Old-Fashioned Love," where Bechet also shows an astonishing physical dexterity on the saxophone with which the stiff slap-tongue playing of Coleman Hawkins seems ludicrous by comparison.

As Gunther Schuller describes it: "The example shows Bechet's characteristic addiction to decorative, almost roccoco, contours stated in free rhythms seemingly disassociated from the beat. Even his on the beat playing seems unconstrained, seems to float above the beat and only occasionally to coincide with it; it is the quintessence of melodic blues."[28]

Recordings made by white bands at this time make very sad listening by comparison with this. One of the earliest examples was Billy Arnold's version of "Stop It" recorded on December 13, 1922 for Columbia. It is obviously an attempt to copy the Original Dixieland Jazz Band, but with none of their dash and flair. The rhythm section of piano and drums has all the retarded momentum of a Model-T Ford being driven with the handbrake on. The sound of the front line is clogged by an alto saxophone which attempts, very inaccurately, to provide a harmony part for the cornet player, who has a tendency to play flat every time he goes above middle C. The clarinet's tuning is even more disastrous, and his skirling phrases against the melody line must be one of the most unmusical efforts ever put on record. Only the trombone player makes a reasonable showing, but even he can do nothing to impart some swing to the corny staccato lead and the tuneless twittering of the clarinet. The personnel for this recording was Charles Kleiner (trumpet), Billy Trittel (trombone), Harry Arnold (soprano sax and clarinet), Harry Johnson (alto sax), and Chris Lee (drums).[29]

To be fair, it should be pointed out that when three years later Billy Arnold recorded his version of "Louisville Lou"[30] it was much better than "Stop It." The band is in tune, and the addition of a banjo does a lot to correct the fluttering beat of the earlier record. Even so, the opening chorus where the soprano saxophone and cornet double the lead still sounds corny even by the not very advanced standards of the day, and the trombone player does not seem to have a very clear idea of his role. He improves in the second sixteen-bar strain, where he plays what is presumably a written lead. The cornet then takes over in the restatement of the original theme, and does so with a fair degree of drive and a good tone. The saxophone player dominates the final chorus and manages some well-timed breaks. However, the homophonic arrangement of the piece is generally a long way from the excitement of even the more old-fashioned black bands of the time.

All this is important in view of the fact that it was Billy Arnold, not Sidney Bechet, who was attracting attention in both Europe and America as an exponent of jazz. Jean Wiener was a young concert pianist who, by 1920, had established a reputation as a performer of music by all the most modern composers. He recalls:

I was a young classical piano player who was fascinated by the music of "Les Six" – Auric, Milhaud and the rest. I also knew Eric Satie and Stravinsky. . . . Anyway, for several years I gave concerts which were the first to feature this music – also Bartok's music and Prokofiev's. I was in on the beginning of Diaghilev. But what interested me most was jazz. Not the fact that a piece was called "I Love You, You Love Me," but the influence of jazz on the music of Milhaud, Stravinsky, etc. So the only important thing I could do in music was to get jazz introduced into serious music circles, and I think I had a certain success. For example, the first time I did it was with a band called Billy Arnold's Band. They were in Paris playing in a dance hall on one of the grand boulevardes. Somebody told me about it and said, "You simply must go and hear these people – it's extraordinary." They were five or six Americans. So I went to hear them and I was amazed because I had only heard records, and these people were not only musicians, they were clowns and acrobats. They slid down banisters while singing songs and so on.

At that time, I gave concerts which were very well attended by the snobbish intellectual set. So I asked this band if they wanted to come and play at one of my concerts. They didn't properly understand at first, and asked if they should come wearing all their funny hats and such like. So I told them, "No, come in evening dress and play for about twenty minutes." They were to appear in the middle of a concert of music by Stravinsky, Milhaud and a Bach concerto. And they played five or six numbers in the middle of this. . . . And what was interesting about this concert, which was held in the Salle des Agriculteurs, was that you had all the musicians who were then in Paris. You had Ravel, you had Albert Roussel. These were the two great living musicians at that time. . . . And when they started to play jazz – the room was absolutely crowded – Albert Roussel got up and ostentatiously stalked out slamming the door behind him. Ravel, on the other hand, came up at the end and said, "How right you were to put that on. It was marvelous." That was typical of the difference between the two men.

Admittedly, there were better white bands than Billy Arnold's. One was a group sent over from America by band leader Art Hickman. Hickman did not come himself but the five-piece band which arrived under his name seems to have been a good one. Billed as Art Hickman's New York London Five, they recorded several titles for HMV. The 1921 version of "I Wonder Where My Sweet Daddy's Gone" suggests that this was an attempt to recreate the success of the Original Dixieland Jazz Band – and a fairly creditable one at that. Although the band lacked the fierce attack of Nick La Rocca's group, as a whole they were able to phrase around the beat rather than squarely on it, and the individual musicians were technically accomplished and well attuned. The line-up of cornet, alto saxophone and trombone seems to be arranged throughout, but each voice had its recognizable part to play. The number, which is in the standard form of alternating sixteen-bar strains inherited from ragtime, is arranged for a number of instrumental breaks. Unfortunately, even though these seem to have been worked out beforehand, both alto and trombone manage to lose the time occasionally. The orchestra maintained a lingering influence on European dance music in the person of sax player Jack Howard, who stayed on there and led a number of successful dance bands in the twenties and thirties.

By 1924 we are reaching the stage where personal reminiscences can be positively verified by recordings. One of the most interesting examples is the Original Capitol Recording Orchestra, who also recorded in London, this time for Zonophone. Despite their little-known personnel, it is worthwhile comparing their recording of "Tiger Rag," made in February, 1924, with Bix Beiderbecke's version with the Wolverines of June the same year. Both are taken at the same tempo and are in the same key. Surprisingly, the Original Capitol Orchestra's version is in some ways superior. Their phrasing is tighter than the Wolverines', whose irritating habit of phrasing everything in dotted quaver patterns is both untidy and monotonous. The Wolverines' decision to use an alto saxophone instead of a trombone – on this of all numbers – was a mistake rubbed even further in by an impeccable trombone performance on the Capitol version. Again, their clarinet player, Tracy Momma, has a warm liquid tone which recalls Leon Rappollo, and is a delightful contrast to the thin, slightly querulous sound of Jimmy Hartwell with the Wolverines. Finally, whereas Beiderbecke phrases consistently on the beat, Vic Sells, particularly on the introductory bars, plays a cornet lead which has a casual fluency surpassing Bix's, and which, at times, even stresses the second beat in the bar – an unusually daring device for a white musician in 1924.

It seems that these musicians had been inspired by hearing the New Orleans bands on the Mississippi riverboats which came up to Davenport, Iowa, a fact which explains why they so unhesitatingly knew what they were about. In fact, they were old musical colleagues of Bix and the other members of the Wolverines. According to Brian Rust, there is a story that Beiderbecke once worked with the Original Capitol Recording Orchestra, but was replaced by Vic Sells over a dispute about his union card. It is interesting to speculate that Bix might have come to Europe. Had he done so, he would not have formed the Wolverines who, ironically, cut their first records on February 18, 1924, almost the very day that the Capitol Orchestra made this version of "Tiger Rag" at Hayes in Middlesex.

By an extraordinary coincidence, in 1924, Leo Vauchant was playing cello in a tango band opposite a Dixieland group who had recently arrived in Paris, calling themselves the Chicago Hot Spots. Shortly after opening, the Hot Spots trombone player returned to America, and the band asked Leo if he could find them a replacement. Hiring a "dep" for the tango band, he joined them himself. The Chicago Hot Spots were none other than the old Capitol Orchestra with two new additions – Vance Pybrock on alto saxophone in place of George Byron Webb, and Freddy Flick on banjo instead of Les Russick. Vauchant recalls:

> It was a band that used to play on the Mississippi riverboats. It was real Dixieland, but good. The Americans were in quite a different league to the French, and everybody learned from them. They probably played more jazz – more solos – than anybody else around at that time. There was a man called Frank Guarante who had a band called the Georgians, and they were good too, but it was more ensemble playing than solos. With the Georgians it was mainly the sound that was different – the tone and the vibrato. But those Chicago Hot Spots were good. They had numbers like "Sensation Rag," "Panama," and tunes that were known in that style. Actually they played them wrong. They should have harmonized them from the chords. But instead they moved up and down a third away from the melody – atrocious! But that's the way they played them you know. Anyway, the solos were the hottest thing in town.

The Georgians were another influential white band at that time. The leader, Frank Guarante, was from New Orleans, and according to Harold Smith, drummer with the Lido-Venice Band, he had influenced Bix Beiderbecke. Guarante's fine tone and excellent technique made him New Orleans's top white cornetist. It seems he was a friend and admirer of such great black trumpet players as Freddie Keppard and King Oliver, and it is obvious from their records that the Georgians were trying to copy Oliver's style of collective improvisation. There are times when the band rides into the closing ensembles of a number in a way which captures something of the balanced, integrated polyphony of King Oliver's Creole Band.[31] This multi-faceted texture is the particular beauty of New Orleans music, and it is interesting that Guarante's musicians restrained their considerable technique in order to preserve this and, like Oliver's band, confined their solo contributions to instrumental breaks. The only time these 1922–3 recordings come unstuck is when Johnny O'Donnell plays alto instead of clarinet. On the latter, he at times sounds uncannily like Johnny Dodds, but his saxophone playing has a fatal tendency to double the lead and so confuse the overall polyphonic effect.

Sadly, Guarante's New Orleans influences seem to have faded as the band stayed on in Europe. Robert Goffin noted that "the band was so successful . . . that they remained here long enough to lose all contact with America." According to Goffin, the band's personnel included "many front-rank musicians such as Russ Morgan and Buck Weaver, whose trombone solo on 'Doodle Doo Doo' in 1923 pointed the way for those that followed . . . Joe Murray was an excellent pianist . . . the banjo player was Freddy Flick, a player of extraordinary ability. . . ." He concludes: "Guarante's conception of jazz was actually very close to that of the great band leaders of today, such as Benny Goodman and Glenn Miller, and the Georgians had a sense of swing which far outdistanced the white bands of the pre-1923 era."

The last important small white jazz band was a group called the Lido-Venice Band. The orchestra included Henry Nathan (trumpet), Bill Haids (piano), Davie Davidson (banjo and clarinet), Freddie Morrow (alto-sax) and Barney Russell (trombone). The band was led by Harold Smith, the drummer. Goffin writes:

The orchestra played only hot; a crisp lyricism gripped them all as acrobatic solos succeeded sinuous ensembles. They were individual to such an extent that after one of them had played a particularly fine break, the musicians all laughed and applauded, or else made the very American gesture of striking the right fist into the left palm.

The Lido-Venice boys improvised to such an extent that we were sometimes surprised to find that we failed to recognize a number which we ourselves played.[32] The strange perfume of their playing still haunts me after all these years. I still remember "Southern Roses," "Yes Sir," "I'm Going South," "Please Don't Shimmey While I'm Gone," "Some of These Days," "Hard-Hearted Hanna," and especially "Somebody Stole My Girl," which Barney used to sing in his nasal, froggy voice, that old

74

and very American tune which had such incomparable success with all the bands. . . . Jazz critics who never heard this band have really missed something, for I place it in the first rank of bands which relied on pure improvisation. . . . It is strange that none of these musicians acquired fame. . . . Circumstances were against them. When they arrived in Europe, there were only a few of us who understood their message. Each afternoon, this faithful handful stuck to their posts, entranced from the first note to the last. Judging from the comparative impression that I felt these were the most immortal moments I ever spent.

After their short stay in Brussels, the Lido-Venice Band moved on to Berlin, and then to the Four Hundred Club in the Rue Daunou in Paris, where I heard them for the last time. At this time [1925], when all the dance halls in Brussels were demanding hot orchestras, the Paris market wished only melodic jazz. After only a few days, the Lido-Venice was replaced by Sleepy Hall's orchestra which had, on saxophone, Rudy Vallee. . . .

It is hard to assess the extent to which Europeans in 1925 had absorbed elements of jazz presented by such American bands. Only a small number of Europeans recorded before the mid-twenties. Many of those records are hard to find today and may well not represent the best available talent. However, some indication is given by records made in Paris by the pianist Tom Waltham between 1925 and 1928. Waltham was an Englishman who had picked up ragtime piano from American soldiers during the war. According to Leo Vauchant, who knew him well, Waltham's piano playing combined unusual rhythmic drive with a good harmonic sense. Unfortunately, the few recordings which survive give little indication of this. To take a few random examples, "C'est Bouche à Bouche," recorded in October, 1925, has almost nothing to recommend it. The trumpet player makes a feeble attempt to play a hot "wah-wah" chorus and the bass saxophone solo, which follows it, gives an appalling rendering of the tune which is both stiff and inaccurate. The piece completely fails to swing as none of the musicians can play four even beats to a bar. Instead this two-beat rendering gives a stiff, corny feel to what is a very uninspiring tune in the first place, and is quite at variance with the spirit of jazz. In "Charleston Dolly" and "Raymonde," recorded in 1926, we are spared the disastrous solos of the earlier number, but the rhythmic feel is still absurdly tight and jerky. This fact is aggravated on "Raymonde" by a tempo which is clearly too fast for the musicians to handle.

Two years later, Tom Waltham's Ad Libs recorded "Tipsy" and

"Sweetie." The same problems persist with "Tipsy," which is not only over-arranged but stiff and dated. "Sweetie," on the other hand, is much better. The band has more precision and a looser feel. However, the revelation is Waltham himself. His piano playing is in marked contrast to everything we have heard before. It swings along, solidly based on four even beats to the bar, and is well supported by a firm and accurate left hand which reveals influences of a stride style perhaps acquired from listening to early records by Fats Waller.

Perhaps it was inevitable that, as jazz developed from a gimmick into real music, it would decline in popular appeal. Even so, it is ironic that hardly had jazz established itself as the dominant new force behind European popular music than interest in the real thing waned to the point where it was just short of being a musical fringe benefit supported by a handful of musicians, critics and intellectuals.

Up until 1923, jazz had constituted a veritable musical revolution. Inevitably though, as is the way with revolutions, this soon reached a state of compromise. The young in America were more interested in expressing their personal emotional needs than in discovering a new music. It was one thing to look to the subculture for something fresh and vital, but it was quite another to take to the music of King Oliver, even if the racial situation had permitted them to hear it. As the novelty of the corny effects and furious tempos of the first Dixieland bands wore off, it became increasingly likely that there would be a trend towards presenting the music in a more palatable form. This would probably have happened anyway as more and more trained musicians took over from the musical anarchists who had started it all,[33] and adapted jazz to their own techniques and training. It was the peculiar talents and character of Paul Whiteman which rendered that probability a certainty.

Whiteman first heard jazz somewhere around San Francisco in about 1915, a fact which he records in his autobiography *Jazz*. "We first met – jazz and I – in a dance hall dive on the Barbary Coast. It screeched and bellowed at me from a trick platform in the middle of a smoke-hazed, beer-fumed room. And it hit me hard. Raucous? Yes. Crude? – undoubtedly. Unmusical? – sure as you live. But rhythmic, catching as the smallpox and spirit-lifting." Whiteman's first record was made as a test in 1920. It was a version of "Wang Wang Blues" and sounds much like all those other post-Original Dixieland Jazz Band emulations, though not, of course, nearly so good. His next efforts, "Whispering" and "Japanese Sandman," seem to be more influenced by ragtime and have lost all traces of the Original Dixieland Jazz Band. Recordings of "Any Time, Any Place," recorded in 1920, and "My Man" and "Hot

Lips" recorded in 1921 and 1922 respectively, show a different style again, and display some of the first attempts at big band section work. Whiteman's contribution to the European scene was made by two trips, the first to London in March, 1923, where the band appeared in the revue *Brighter London* at the Hippodrome, and also played for the social set at the Grafton Galleries, and the second in 1926, when he again visited London and subsequently Paris, Berlin and Vienna.

Besides being a musician, Whiteman was a brilliant publicist with a rare talent for understanding his audience. His music perfectly captured the dancing mood of the time and the extent to which jazz should be allowed to cater for it. "In America, jazz is at once a revolt and a release," he wrote. "Through it, we get back to a simple, to a savage if you like, joy in being alive. While we are dancing or singing, or even listening to jazz, all the artificial restraints are gone and we are rhythmic, we are emotional, we are natural."[34] At the same time, Whiteman sensed the dilemma of young people who found syncopated music irresistible to dance to, but felt embarrassed by the middle-class tirades against the new "sinful" music which were published in magazines across the country in 1921 and 1922. As Robert Goffin remarked, "Paul Whiteman was the first to find a compromise between real jazz and the prejudices of a bourgeois public, which could not swallow certain of the novelties of syncopated music." Whiteman's symphonic adaptations cleverly reconciled the appeal of jazz with smoother, more danceable orchestrations. When the band opened at Broadway's Palais Royal on October 1, 1920, the *New York Clipper* commented: "Such an attraction have he and his orchestra become, that the owners have found that the place is nightly filled to capacity without the big three thousand dollar a week revue which ran last year. The only attraction at the place besides Whiteman's orchestra is the dancing of Hyson and Dickson.

. . . Whiteman and his orchestra of nine are receiving 2,500 dollars weekly, the record price for such an organization. In addition to playing the Palais Royal, Whiteman is making phonograph records."

As a result, everybody's face was saved. Jazz was beginning to become intellectually as well as socially fashionable. Helen Lowry of the *New York Times* explained triumphantly that jazz "now is arranged and written as for a symphony orchestra, save for the God-given trick of being a master of syncopation. . . ."

Europe in general and France in particular received Paul Whiteman's music as faithfully as they had accepted Dixieland. The unmistakably American style in a European symphonic setting allowed people to match their traditional tastes to a desire for novelty as never before. For the rest of the twenties, "sweet," rather than "hot," was the watchword of European jazz, which, for geographical reasons, was even further removed from the creative sources of the music than white America. But even though it is fashionable to condemn Whiteman's symphonic ambitions as either pretentious, or a cynical manipulation of the public's latent snobbery, it is only fair to point out that his insistence on very high musical standards was an example which all shades of musical taste soon followed. At least some of the most important characteristics of jazz reached the level necessary for their expression, and the development of big band section work was also probably helped by the pioneering efforts of arrangers like Ferdinand Grofe, Bill Challis and Lennie Hayton who worked for him.

THEATER AND DANCE

2

ANY OF THE MOST CREATIVE PERIODS in music were those in which it was a genuinely popular expression rather than something designed for a cultural elite. The music which today we call serious, for instance, was born in the Italian popular theater of the seventeenth century. It would be unnecessary to stress this but for the complete failure of serious modern music to communicate with ordinary people. Instead, the philosophical abstractions which obsess modern composers – and the new wave of jazz players too – encourage them to retire from the world to colleges and universities. There they write music to impress their colleagues rather than to stimulate the public, of whose intelligence and perception they have long since despaired. One result of this is that the use of serious music in the theater has never been more unsatisfactory than it is today. Opera has degenerated into a grotesque nineteenth-century relic, whose irrelevance is emphasized by the outrageous prices demanded for admission. Even in the popular field, the rock operas of Tim Rice and Andrew Lloyd Webber and others are pleasant enough, but they do not compare with the work of Cole Porter, Harold Arlen and George Gershwin. Admittedly, in this television age, theater itself has ceased to be popular entertainment. But this is one more indication that there has never been a wider gap between art and entertainment than now.

Jazz was one of the last expressions of music which was both popular and artistic at the same time. The purpose of this chapter is to examine the ways in which jazz was encouraged in its early days by popular theater. I want to suggest that its artistic development was helped, not hindered, by the very popular nature of that theater, and that it was this which kept it clear of the intellectual pretension which has such damaging results in more culturally introspective societies.

From the early years of this century a network of theater chains covered the black neighborhoods of the United States. Some were well organized, like the famous Keith circuit, or the notorious T.O.B.A. But in addition, there were innumerable small touring companies, as well as carnivals, circuses and minstrel shows. All of these used black musicians.

80

This situation persisted well into the thirties, and it is therefore not surprising that jazzmen of the twenties, like the seventeenth-century Italian musicians, didn't waste their time making fine distinctions between art and entertainment. Those with elitist notions suffered for them. Scott Joplin died penniless and broken-hearted at this failure to make ragtime worthy of serious consideration at the very moment Jim Europe was making a big name and even bigger fortune adapting ragtime to the needs of the dance-crazed American public.

The sudden vogue for all-black theater shows on Broadway, following the success of *Shuffle Along* in 1921, made the theater an even more important center of activity for jazz musicians. Men like Fats Waller, who wrote the music for *Hot Chocolates* among other shows, and J. P. Johnson, who wrote *Running Wild*, thought of themselves as composers for the theater as well as jazz piano players. Others, even if they did not write for the theater, spent a great deal of time working in it. Almost every major jazz orchestra of the 1920s played for theater shows whenever they were not touring the dance halls. It is often said, I think incorrectly, that Louis Armstrong left Fletcher Henderson in 1925 in order to escape the restrictions of a large commercial orchestra. While it is certainly true that Chicago was a more stimulating musical environment for a New Orleans musician like Louis, it does not explain why he immediately joined Erskine Tate's large theater orchestra, whose repertoire ranged from hot specialties to symphonic overtures. Besides his normal musical duties, Louis was expected to appear on stage dressed as the Reverend Satchelmouth, preaching a cod sermon. No one ever heard him, or Sidney Bechet, who also appeared on stage in shows like *How Come* in 1923 and the *Revue Negre* in 1925, complain that such things were unworthy of them as jazz musicians. It is critics, rather than musicians, who have attempted to drive a wedge between jazz and other commercial music. This was a distinction which the early jazz players simply did not understand. It is ridiculous to suggest that jazzmen forsook their art at such times because that assumes they would have had to abandon principles they never held in the first place.

At least one contract for a trip to Europe was secured because of the theatrical element – perhaps even as a result of Louis' success as the Reverend Satchelmouth. Writing in *Jersey Jazz* in May, 1974, piano player Claude Hopkins describes how his band got the job accompanying the *Revue Negre*, which starred Josephine Baker. The show was being financed and promoted by a Mrs. Caroline Dudley Reagan. One night, she called by the Smile-a-While cafe in Ashbury Park near Atlantic City to hear the Hopkins band. Hopkins recalls:

81

When I learned that she was there I put up several novelty numbers that we used. One was a tuba solo on "Oh Katarina," and another was a piano specialty on a number called "Prince of Wales." But our pet was a number which lasted ten or fifteen minutes – "The St. Louis Blues." It was that which clinched us the European tour, so I'll explain the routine.

Our trumpet player, Henry Goodwin, dressed up in an old frock coat, put on a pair of horn-rimmed glasses, and then he was ready to start preaching in the fashion of an old Baptist preacher. It was all done to music. The trombonist, Daniel Doy, and alto sax man Joe Hayman, would imitate the sisters getting happy and shouting as they do in some of the Holy Rollers' Baptist churches. The bass player, representing the deacon of the church, would move in and out of the audience with his battered upright tuba, and money would drop in the bell, simulating the collection plate. The drummer and I kept up the theme of "The St. Louis Blues" throughout the entire number. The act put the audience in stitches, and Mrs. Reagan, who, I found out later, was a very stern woman, was almost hysterical. Watching her, I knew our chances were very good.

The *Revue Negre* seems to have been a small-time show with an almost unknown cast. Claude Hopkins remembers that Ethel Waters was to have been the star, but the promoters could not afford her fee. Eventually, Ada Ward was selected to replace her. The choice had one unusual and important consequence for the history of show business. According to the nightclub owner Bricktop, Ada Ward was a drinker and inclined to be unreliable. In order to balance this risk, Mrs. Reagan also hired the unknown Josephine Baker on the recommendation of Spencer Williams, who had been impressed by Josephine's comic performance in *Shuffle Along*. Others in the show were the novelty dance team of Mutt and Jeff, an acrobatic dancer named Tommy Weeds, the blues singer Maude de Forest, "native dancer" Joe Alex, and a producer known as "Honey Boy." There was just enough plot to link the various songs, comedy routines and dancing acts which were the essential ingredients of the newly fashionable all-black Broadway shows. As usual, the band which accompanied the show contained first-class jazz talent. At the last minute, the great Sidney Bechet was added to the other front-line instruments already mentioned and the rhythm section comprising Claude Hopkins on piano, Ernest "Bass" Hill on tuba and string bass and Percy Johnson on drums, was also exceptionally fine.

The *Revue Negre* opened at the Théâtre des Champs Elysées in Paris in the fall of 1925. It was only a moderate success. Even when the show moved to a smaller theater, it failed to catch on. Several of the cast

82

began to leave as opportunities to return to the United States arose. Nevertheless, for Josephine Baker at least, the situation was saved by the fact that the French, long before anyone else, had already discovered that black is beautiful. Henri Varna, director of the Folies Bergères, was interested in the exotic possibilities of a black act in his show. Auditions were held. Although Varna does not seem to have been very impressed with the endless tap dancing, he realized the potential of the leading lady. Under his direction Josephine Baker became one of the most sensational successes of the Folies and, ultimately, an international celebrity.

Almost at once, Josephine's career ceased to have anything to do with jazz. Admittedly, the Folies Bergères' orchestra was already modeled on Paul Whiteman lines, and a black jazz band played in the front lobby between acts. But the fact that Josephine did her steps to jazz numbers, swinging her sensational naked brown body to blue music, was incidental. Her father's career as a drummer with New Orleans bands working the riverboats around St. Louis, and her own early days touring America with Bessie Smith were forgotten. Instead, she had achieved the unattainable for a black performer – she was glamorous, she was chic, she was a center of attention in a white world. The black varnish of her personality set a special gloss on the French love of the primitive and exotic. With her as its new star, the Folies Bergères was transformed into a kind of glittering safari into darkest America.

Josephine was perfectly cast for the part. She had never been a great singer, and her dancing had always relied more on comedy than rhythm. But, as her fellow artiste Jimmy Daniels remarked, she had even more important qualities than these.

> She had balls! She was born to be a star . . . there was no mistaking it. She was one of the great poseurs of the world. She just knew how to be unique. . . . There were all those beautiful girls in the chorus – but nobody was looking at anybody else but Josephine. In the early days, she'd cross her eyes and do all kinds of crazy things at the end of the chorus line, and these ravishing girls could drop dead because nobody was looking at them. And later on, when she got the chance to show she'd got glamor, she showed it – and how!

As far as jazz was concerned, Josephine was an exception to the rule. She was alone in making a sensational success out of not being a very good jazz singer and dancer. Overwhelmingly, these all-black shows succeeded because of the superb jazz talent displayed by the singers, dancers and musicians who worked in them. A surprisingly large number of the best jazz dancers of the twenties visited Europe as part of one or another of black shows which played here. Mae Barnes toured with a group called Ethel Whiteside and Her Ten Picaninnies between 1919 and 1921. Johnny Nit, U.S. Thompson and Willie Covan were in London with *Dover Street to Dixie* in early 1923. Johnny Hudgins arrived with *Blackbirds of 1926*, and two years later, Bill Robinson followed with the 1928 edition. Many others made solo appearances in theaters and nightclubs, notably Buck and Bubbles, the Berry Brothers and the Nicholas Brothers. The same was true of the musicians. Sidney Bechet was a featured member of the *Revue Negre*. Other reedmen in Europe were Garvin Bushell, who worked in the *Blackbirds of 1926* show, Gene Sedric (later with Fats Waller) and Jerry Blake, who both arrived with Sam Wooding's second European tour in 1928, and Buster Bailey, who came over with Noble Sissle in May, 1929. Among the trumpet players were Joe Suttler, said to rival Louis Armsttong in his Chicago days, who played with the Plantation Days Orchestra in 1923, Johnny Dunn, who was featured in *Dover Street to Dixie* at about the same time, as well as in *Blackbirds* later, Tommy Ladnier who was with both Sam Wooding's 1925 and 1928 European tours, Doc Cheatham who was with Wooding's second tour, and Edwin Swayzee and Arthur Briggs who were both with the second *Blackbirds* show of 1928. Rhythm instrumentalists were equally distinguished. Bass players included "Bass" Hill with the *Revue Negre*, the great Welman Braud, later an important member of Duke Ellington's orchestra, also in *Plantation Days*, and John Warren, who worked with Wooding. Finally, the theater shows introduced Europe to at least three excellent piano players: J. P. Johnson, who wrote *Plantation Days*, Claude Hopkins, who was musical director for the *Revue Negre*, and Freddie Johnson, who worked with Wooding. Finally, in addition to the big-time reviews like *Blackbirds*, there were several smaller shows touring Europe, among them Harry Flemming's *Bluebirds*, Louis Douglass' *Black Flowers* and John Coffie's *Revue*, as well as innumerable song and dance acts which appeared in vaudeville. Among those who worked for such shows were Roy Butler, Cle Saddler, Cricket Smith, Herb Flemming and Al Wynn.

Such shows were in Europe as an extension of the fashion for all-black entertainment which began in 1921 with Noble Sissle and Eubie Blake's extraordinary Broadway success, *Shuffle Along*. Dozens of imitations followed throughout the twenties, some of which came to Europe. Musicians and performers jumped at the chance to go abroad. "It was an opportunity to travel, to get away from the race problem and to see the world," recalls blues singer Edith Wilson, who starred in *Dover*

Street to Dixie and *Blackbirds of 1926*. "The musicians used to like working the shows with all those girls. So there'd be a lot of jazz musicians in the orchestras. Johnny Dunn – I'd put him first. He was a great jazz-man. Garvin Bushell – he was good too. Then there was Tommy Ladnier and a lot more. Put them all together and they made their presence felt."

The fact that so many first-rate jazz players worked in these shows meant that their music was introduced to audiences who would never otherwise have heard them. This was certainly how Spike Hughes, one of the best European jazz writers and musicians of the pre-war period, was first exposed to Afro-American music. He wrote of the 1926 *Blackbirds*:

> I was hearing, for the first time, Negro music played with all its characteristic colorfulness and vitality. The initial impact of the orchestra was rather strange; here was a group of wind and percussion players using long familiar instruments such as trumpets, trombones, saxophones, clarinet, piano and the rest, who played tunes with the most elementary harmonic sequence, who yet succeeded in sounding entirely new. . . .
>
> I believe the novelty lay in the unfamiliar use of familiar instruments. Whereas the European convention demands that brass instruments should be used in orchestras only for festive or solemn moments in music, here was a band which used them for gay, farcical and sentimental purposes so that the lions we knew could roar could also coo gently as any sucking dove.
>
> Above all things, though, I learned from the *Blackbirds* orchestra that the music which cathedral organists and ill-informed writers of letters to the newspapers described as "barbaric", "undisciplined," "crude," and "atavistic," was in fact based on a remarkable technical precision of execution in ensemble passages, and a strict, unalterable set of rules governing all improvised playing.[1]

For some Europeans with enough musical knowledge to understand what was going on, their initiation into black music was profoundly moving. The concert pianist Angus Morrison has described the "irresistible blend of blatancy and sweetness" of Johnny Dunn's playing in the show *Dover Street to Dixie*. Morrison went to see the show with his close friend Constant Lambert, on whom it seems to have made an even more overwhelming impression. Morrison wrote later,

> Without doubt, this performance was one of the key experiences of his life, beginning not only his long preoccupation with jazz and the possibility of

blending many of its rhythmic inventions and subtleties into the texture of more serious music, but also moving him in a far deeper way emotionally than any music he had hitherto heard. Later he went (often in my company) very frequently to see and hear the same players in *Blackbirds*, but by then his interest in jazz was much more conscious and formulated, fully aware of all the complex technical processes and determined to master them for his own uses. The early experience was the truly formative one. I am convinced that the first time he saw *Plantation Days* was a moment of true inspiration – a moment he sought to recapture over and over again in his own music – in the "Rio Grande," the slow movement of the "Piano Sonata," the "Piano Concerto," the "Elegiac Blues" and even that exquisite piece written many years later, "Aubade Heroique."[2]

The relationship between jazz and the theater was much more complex and significant than a simple connection between certain musical skills and their most convenient outlet. Jazz achieved its effects in a uniquely theatrical way. The exhortatory, vocal styles of all the great jazz players were *dramatic* in a way which was almost shocking to white audiences, taught to admire refinement above everything else. One of the most remarkable things about the shows, in both Europe and America, was their inheritance of the tradition of African tribal song and dance.

What were these shows actually like? Reading the reviews it is clear that, apart from the novelty of seeing black performers on Broadway at all, their most sensational feature was the dancing. After seeing *Liza* on Broadway in 1922, the critic Heywood Brown wrote, "We have the vague impression that all other dancers we ever saw did nothing but minuets."[3] Reviewing Eddie Rector's performance in the same show, the *New York World* wrote, "We can recall no other male dancer in town to equal him." The high point of J. P. Johnson's *Running Wild* in 1923 was the charleston, presented by the Chorus Boys (billed as the Dancing Redcaps) to the accompaniment of hand-clapping and foot-stamping. "The effect was electrical," wrote James Weldon Johnson in *Black Manhattan*. "Such a demonstration of beating out complex rhythms has never before been seen on a stage in New York." This was understandable since the Redcaps included Pete Nugent and Derby Wilson, both of whom went on to become great dancers in their own right. There was equally extravagant praise for *Dixie to Broadway*, which developed out of Lew Leslie's success in London with *Dover Street to Dixie*. Heywood Brown remarked, "When I see a Negro child two or three years old, come out and dance a little better than anybody at the New Amsterdam or the Winter Garden, I grow fearful that there must be certain reservations in the theory of white supremacy. . . . *Dixie to Broadway* is the most exciting of all the musical comedies now current in New York" – a list which included *Lady be Good* with Fred and Adele Astaire.

It was therefore the theater which first demonstrated the natural ability of black people to unite complex counter-rhythms within an unchanging pulse of two or four beats to the bar. Within ten years the extraordinary rhythmic feats of U. S. Thompson, Willie Covan, Eddie Rector and Bill Robinson had developed into the tensile, buoyant genius of Baby Lawrence and the Nicholas Brothers.

In America, the way had already been prepared for this to some extent by the general public's continuing interest in dancing. Many of the great black dancers gave private lessons. "Many times I'd be asked to give private tuition in homes along Park Avenue," remembers U. S. Thompson. "Our steps seemed quite new to white people." Producers were quick to exploit this commercially. Among the many black dancers who coached white chorus lines, or the stars themselves, were Charlie Davis, Lawrence Dees, Willie Covan, John Bubbles and Buddy Bradley. None ever got due credit for their remarkable innovations. John Bubbles remembers teaching Fred Astaire in the thirties. "I didn't mind – I got paid for it," he remarked "but he wasn't very apt to catch the steps you know. He wasn't very quick. So he brought his friend Marilyn Miller along too. She was really quick. So the way round it was, that I'd teach her, so she could teach him. Because I didn't want to take all day to show him something he couldn't remember. I'm just wasting time at that."

Not content with simply enlisting the aid of teachers like this, producers scouted Harlem for ideas and sometimes lifted whole routines. "They tried to take everything from us," recalls singer Edith Wilson. "But as soon as they'd get it we'd change it all into something different. Sometimes on Broadway, they'd take your whole act. . . . Made you mad as hell! You're getting ready to do something, and somebody goes right out ahead and does it before you." These acts of piracy were all the more scandalous for the fact that no black dancer achieved stardom in the twenties, and only very few made it in the thirties when far less talented white dancers were earning fortunes in Hollywood. Even though the need to keep ahead of predatory white producers probably did a lot to stimulate the already remarkable black talent for invention, it is incredible that the genius which did so much to lighten the leaden, earthbound meanderings which still pass for dancing in the white world should have continued to be ignored until it had already passed into history.

In Europe, where dancing was traditionally more in line with military maneuvers than music, the situation was even worse. If, by 1925, improvisation had been lost to European music for over a hundred years, improvisation in dancing does not ever seem to have existed. Confronted by the incredible feats of ingenuity performed by the dancers in *Blackbirds* and other shows, European audiences applauded them as they would an artiste on the high wire, and considered them as scarcely more relevant to their daily experience. However advanced the European musical tradition was in matters of harmony, rhythmically it was sadly impoverished. As Sam Wooding pointed out: "You Europeans only had two time signatures. You had 2/4 and 3/4. You didn't know anything about 'slow drag' and 4/4 – four beats to the bar and all that. You didn't know that. Therefore that was in opposition to us, because we came with rhythm and time, and this was the new angle."

It is easy to take these remarks by Sam Wooding for granted: there are no longer any prizes for guessing what "all God's chillun" have got. But taking black rhythm as a matter of course is one way of ignoring it. Oblivious to the promising, though daunting, possibilities for invention presented by the Afro-American dances seen on the stage in the early years of the twenties, British ballroom managers were busily commissioning people like Victor Sylvester to standardize dance steps. *Sylvester's Ballroom Textbook* – the bible of strict tempo – ran to fifty-five editions, made its author a fortune and slammed the door on any possibility that Europeans might finally discover that dancing was a creative activity with at least as much to do with art as exercise. No wonder reviewers of shows like *Blackbirds* reacted in disbelief. The *Tatler* for October 13, 1926 wrote, "Gracious, but these colored gentlemen are some 'steppers!' I had decided that Hal Sherman was the cleverest character dancer I had ever seen, but in this colored show there are at least three performers who run him neck and neck – Lloyd Mitchell, U. S. Thompson and Johnny Nit. To watch what these three dancers can express by their feet and body movements is to be educated. Indeed, you might think it unbelievable if you had only watched the ordinary step dancers."

Edith Wilson sang most of the jazz and blues numbers in the same show.

Rhythm. That was it. Over there in Europe they didn't have that rhythm. They weren't used to that, and that's what made it interesting. . . . We had

88

some boys that did all kinds of steps – taps, kicks and all sorts of things. They'd mix up some of the European style with their own. . . . The dancing always stopped the show. This was the show the Prince of Wales used to come to all the time. He used to dance. I used to do a number on stage, and he'd do it right along with me. He'd be in the box – they had curtains you could draw so you couldn't see in from the side – and he'd be dancing right along with the show. He used to have himself a ball!

Most of the critics who reviewed the black theater shows of the twenties agreed that the dancing had something – no one was quite sure what – to do with jazz. In fact, conversations with dancers and musicians who were performing at the time indicate that jazz and dancing were intimately related, and it is surprising that students of jazz have been so slow to make this important connection. One proof of this is the large number of recorded jazz tunes which are named after dances. Louis Armstrong, for example, recorded "Struttin With Some Barbecue," "The Georgia Grind," "Georgia Bo-Bo," "Sugar Foot Strut," "Irish Blackbottom" and "Stratic Strut," among many others. Jelly Roll Morton recorded "Turtle Twist," "Shoe Shiner's Drag," "Seattle Hunch," "Blackbottom Stomp" and "Georgia Swing." Duke Ellington, whose band made such a sensation playing for dancing at the Cotton Club, recorded titles such as "The Creeper," "Doin' the Frog," "Jubilee Stomp," "The Mooche," "Rockin' in Rhythm," "Jazz Convulsions," "Birmingham Breakdown" and "Snake Hips Dance."

This was not only because the American public danced for amusement and wanted music which catered for their tastes. In fact, it is extremely probable that many of the rhythmic ideas developed by dancers were only later taken over by jazz players. This is critically important, because the dynamic tension and swing derived from the jazzman's ability to lay counter-rhythms over a steady pulse is probably the only entirely original element which jazz added to music. Jazz dancer Willie Covan is one who is quite convinced that jazz was inspired by dance, and not the other way around.

Jazz came into existence as music playing for shows. The dance bands, when they started playing for the jazz dancers, learned a lot of tricks from the dance steps. They couldn't play straight music anymore. They could hear the dancers go off straight rhythm and doing syncopations and they began to put that into the music. . . . Take tap dancing for instance. It was a long time before they wrote music for that. You'd get mostly straight music. In ballet, on the other hand, they always wrote for the dancers. But the bands at that time didn't help you with that rhythm – you had to do it all yourself.

So when we first started we used to tell the drummers a lot of licks to make. They didn't know that. They were just playing straight drums. They never made "off licks." You had to tell them to do that. You'd say, "Give me the cymbal, or make such and such a break here." You had to explain to them. Sonny was the best of the lot – Sonny Greer. Sometimes, I'd tell a drummer, "Give me so and so," and I'd make the lick, and the band would fall out laughing because they'd never seen that before. They'd been playing straight.

Such experiences were not unique to Willie Covan. Dancer Mae Barnes made her professional debut at the age of twelve, touring Europe with a group called Ethel Whiteside and Her Ten Pickaninnies. She also remembers having problems with drummers in the early twenties.

I had a lot of rhythm, so I used to change the rhythm all the time. There was only one drummer who could keep up with me at that time. He was called "Battle Axe" [almost certainly "Battle Axe" Kenny]. He was the greatest drummer in the world. He could put a show over on his drumming alone. I had so much rhythm in my tap dancing that he'd put in all kinds of things behind me to see if he could throw me off. And I'd never pay any attention, and he'd get a kick out of that because he could really cut loose. . . . There's some drummers that'll catch anything. If you sneeze they'd catch it. But in those days, there were a lot of others that if you change your steps, they got lost.

John Bubbles was even more emphatic. "The dancers helped the drummers a lot, especially the white ones. I remember teaching Gene Krupa a whole lot of licks up in the Congress Hotel in Chicago in the twenties. He was working with Benny Goodman then, and I was teaching Gene some good licks on his rehearsal pad up there in the dressingroom – they made him famous! And there was another one – Buddy Rich. I helped him too, later on."

Many of the problems described by these dancers were no doubt the result of technical rather than inherent limitations. The whole history of jazz suggests a strong link between an increasingly refined sense of timing and sufficient technical skill to execute it. Since black people often had difficulty in acquiring and learning to play instruments at that time, the superior skill of the dancers is easy to explain. As Marshall Stearns has pointed out, John Bubbles was anticipating the rhythms of the Count Basie band nearly ten years before they were heard in New

90

York. "By 1930, besides his highly unusual accenting of off-beats with his heels, he was already working out rhythmic patterns which extended beyond the usual eight-bar units. In doing so, he was looking ahead to the prolonged melodic lines of cool jazz fifteen years later."[4]

Presumably because rhythm had traditionally been the weak link in Western music, the element of "time" in jazz has been consistently underestimated, particularly in Europe. Europeans are now well aware that jazz musicians improvise, even if they do not always understand the precise application of melodic invention within a given harmonic sequence. They also understand that jazz has borrowed from the blues the tendency to flatten the third, seventh and fifth intervals of the scale. All this is perfectly correct as far as it goes, but it ignores the fact that the rhythmic innovations of black music are even more important than these as determining characteristics of jazz. The dancers and musicians who developed jazz in its early days prove this by the frequency with which they specifically define jazz in terms of time. Saxophone player Roy Butler, who worked as a professional musician around Chicago between 1918 and 1928 (when he came to Europe accompanying a dancing act), carefully distinguishes between Dixieland beat, by which he appears to mean white imitations, and jazz: ". . . Dixieland originated out of New Orleans. It's a two-beat kind of music. Sometimes we would take an ordinary kind of number, and play it Dixieland style, which would mean two beats to the bar. But in our groups we generally featured jazz, which was four beats."

This brings us back to John Bubbles. "Jazz is music in double time. You may get certain amounts of music – say it's four bars – of two beats to a bar. Then you get four beats to a bar. Then you get eight beats to a bar. It's different tempos that you set up to point out the idea of jazz, because you couldn't play it if you didn't double the tempo. You couldn't do it otherwise – that's my idea of jazz. So that for every beat you get two or four or eight, according to the tempo."

When he talks about doubling the tempo, Bubbles does not, of course, mean doubling the speed at which the number is played. On the contrary, he means doubling the time within which the piece achieves its harmonic resolution. The idea of splitting each beat into two or four is not a concept which has any direct relationship to tempo. A useful demonstration of the difference is to hum the French song. "Frere Jacques," with the traditional two beats to the bar emphasis:

1	2	1	2		1	2	1	2
Fre —	*re*	*Jac —*	*ques*		*Fre*	*re*	*Jac —*	*ques*
Dor —	*mez*	*Vous?*			*Dor —*	*mez*	*Vous?*	
Sonnez	*les Ma*	*— tin —*	*es*		*Sonnez*	*les Ma*	*— tin —*	*es*
Dor —	*mez*	*Vous?*						

The fast and jerky rhythm has an entirely different emotional feel when the two beats to the bar are increased to four. This contrasting smoothness is an essential element if jazz is to swing.

1	2	3	4		1	2	3	4
Fre	—	*re*			*Jac*	—	*ques*	
1	2	3	4		1	2	3	4
Fre	—	*re*			*Jac*	—	*ques*	
1	2	3	4		1	2	3	4
Dor	—	*mez*			*Vous?*	—		
1	2	3	4		1	2	3	4
Dor	—	*mez*			*Vous?*	—		
1	2	3	4		1	2	3	4
Son-nez les		*Ma-*			*tin*	—	*es*	
1	2	3	4		1	2	3	4
Son-nez les		*Ma-*			*tin*	—	*es*	
1	2	3	4		1	2	3	4
Dor	—	*mez*			*Vous?*	—		
1	2	3	4		1	2	3	4
Dor	—	*mez*			*Vous?*	—		

When Bubbles talks about "double time" we again come to Gunther Schuller's term "the democratization of the beat." Its simplest expression is the jazzman's habit of clapping or otherwise stressing the weaker second and fourth beats in the bar, against the stronger first and third, on which most Western melodies are constructed. This kind of rhythmic emphasis in contrast to the main one is the way in which the American black musician tries to reconcile his inherited polyrhythmic approach to playing with the European habit of trying a melody to a single time signature. There is overwhelming evidence that jazz took the basic four to the bar beat from European music, but that blacks found the resulting monotony too much for them. They therefore used their wonderful sense of time to lay counter-rhythms on top of it. The competition between these two rhythmic pulses is what gives jazz its tension and excitement, and is the pivot on which the music swings.

92

The cast and orchestra of *Shuffle Along*, New York, 1921.

RIGHT Noble Sissell and Eubie Blake, the composers of *Shuffle Along*.

BELOW The Four Harmony Kings in New York, *c*. 1924. Ivan Browning is second from right.

LEFT Leighton and
Johnson in the late
1920s.

BELOW Charlie Davis
(on horse) and Ivan
Browning (extreme
right) in *Chocolate
Dandies*, 1924.

TOP Buck and Bubbles in the early 1930s.

ABOVE Browning and Starr in the mid-1930s.

The Cotton Club, New York.

TOP Evelyn Dove in Europe, 1930.   ABOVE The Bon Bon Dancers in *Hot Chocolates*, New York, 1924.

ABOVE LEFT & RIGHT
Adelaide Hall in
Blackbirds, 1928.

LEFT Bill Robinson in a
New York show.

OPPOSITE Josephine Baker in Paris in the late 1920s.

LEFT Success in Europe for Josephine Baker, *c.* 1931.

Revue Negre, Paris 1925 – ABOVE Josephine Baker is doing the splits at the front, Sidney Bechet is behind her on soprano-saxaphone, Percy Johnson on drums, Henry Goodwin on trumpet and Daniel Doy on trombone.

101

Alberta Hunter RIGHT
leaving Orly Airport,
Paris, for London in
1930 and BELOW
starring in a Paris show
during the same period.

In this respect, the differences between African and European music are absolute and fundamental. The two rhythmic approaches can best be described by the terms "additive" and "divisive." All Western music is rhythmically "divisive." A conductor stands in front of an orchestra and physically divides the time into so many beats to the bar with his baton. African music, on the other hand, is additive. In this the beat is irregular in time so, in effect, the musicians are adding together bits of time of unequal length.

Jazz is therefore a sort of compromise between these two rhythmic concepts. Although he is much less skilful, the jazz musician has developed some of his African ancestor's ability to play complex additive time without losing the place. This process becomes easier as the basic unit of time is broken down into a greater number of units. The reason why John Bubbles emphasizes doubling the number of beats in the bar is that doing so gives the performer more scope for improvising cross-rhythms. For this reason, the first step which jazz took towards being able to swing was to exchange a two-beat conception for a four-beat one. From here, the American black musician went on to develop the capacity to feel the eighth note as the basic rhythmic unit. As a result, he has greater freedom to impose his own counter-rhythms over the basic beat without losing his place in the melody.

White European musicians have great difficulty in this respect. All the great jazz soloists have been able to construct their melodic lines, not only on the weak beats, but on subdivisions of weak beats, and it has been the special achievement of modern jazz to refine this process to a supremely complex and subtle level. Anyone who plays a Charlie Parker solo at half speed and listens attentively will recognize that he is thinking in eighths even when he is playing in quarter notes. Consequently he is able to build phrases with absolute precision on micro-beats which fall between the main beats, and are sometimes separated from them by time lapses of as little as a tenth of a second.

TRANS. BY BERNARD CASH, 1976.

Although, by European standards, Parker's "Bird of Paradise" solo shows incredible rhythmic subtlety, his sense of time is simpler than that of a good African master drummer. The eighth-note technique of jazz is only a simplification of the "additive" approach of African music. Father A. M. Jones has written one of the best books on African music.

104

As he has pointed out: "Africans do not use this eighth-note technique when they drum or clap three against four rhythms. You can work out this procedure on paper using basic eighth notes, but it is really cheating because the African uses fractions of eighth-notes." In the example he gives and which is quoted below, "the four dotted crotchets ought to be four plain crotchets, which is how the African would conceive them. But in that case, insoluble problems result in dealing with the second clap or counter-rhythm – all of which is an excellent example of how writing music down can limit it."

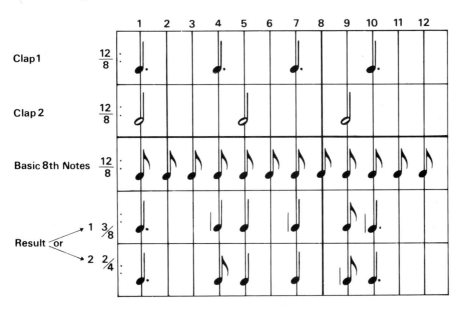

This shows a rhythmic skill which European players can only approach by conscious imitation and which, Father Jones insists, is the crucial difference between African and European music.

> We have to grasp the fact that if, from childhood, you are brought up to regard three against two as just as normal as beating synchrony, then you develop a two-dimensional attitude to rhythm which we in the West do not share. This bi-podal conception is so much part of the African's nature that he can not only with ease play a broken pattern in time relation of three against two, but he can do this when the bar lines of his short triplets are staggered permanently with the duple bars and, still further, he has no need to regard his short triplets as triple at all and can perfectly well plan a duple pattern at the speed of the individual notes of these short triplets. . . . [African music's] very characteristic treatment of polyrhythms demands a

105

specially acute rhythmic sensitivity for its execution. Only those peoples possessed of this faculty could possibly perform it. For this reason, we do not think that the African musical system could ever take root, for instance, among the peasant peoples of Western Europe. We find it hard to believe that its prevalence in Africa could have been due to cultural assimilation. The only alternative seems to be [to maintain] that the peoples of the world fall into two classes – those who think in terms of staggered polyrhythms, and those who do not: and that all the African peoples whose music exhibits this trait happened, in the past, to belong to the former group.[5]

Arguments like these drive a long, straight nail through the heart of all those basically white supremacist arguments which, while they pay lip service to the rhythmic inheritance from Africa, always lapse back into the comforting philosophy that somehow jazz owes as much to European as to African culture.

There is ample confirmation of the fact that the principle of three against two is basic to Afro-American music available to anyone who looks for it. As James Lincoln Collier records in his book *The Making of Jazz* (pp. 24–25) "There is in the Library of Congress Archive of Folk Song a remarkable game song called 'Old Uncle Rabbit,' in which one child is singing in three over an answering voice in two, something which no child raised in the European tradition could do without training." He adds, "These variations on three-over-two figures are abundant in transcriptions of black American music. They are obviously drawn from African music, where they are a commonplace."

This digression is more relevant than it might appear. Jazz only began to develop quickly after Louis Armstrong had pointed the way with his first Hot Five recordings in 1925. Although his tone, range and melodic ideas were remarkable, the careers and reputations of players like Jabbo Smith and Joe Suttler suggest that they were not completely unique. What distinguished Louis from all his contemporaries was his incredible rhythmic freedom and swing. This was something which dancers had already developed by this time. Jazz dancing was already established as a well-developed art when Louis' first recordings under his own name began to appear. The rhythmic subtlety of the black dancers was part of the same inventiveness characterizing all black performance; it is also considered, because of its basis in improvisation, to be the hallmark of jazz. If jazz dancers were already applying principles to their individual routines, it follows that they were the first jazz soloists.

There seems to have been a lot of confusion on this issue, particularly

106

among European critics. Most of it derives, I believe, from an arbitrary distinction made between melody and rhythm. The one quality which all the great jazz players and singers have in common is the ability to achieve melodic effects by no more than the clever use of rhythm. Billie Holliday, for instance, improvises rhythmically as much as she does melodically. Her special skill is to phrase so that melody notes do not fall on the expected beat, but are lodged in the cracks between them in a way which brilliantly concentrates dramatic tension. Similarly, Louis Armstrong recast the emotional effect of a song by his ability to rephrase the melody, thereby turning what may be a sentimental little lyric into something either funny or deeply moving. The methods he used were extremely economical, perhaps nudging a familiar phrase slightly ahead of the beat, or leaning on a note which is not usually stressed. In short, the black musician seems to think rhythmically before he thinks melodically. Listening to Charlie Parker's "Bird of Paradise"[6] Father Jones remarked that it was the closest thing he had heard in jazz to what an African master drummer does when he proves his skill by laying the most complex rhythmic ideas over the original pattern without ever getting lost. In this respect, it is also interesting to recall Mae Barnes' account of how Battle Axe Kenny would try to throw her with complicated cross-rhythms, and how delighted he was to be unable to do so.

Black theater of the twenties was important because it put these astonishing rhythmic talents on show for the first time. Black musicals seem to have been tailor-made to express the virtues of black performance. Indeed "performance" is the key word. The need to make every performance a personal one – original and distinct from all competitors – is what turns the black artiste into an artist. Whereas the European tradition aims at organization, uniformity and discipline, the African tradition strives for the opposite. The direct statement in either music or speech is considered crude and unimaginative. Relating this more specifically to dancing, Father Jones notes in *Studies in African Music* that "Dancing is a very important activity of the [religious] cults, and every priest of the Yeve cult wants his members to dance better than those of any other Yeve branch. This spirit of emulation should be noted. We believe that it is quite an important element in African dancing as a whole. In fact, 'showing off' seems to be one of the vitalizing factors in good dancing." (He could equally well have added: "in good jazz too.") Later on in his book Jones elaborates on this overwhelming urge to perform: "When asked, 'Why do you put on fancy dress?' the answer is, 'To show the people.' Similarly, a new club having well rehearsed the dance, the leader will say, 'Now we'll show the people," and the club will be keen to display what fine dance steps, drumming and dress they have got."

This intensely exhibitionistic streak is what made shows like *Shuffle Along* and *Running Wild* so exciting. Even though the process of inheritance is still not clear, the characteristics shared with African tribal song and dance are too obvious to overlook. The furious pace, the spirit of exuberant competition and the driving swing of the American black are all qualities of performance which go right back to the land of his ancestors. As a result, shows like these were popular entertainment in the fullest sense of the word, uniting poetry, music, dancing and drama in a way which no contemporary white theater could match.

In this, they were helped by characteristics of language which also derive from Africa. The fact that African languages are tonal to the extent that a difference of pitch will completely alter the meaning of the word indicates that there is a very close connection between music and speech. There is overwhelming evidence that the smears, glissandi, muted effects and other "illegitimate" characteristics of Afro American music are inherited from the same qualities of African speech.

The dramatic affinities of Afro-American music were most obvious in the blues, and it was the special function of the theater to introduce these to white audiences for the first time. Europe was particularly fortunate in that Sidney Bechet, certainly one of the greatest blues players in the whole history of jazz, was part of the *Revue Negre* which arrived there as early as 1925. Trumpet player Henry Goodwin, who was also with the show, has described Sidney's part in the production:

> Part of the *Revue* featured an act by Sidney Bechet. He would come on stage wheeling a fruit cart with imitation fruit piled on it, and dressed in a long duster. He'd come out shuffling along slow, and then he'd leave the cart and start to play the blues – and he could really play the blues. I learned a lot from Bechet about the blues. Sometimes, Bechet wouldn't be there for the show, and I would take his place. Bechet kept asking me to come with him, but I didn't do it then.[7]

The passionate statements of the blues, which were both simple and direct, made natural theatrical material, and it is therefore not surprising that they were a basic ingredient of black shows on Broadway.

Given the vast differences which separate African from European culture, it is not surprising that almost everyone concerned was slow to appreciate the precise significance of what they were seeing. Not only were white audiences often confused by the Africanization of their own theatrical traditions, the black performers and producers themselves

108

complicated matters by an understandable tendency to play down the kind of material they were best at, in the hopes of pleasing their white audiences. Even the best black shows were often compromised by disastrous attempts to copy the lavish productions and sentimental story lines of the old-style Broadway musical comedies.

The English musician and critic, Spike Hughes, was one of the first to notice the way in which black theater tended to get lost in productions which were more emulative than original. He wrote of *Blackbirds of 1926*:

> In one respect, I was rather disappointed by *Blackbirds*. I never really found that Florence Mills was my cup of tea. I thought she was charming and had an enormously strong personality, but, in an inexplicable way, I felt she was somehow too refined. I had made no great study of Negro music at that time, but I believe that if I had shut my eyes while Florence Mills was singing, I could not have told whether she was white or colored; in short, she was a song and dance artiste who might have come from either side of the Atlantic.

Perceptively, Hughes noted that it was the black elements which were the interesting ones.

> . . . [The] part of the *Blackbirds* which appealed to me most was the singing of Edith Wilson, who came before the curtain and sang: "If You Can't Hold the Man You Love, Then Don't Cry When He's Gone." This was a raucous twelve-bar song written and sung in the manner peculiar to the Bessie Smith school of blues singing, a typical cautionary tale, brimfull of cynical philosophy and good advice with its roots deep in the tradition of secular Negro song.
>
> Edith Wilson was no Bessie Smith, but she had some of her attack and rough sincerity and I remember the song she sang while I can no longer hum more than the first bar of anything sung by Florence Mills.

All too soon, black theater began to suffer from the efforts of both white and black producers to legitimize them, and so bring them more into line with what it was believed white audiences would most enjoy. Time and again, it was only the miraculously inventive dancing which rescued shows from the sugary confections of Broadway musical comedy.

A typical example was the *Blackbirds of 1928*, panned by most critics as a worn-out duplicate of Times Square usages; according to the *Tribune*, it was "bound up in the red tape of its own monotonous traditions." Alexander Woollcott described it in the *New York World* as ". . . just a third-rate Broadway show, tinted brown." Nevertheless, the dancing of Bill "Bojangles" Robinson and Earl "Snakehips" Tucker made the show a resounding success which ran for a total of 518 performances. Another example was the show *Brown Buddies*, which opened in New York on October 7, 1930. The plot, songs and jokes were all described as poor. The *Tribune* called it "cheaply pretentious," and the *World* voiced a common objection, remarking: "How near they are to Broadway which used to copy them, and which they now copy in return." Yet, the applause for Bill Robinson recorded in the *Tribune* "has not been equaled since the first night of the *Merry Widow*." Critic after critic was delighted by the manner in which Bojangles watched his feet. "He has a trick of watching his feet while he dances," wrote the critic for *Commonweal*, "as if he were talking to them gently and coaxing them to do the impossible. When they obey, as they always do, he beams with delight. . . ." As a result, black theater had been purged by 1930 of what can only be described as its jazz elements. Perhaps the innovations of 1921 were too daring to be sustained. Whatever the reason, the result was a loss to both the theater and to jazz. Soon the dancing was all that remained to demonstrate the natural creativeness of the black. The critic Robert Garland of the *Telegraph* wrote of *Blackbirds of 1930*: "The whole show stops when there isn't any dancing."

All this was probably understandable enough. Blacks were bound to react angrily to the kind of cultural ghetto to which they were banished by the dominant white traditions, and to do so by trying to match their achievements. W. C. Handy and Will Marion Cook, for example, both set out to show that black musicians could play anything. Unfortunately, the more original contributions which black culture had to make were sometimes overlooked in the process.

Presumably the fact that black theater declined as fast as it did explains why its connection with jazz has waited so long to be recognized. Nevertheless, it is clear that the black theater of the twenties has an honorable place in the history of jazz. It was the place where the popular song – the "standards" of the jazz repertoire – were combined with both the inflections of the blues and the supremely sophisticated rhythmic sense of jazz dancing. The theater also encouraged all those inherently individualistic qualities of African song and dance – a larger than life sound, an openly emotional approach and unique personal projection. All these are characteristics of the great jazz musician too. There is a clear parallel between what Father Jones has to say about the African performer's "exhibitionism" – something which undoubtedly made Afro-American theater so lively to watch – and the approach of the jazz soloist, who seeks out his colleagues in jam sessions and deliberately

110

tries to out-play them in order to prove, and improve, his own creative powers. These were all qualities which were displayed by the all-black shows of the early twenties. In short, if jazz was not born in the theater, it was most certainly weaned there.

The effects of black theater were naturally much more diluted in Europe than they were in America. But, for this very reason, Europe provides, in microcosm, a simplified example of what was also happening in America. The jazz elements of black musical shows were even more of a novelty there than back home, and their fate was correspondingly more rapid. Having no European roots, those musicians and performers who stayed for any length of time were quickly conditioned by the prevailing attitudes of their audiences.

Sam Wooding, who first arrived in 1925 with an orchestra which was to accompany the show *Chocolate Kiddies*, is a notable example of someone who suffered in this way. During the three or four years during which he was almost continuously away from America, Wooding increasingly turned his back on his Afro-American roots. He stopped playing for shows and even for ordinary dancing, and became obsessed with the European idea of the concert orchestra. He notes with pride:

> I didn't play for dancing much. . . . I was there three years. I played the Casino in Biarritz. I did that four seasons. I played two or three big jobs in Paris – the Ambassadeurs and the Embassy Club among others. But I didn't play in Montmartre. That's where the little fellers played. I didn't bother with that – just like you wouldn't hear Guy Lombardo playing in Greenwich Village. . . . Anybody can play for dancing. But not anybody can give a concert. If you're going to stay on top, you gotta be first, not playing some little place for dancing, because people didn't pay any attention to dancing. They're listening to the rhythm, and it's one of those things where they are entertaining themselves. A man goes with a girl and he doesn't sit there listening to "Oh, What a Beautiful Spring," that saxophone player's putting down. He'd rather look into his girlfriend's eyes and see what they're saying.

While this was a perfectly natural snobbery in a black American who had recently escaped from the cultural quarantine of Jim Crow, Wooding's decline into obscurity on his return to the States speaks for itself. The increasingly pretentious nature of his music indicates that there were very few genuinely Afro-American influences left.

Meanwhile, jazz continued obstinately to prove that it was a people's music. Most of the new ideas continued to come from bands, particularly those working the south-western areas of the country, which

111

played almost exclusively for dancing. When Wooding returned to America, he discovered to his amazement that people were much more interested in whether his band could out-swing Fletcher Henderson than in how many important European aristocrats he had entertained. By 1935, he had left full-time playing altogether, and was studying for a music degree at Pennsylvania University. Within six years of being one of the three most important figures in big band jazz, Sam Wooding had passed into history, a sad proof of the fact that art is most healthy when it is least suspected of being artistic.

THE SERIOUS COMPOSERS MEET JAZZ

3

ARLY IN 1924, the young French trombone player Leo Vauchant began an extraordinary series of weekly meetings with
Maurice Ravel which went on until 1928. The celebrated
French composer had heard Vauchant playing trombone with
the band at Le Bouef sur le Toit. Impressed and curious to
discover the secret of his spontaneous improvisations, he invited him to
visit him at his house outside Paris. Vauchant recounts:

So I went there the first Friday with the trombone. He said, "Look, I
know what you're doing. You're playing around the melody. But the
notes you play, how do they come to you?" "Well," I said, "it's a style, like
the Hungarians do. The Jews have their way too. . . . They are modes that
apply to racial background or something. And if you like it, it grows into
you, and you apply it to whatever you want." He said, "OK, I'll give you a
C scale. What are you going to do?" I said, "Well, I know what I am not
going to do," because all the fellows I know, the violinists, even some of the
great ones, would take a C scale and just play the seventh arpeggios based
on the notes of the scale. "The first note I would play on a C chord is E♭."
He said, "How come?" "Well," I said, "it's the augmented ninth. Since
you have a tenth, it could be a flattened tenth. You have both intervals, but
you have to say raised, although it's really flattened because you get off it
and come back, but it doesn't lead upward." He said, "Yes, I've noticed in
Gershwin there's a lot of that. But where did he get it?" I said, "It comes
from the blues – American stuff." He said, "OK, I'm going to play a
piece." And he played one of these billets-doux from one of those horrible
farces. So he said, "I'm going to play the melody, and on the second
chorus, I will only play accompaniment. See what comes to you." And I
said, "Well, I'll do one around the melody, but played with syncopation. . . .
Then the next thing, you play the lead and I'll blow a straight chorus over
the top of it." And he was happy. He said, "Why has nobody thought of
this before?" I said, "You'd be amazed how many people are doing it." He
was out of his cocoon you know. He had no idea how many people were
aware of those things and, consciously or not, were using it. To him, it was
a big discovery.

114

The twenty-year-old Leo Vauchant had driven from Paris to "Le Belvedere" – Maurice Ravel's house at Montfort L'Amaury. His bright red Bugatti, recently bought from Maurice Chevalier, seemed an appropriately stylish reward for someone who was so successful in the flashy, fashionable world of jazz. Not only was jazz enjoying the first of its short and infrequent bouts of popularity, but the interest of several "serious" European composers seemed to confer more than a hint of intellectual respectability. These meetings prove that Ravel's musical curiosity was more genuinely aroused than that of other French composers who, like Milhaud and Auric, abandoned jazz as soon as its usefulness and novelty wore off. Even so, this was only a comparatively brief honeymoon period. Ironically, the dense, impacted sounds of the "blue" thirds and sevenths of jazz turned out all too soon to be less a revolutionary source of inspiration than a dissonant expression of two musical worlds in collision. The considerable efforts made by Ravel, in particular, to understand the language of jazz, in the end only proved the contrasting aims of the classical and jazz worlds.

Nevertheless, Paris in the early 1920s seemed the natural headquarters for a European jazz cult. This was not because of any special French feeling for Afro-American music; in fact, it probably reflected more of an interest in cults than jazz. For almost fifty years Paris had enjoyed a self-perpetuating reputation as a center of artistic activity. It was Nietzsche who observed that the loss of the Franco-Prussian War seemed to have turned Paris into the intellectual capital of Europe. Since that time it had produced many of the latest developments in painting, literature and music. It was the home of Debussy, Fauré and Ravel, Matisse, Renoir and Rodin, Mallarmé, Proust and Gide. It was the adopted home of Stravinsky, Prokofiev, Falla, Picasso, Modigliani, Wilde and Stein among many others. There was also a remarkable exchange of ideas as painters, writers and musicians met in select intellectual circles. Mallarmé held his famous "Tuesdays" at this apartment in the Rue de Rome. Later, a similar group calling themselves "Les Apaches," to which Ravel, Stravinsky, Manuel de Falla, Tristan Klingsor, Florent Schmitt and Paul Sordes all belonged, anticipated the gatherings of Jean Cocteau and "Les Six" in the 1920s. By 1925, Paris had seen three major revolutions in painting – impressionism, cubism and surrealism – and a bewildering variety of musical styles, including the lyricism of Fauré, the neo-classicism of Saint-Saens and the pioneering work of Eric Satie, who in turn influenced Debussy, Milhaud, Poulenc and Ravel.

So much intellectual curiosity and experiment was almost bound to produce an interest in something as exotic as jazz when it finally came along. Indeed, looking back, it is possible to see forces at work which virtually guaranteed it a favorable reception. The first of these was the discovery of West African art in the early years of the century. Gauguin was probably the earliest inspiration for this when he returned from Tahiti in the 1890s and began making pseudo-primitive carvings which set a fashion for the primitive and exotic. By 1907, painters such as Matisse and Picasso were displaying similar influences – notably those of Negro culture – in their paintings, and a vogue for African art was firmly established. This persisted until the twenties, by which time several important exhibitions had been held in Paris. The other tendency, which was more general, was a kind of self-conscious avant-gardism, evident in a growing impatience with artistic conventions. The most extreme form of this was expressed in the "anti-art" of Dada. But a milder version of the same thing inspired some of the surrealist painters, and even extended to music, where a full-scale revolt was being led by Jean Cocteau against the German symphonic traditions dominating European music.

To the young French composers of the twenties, the rather overblown orchestrations of German composers like Mahler, Strauss and Wagner seemed to constitute a kind of musical obesity. Such composers had greatly increased the range of their harmonic ideas, and so the size of their orchestra. The results were to make the music grandiose but rhythmically unwieldy. As Henry Pleasants has pointed out in *Death of a Music*, "Music moved less easily because there was more of it to move."[1] The younger French composers were trying to get away from the pretensions of the German symphony. They wanted a leaner, more economical style, permitting not only more angular, dissonant harmonies, but greater rhythmic freedom. This, they hoped, would restore clarity and precision to music which was drowning in a sea of sound. Instead of writing symphonies, they concentrated more on short descriptive pieces and ballet music.

All this combined to produce an intellectual climate which, for a while, was uniquely suited to a favorable reception for jazz. For a start it appeared to sound an appropriately irreverent note to people who had recently passed through hell and survived. It appealed to the rather phony "populism" of men like Jean Cocteau; its "primitive" sound and "savage" quality attracted the surrealists; and the musicians adopted it as a way of thumbing their noses at the ponderous pretensions of the Wagnerian school. It was therefore quite in keeping that Paris should produce the first jazz club, and entirely fitting that it should be given the surrealist name Le Boeuf sur le Toit. This became the main meeting place for all the leading intellectuals of the day, particularly the younger ones, for whom jazz had become an almost obligatory intellectual affectation. It was here that Ravel was first introduced to jazz by the piano duo of Jean Wiener and Clement Doucet early in 1922. It was here also, two years later, that he met Leo Vauchant. He relates:

> In that place, there were four other men besides Ravel who met regularly in 1924. Honegger, aged thirty-two, Darius Milhaud, same age, Poulenc, twenty-five, Auric, twenty-five, Ravel was forty-nine then, and I was twenty. I'm not taking an ad on myself now, I'm just telling you things the way they were. I know that those four guys were intrigued by what I was doing with the trombone. We were playing a jazz that was saccharine-coated by Wiener and Doucet. And the one who caught on the best was Maurice Ravel who was forty-nine – the others were thirty-two and twenty-five – and he caught on better than any of them. He asked me one day – I played on a trombone that was bigger than French trombones, bigger in bore – "It's amazing," he said. "Is that a tenor trombone?" I said, "Yes." "How come you play an octave higher than any other trombone players I've heard, with a bigger instrument?" At the time I remember that I said: "I am ambitious." He laughed. He was known for having a good sense of humor, so I thought I'd throw things at him, you know. Also, I used to play drums every now and then. The drummer played an alto sax – not too well you know. So he'd play and I'd sit in and play drums. And I used to play a mess of drums, let me tell you – I mean on things that he, Ravel, would dig, you know. So he said, "Look, I'm open on Friday, because usually I come to town. Could you come? You take the bus. . . ." I said, "I've got a car." Anyway, he explained to me how to get to the Belvedere at Montfort L'Amaury where he lived. He asked me, "Could you spend the afternoon with me?"

Le Boeuf sur le Toit seemed to characterize French intellectual life in the twenties. The prevailing philosophy was not so much non-conformist as anti-conformist. The result was an odd mixture of wit and childishness, indulgence and discipline, idealism and iconoclasm to be found there. The qualities which have always encouraged the French to air their intellectual preoccupations publicly in cafés and restaurants gave the place a slightly narcissistic air. Almost overnight, Le Boeuf became the place to see and be seen. All the leading Paris intellectuals were to be found there nightly: painters like Picasso, Picabia, Derain and Marcel Duchamp, writers like Radiguet, Cocteau, Max Jacob and André Breton. Most evident of all were "Les Six": Arthur Honegger,

Louis Durey, Germaine Tailleferre, Darius Milhaud, Georges Auric, François Polenc – the half-dozen young French composers who had collected under the intellectual stage management of Jean Cocteau.

The idea for Le Boeuf came from the concert pianist Jean Wiener. Quite soon after the Armistice, Les Six and their friends began holding regular Saturday evening dinners in a little restaurant on Rue Blanche. Wiener suggested that they change their rendezvous to the Bar Gaya where, as a way out of financial difficulty, he was playing nightclub piano. He had already heard ragtime and jazz played by British and American soldiers during the war, and he was fast developing a reputation for his own interpretations of George Gershwin, Jerome Kern and other American composers. His own compositions already included a "Franco American Concerto." While such famous meeting places as La Rotande, Le Dôme, and La Coupole continued to cater to the more conventional, the Gaya soon became the headquarters of the young avant-garde. Here Jean Wiener introduced them to the music to which their increasingly anarchic philosophical views seemed to predispose them – jazz. "I was engaged to play piano every day from seven till two AM. And I had an American Negro called Vance Laurie, who played banjo and saxophone marvelously. There was also a drum set that Stravinsky had lent me. And from time to time, Cocteau used to come along and hit a beat or two on the snare drum, and all the women were delighted. We had all the American music – Cole Porter, Gershwin and so on. Within three days, you couldn't get a seat."

Everyone claiming to be chic flocked there nightly and the fame of the Gaya increased. One memorable evening, the Prince of Wales arrived and sat with Arthur Rubinstein and Princess Murat, listening to Jean Cocteau playing the drums, while a crowd of disappointed social climbers clamored to be let in.

The proprietor, Louis Moyses, soon recognized the advantages of larger and more centrally located premises. On December 21, 1921, he opened a new establishment at 28 Rue Boissy d'Anglais. He took the name Le Boeuf sur le Toit from the title of a ballet devised by Jean Cocteau. Darius Milhaud had been inspired to write the music by the Brazilian folk dances he had heard while working at the French Embassy in Rio during the war. Jean Wiener, who was immediately installed as the resident pianist, recalls that "there were two places next door to each other. One was a bit like Maxims, and the other connected to it, where the artists used to go. Everyone could go from one to the other. It was only that in one you got food for millionaires, and in the other you sat around and drank whiskey saying you would pay tomorrow."

The reputation of Le Boeuf as the comfort station of the avant-garde continued to grow. Surrealist attempts to provoke and shock pervaded even the decor. A monstrous picture by Francis Picabia called *L'Oeil Cacodylate* dominated the bar.[2] The canvas was daubed with inscriptions: "My name has been Dada since 1892," wrote Darius Milhaud; "I like Salade," was Poulenc's contribution, punning on the word "salade" which also means chaos. Beside this hung another, to which were fixed a matchbox, a piece of string and an out-of-date invitation to a party given by Marthe Chenal. Across it all ran the startling legend, "Merde a celui qui le regarde."

Wiener worked at the Boeuf as part of a duo with the Belgian pianist, Clement Doucet. Together they made a formidable team. Besides his interest in jazz, Wiener was already famous for his determined efforts to promote and perform works by all the most modern composers, such as Schönberg and Stravinsky. Doucet seems to have had a special talent for American popular music. His technique of tracing melody with the thumb of his right hand, while his other fingers filled in the harmonies and his left hand marked an unfaltering rhythm, astonished musicians who came to Le Boeuf. His performances were all the more legendary, so the story goes, for the fact that he used to read detective stories while playing. Somehow, he managed to turn the pages with his left hand without losing the beat.

This was the intellectual kingdom over which Cocteau presided, and it was one in which jazz played a much more than ornamental part. In 1918, he published a sort of notebook of philosophical jottings about art in general, and music in particular, called: *Le Coq et l'Arlequin*. The style is random, pretentious and arrogant, but despite its lack of maturity, its attack on elitism in art made a big impact in post-war France. He insolently dismissed the admittedly gross symphonic traditions of Germany, where music "is dying of approbation, carefulness and application of a scholastic vulgarization of aristocratic culture," and called for a "music for everyday," a music which did not demand to be listened to "head in hands." Instead, he proposed the rather hopeful theory that "the opposition of the masses to the elite stimulates individual genius."[3] He indiscriminately lambasted the heaviness of Mahler, Strauss and Wagner, the romanticism of Rimsky-Korsakov and Mussorgsky, and the impressionist refinements of Debussy and Fauré. His ideal composer was the much less well-known Frenchman, Eric Satie, who "teaches what, in our age, is the greatest audacity, simplicity. Has he not proved that he could refine better than anyone? But he clears, simplifies and strips rhythm naked. Is this once more the music on which, as Nietzsche said, 'the spirit dances,' as compared with the music in which the spirit swims? Not music one swims in, nor music one dances on; *music on which one walks.*"

Cocteau's search for a "music for everyday" led him to the circus, the fairground, and the music-hall. It was there that he discovered jazz. It seemed tailor-made to fit his intellectual scheme of things. There was none of the heavy solemnity of German symphonic music with its interminable developments, nor did it have the soft diaphanous quality of Debussy. Jazz was unquestionably music of the people, with the added attraction of being exotically Negroid. It was rhythmic, percussive and, above all, economical – all qualities admired by his hero Eric Satie.

Satie was certainly one of the first European composers to incorporate Afro-American influences into a longer work. In 1917 he wrote the music for a ballet called *Parade,* which had been devised by Cocteau as a setting for all his favorite fantasies. The title refers to the parade of turns performed outside a fairground to attract customers. As far as jazz was concerned *Parade* was of more historical than musical interest and includes only one scene depicting an American girl who imitated Charlie Chaplin and danced a sad little ragtime. Today the score seems conventional enough, but was nevertheless punctuated by such unusual interruptions as a ship's siren, a roulette wheel, a typewriter and several revolver shots. At the opening performance, long before the final curtain, the theater was echoing so loudly with cat-calls and shouts that Ernest Ansermet was hardly able to conduct the orchestra.

"Tact in audacity," wrote Cocteau in *Le Coq et l'Arlequin,* "consists in knowing how far we may go too far." This remark is central to his thinking. It suggests that his philosophy was almost as much an attempt to discredit as to enlighten. For all his talk of "a music for everyday," Cocteau was more concerned that music should discharge its philosophical obligations rather than be an effectively moving experience for the listener. The results were usually the exact opposite of "music for everyday," which, by implication, ordinary people could enjoy. Since the public is certain to be disconcerted by an art reduced to its bare essentials, Cocteau advised the artist to cultivate elements in his work of which the public disapproves, since the distance between the artist and his audience is the best measurement of his worth. Even so, the music which Satie wrote for "Parade" was effective, simple and at moments even sentimental. Ironically, he had produced a perfect example of "music for everyday," and one which was only encumbered by pistols, foghorns, typewriters and other items of Cocteau's intellectual lumber.

It is difficult to examine Cocteau's ideas for a "music for everyday" without concluding that they were as hollow as a jug. This is sadly evident in his attitude to jazz. He had already correctly observed that jazz combined a remarkable lack of pretension with great rhythmic subtlety and melodic invention. By his own aesthetic standards it seemed the ideal "music for everyday." Instead, however, it appears that Cocteau's interest was a form of artistic slumming, modishly adopted as a gesture of contempt for the musical establishment. Before long, it was clear that the sudden popularity of jazz was quite incompatible with his general contempt for public taste. As jazz developed as music, so its value as a provocative pose declined. By early 1920, the interest of Cocteau and his young protégé, George Auric, was already waning. In the February edition of *Le Coq et l'Arlequin*, Auric wrote that although jazz had been an important element in the new musical reawakening, its work was now done: "Let us stop our ears so as to hear it no more." So, now that its usefulness was at its end, jazz was to be abandoned regardless of its intrinsic merits.

Jazz would have probably never had more than a superficial impact on European classical music if it hadn't been for the sustained interest of other more important composers. In 1918, Stravinsky wrote a piece called "Ragtime," of which he wrote:

Before talking of my return to life after this long and depressing illness [Spanish influenza], I must go back a little to mention a work I composed directly after finishing the score of the *Soldat*. Its dimensions are modest, but it is indicative of the passion I felt at that time for jazz, which burst into my life so suddenly when the war ended. At my request, a whole pile of this music was sent to me, enchanting me by its popular appeal, its freshness and the novel rhythm which so distinctively recalled its Negro origin. These impressions suggested the idea of creating a composite portrait of the new dance music, giving the creation the importance of a concert piece, as, in the past, composers of their periods had done for the minuet, the waltz, the mazurka, etc. So I composed the *Ragtime* for eleven instruments, wind, string, percussion, and a Hungarian cymbalom.[4]

Stravinsky's "Ragtime" must be taken much more seriously than other jazz pastiches of his time. The piece bears the unmistakable stamp of genius, which turns even the most obvious borrowings into something entirely original. Whereas Milhaud in his *Creation du Monde* and Satie in *Parade* transposed cliches from blues or ragtime and called it jazz, Stravinsky succeeded in dressing ragtime syncopations in his own unique style. The harmonic dissonances are clearly Stravinsky but,

121

nevertheless, they are also extensions of the things which Earl Hines and J. P. Johnson were to do ten years later. In short, it is a brilliant work which is only spoiled by the often niggardly attitude of classically trained performers to the dotted quaver, which lends a pinched, subtracted quality to their rhythmic effort, and which deprives the music of any possibility of swing.

All European music which claimed jazz influences before 1920 was in fact inspired by ragtime. This, in its pure form, was written music, usually performed on the piano. Even instrumental renderings did not have the earthier, vocal influences of later jazz and blues. Europeans usually received their "jazz" in the form of sheet music transcriptions in a ragtime style. African influences were limited to syncopation, and cross-rhythms played over a basic meter usually at a medium tempo. These were the influences for such pieces as Auric's "Adieu New York," and Milhaud's "Caramel Mou," written as a "shimmy for jazz band" and included in *Le Piege de Medusa*, yet another of Eric Satie's adventures in Dada rigmarole. Although some of the rhythmic ideas for even this rather simplified music were revolutionary by European standards, such pieces were inevitably pastiches of no real importance either as jazz or anything else.

The music written after 1920 had a more genuine jazz influence and was therefore more interesting. In the late summer of that year, Milhaud and Cocteau traveled to London where their latest "music-hall ballet," *Le Boeuf sur le Toit*, was to be performed at the Coliseum. The music had been inspired by the Brazilian maxixes, sambas and fardoes, which Milhaud had heard while working at the French Embassy in Rio. His intention was to produce something along the line of silent film music. It was Cocteau who siezed on it as the accompaniment for a ballet. In Paris, *Le Boeuf sur le Toit* provoked the usual outcry associated with works in which Cocteau was involved. But in London, where the audiences were less familiar with the infuriating posturings of *L'Enfant Terrible*, and therefore, less sensitive to ridicule, it was very well received. While there Milhaud found the time to make frequent trips to the Hammersmith Palais, where Billy Arnold's jazz band, recently arrived from New York, was playing to packed houses. He wrote:

By going often to Hammersmith and sitting close to the musicians, I tried to analyze and assimilate what I heard. . . . Here (in contrast to the trendy sweetness of gypsy music or the crudity of the bals musettes) there was a very subtle understanding of the art of timbre: the use of the saxophone, destroyer of dreams, of the trumpet, alternatively langourous or dramatic, of the clarinet, often high in the upper register, of the lyrical trombone bending the notes a quarter of a tone with the slide on the crescendos, all intensified the feeling. Meanwhile, the piano, together with the drums, whose complete and subtle punctuations provided an inner pulse indispensible to the life of music, held this diverse but never disjointed ensemble together. Their constant use of syncopation in the melody was done with such contrapuntal freedom as to create the impression of an almost chaotic improvisation, whereas in fact, it was something remarkably precise, requiring daily practice. I got the idea of using these rhythms and timbres in a work of chamber music, but first I needed to go more deeply into this new musical form, whose techniques still troubled me.[5]

Milhaud had to wait until his tour to the United States in 1922 to continue his jazz education. He was invited to tour there by Robert Schmitz, who, since moving to New York, had done everything he could to promote the interests of modern music in general and French music in particular. Within days of his arrival in New York Milhaud caused consternation in American musical circles by boasting of the jazz influences in European music. One band which particularly impressed him was the group led by Leo Reisman at the Hotel Brunswick in Boston. Milhaud noted that Reisman's orchestra had an extremely delicate quality "with murmurous sounds from gently strummed chords, the whisper of tightly muted brass and strange plaintive sounds, only half formulated by the saxophone. The drums discreetly dominated the rhythm, which supported the delicate lace of the sound so delightfully produced by the thin tones of the violin. This was all in strong contrast with the live orchestra of Paul Whiteman which I had heard some days before in New York, and which had the elegant precision of a well-oiled machine, a kind of 'Rolls-Royce of dance music' but whose effect remained pedestrian and predictable. . . ." It is clear from this description that Reisman's music had very little to do with jazz. It was the French singer Yvonne George who first took Milhaud to Harlem. He wrote:

The music I heard there was quite different from anything I had known before and was a complete revelation to me. The melodic lines, dominated by the drums, interwove with each other in a breathless mixture of broken, twisted rhythms. A Negress whose gravelly voice seemed to issue from the depths of time, sang at each table in turn. With a dramatic, despairing expression she endlessly repeated the same refrain, backed by the jazz which provided a constantly changing accompaniment. This authentic music was rooted in the most obscure elements of the black soul, no doubt

123

the traces of Africa. I was so struck I couldn't tear myself away. From then on, I frequented other black theaters and dance halls. In some shows the singers were accompanied by a flute, in others a clarinet, two trumpets, a trombone, a complicated drum kit grouped for one player, a piano or a string quintet.[6]

Milhaud was completely captivated. He returned to France, equipped with a portable record player and a stack of "race" records on the Black Swan label which he bought in Harlem, more determined than ever to write a chamber work incorporating jazz.

The opportunity came quite soon. Parisian intellectuals had been interested in Africa ever since the cubist painters had discovered West African sculpture in the early years of the century. In 1922, inspired by an anthology of black writing he was compiling, the writer Blaise Cendrars proposed the idea of a ballet based on the creation of the world as told in African legend. Rolf de Maré, who, as director of the Ballet Suédois, was competing successfully with Diaghilev, agreed to produce it. Fernand Léger was appointed as designer, and soon he, Cendrars and Milhaud were touring the Antillian quarters of Paris looking for ideas. Léger, who was determined to make the spectacle as engagingly primitive as possible, suggested that models of birds and animals be inflated with gas so they would float away at the right moment during the performance. To Milhaud's evident relief, "this idea proved unfeasible since it required complicated installations for storing gas in each corner of the stage, and the noise of inflation would have drowned the music."[6] Eventually, Léger settled for animal costumes modeled on those worn by African tribesmen during religious ritual.

La Création du Monde, as the ballet came to be called, was, at last, the opportunity that Milhaud had been waiting for to combine jazz elements with a more extended classical form. The simple but dramatic story in its African setting was the perfect occasion for a ballet based on jazz. The action portrays the three gods of Creation who conjure up spirits that will bring the insects, birds and animals into the world. The animals dance with their creators as the ballet builds to a dramatic climax. This ends with the birth of man and woman, who discover each other and embrace as the world enters its first springtime.

Milhaud responded brilliantly to the challenge of the powerful events depicted. His choice of the seventeen solo instruments required for the score was dictated by his Harlem experiences, and included saxophone, piano and percussion, and prominently featured trumpets and trombones, whose versatile use by jazz players had always astonished classical

124

musicians. The music begins with a sedate little melody picked out by the flutes and saxophone while the piano sets an evenly accented medium tempo. Against this the trumpets and trombone introduce a brief syncopated figure which rocks along gently on the second and fourth beats. Suddenly the trombone returns and rudely smears the melody with a crude, sliding counterpoint, so dissonant as to almost suggest a different key. This builds to a new climax as the trumpets play a fanfare. There is a brief reiteration of the original syncopated figure by the flutes before the double bass introduces the famous blues theme around which the rest of the ballet is constructed. Milhaud clearly understands the uses of the changeable third which so distinctively connects the tonic and subdominant chords of the blues. This is the most obvious, even corny, of all the blues devices, but Milhaud rescues it from parody by turning it into a fugue, which superimposes trombone, clarinet and finally trumpet statements of the theme. This never fully resolves, but constantly changes direction as each resolution to the subdominant is reharmonized as a tonic which in turn implies a new subdominant. This is finally condensed into a riff figure suggested by the clarinets, and then elaborated in turn by the trombone and the trumpets, which play the kind of strident role which so impressed Milhaud in the speakeasies along Lennox Avenue. The counterpoint is so clever here that it seems as if the tailgate figure played by the trombone is stressing the weak second and fourth beats, whereas in fact it falls on the first and third, just as the New Orleans tailgate tradition dictates it should. At this point, there is a gentle modulation to a new key as the clarinets play a languorous little tune. Tentatively, the original blues theme returns in the new key and is worked to a last happy climax before achieving its peaceful conclusion.

Milhaud's success with *La Création du Monde* was due largely to the fact that he chose to use jazz for a ballet, rather than in the more abstract form of a symphony or concerto. Consciously or not, this was how Milhaud got around the problem of using jazz, whose popularity as dance music in the twenties encouraged the conventional view that it was merely "pop" music, in a more serious musical context. While touring America in 1922, Milhaud had rather smugly criticized the musical establishment there which "did not understand the artistic significance of jazz and relegated it to the dance hall." His remarks seem arrogant, given that the jazz influences of which he boasted in Europe were both exaggerated and misunderstood. In particular, there was the same tendency to deny the importance of any music not produced in the sanctity of the conservatoire or concert hall. In fact, it made no sense to separate jazz from the dance hall, which was the source of its rhythmic invention and swing, and it was precisely these qualities that were lacking in European music. Given that the rhythmic excitement, the varied timbres and vocal qualities make jazz uniquely suitable to the descriptive purposes and dramatic needs of a ballet, Milhaud's decision to use it in *La Création du Monde* was fortuitous.

When *La Création du Monde* was presented by Rolf de Maré's Ballet Suédois on October 23, 1923, it shared the bill with another interesting novelty. De Maré, too, had recently returned from a tour of the United States, which had so impressed him that he wanted to produce an authentic American ballet. It was Milhaud who had suggested that a young American he had met at the house of Princess de Polignac should compose the music. His name was Cole Porter.

Within the Quota was accordingly written by Cole, in collaboration with the American painter, Gerald Murphy. It describes the encounters of a young Swedish immigrant to America with an heiress, a "jazz baby," a cowboy, a "colored gentleman" and "The Sweetheart of the World." Between dances with each of these, he is visited by a character who seems to represent the Puritan spirit of Prohibitionist America, who warns him of the temptations to which he is exposed.

Within the Quota is a far less significant work than *La Création du Monde*, which is probably Milhaud's masterpiece. Its very different style and approach is not only an interesting example of contrasting European and American attitudes to jazz: a comparison of the two clearly reveals the irreconcilable differences separating both American and European traditions from music influenced by Africa.

La Création du Monde fails in the end, less because Milhaud did not properly understand what he was doing than because he was attempting the impossible. Many of his ideas are bold attempts which almost came off. He seems to have had a better understanding of jazz rhythm than Ravel, for example, who often confused irregular accents with jazz rhythms. Except for two or three momentary changes, the whole of *La Création* is written in 2/2. If the rhythm of the fugue is rather stiff, jazz players of 1925 also often had rather stiff rhythmic ideas. In the hands of a good jazz musician the fugue theme could swing. There are sections of the piece where Milhaud's considerable understanding of the "back beat," which is the basis of swing, comes through. Ironically, there are even moments when his counter-rhythms work so strongly against each other that they suggest the polyrhythmic nature of African music more than jazz does. But, in the end, the problems prove insurmountable. The dramatic requirements of a ballet

126

require constant changes of tempo. The moment the steady pulse, which is the essence of jazz, is lost, the music ceases to swing. Even more fundamental was the fact that Milhaud, like Stravinsky, Ravel and all other composers who tried to write music "in the style of jazz," used wrong notations in his scores. The jerky rhythm with which classically trained musicians always seem to play jazz was encouraged by his way of writing triplets, made up of a dotted quarter note, and a sixteenth instead of a quarter note and an eighth. This is just one expression of the general rhythmic weakness of European classical music. The problem is that Afro-American music is too subtle rhythmically for European notation, which indicates *what* is to be played adequately enough, but not *how* it is to be played. Unlike Afro-American music, where the beat is the thing upon which all else depends, the percussion parts of a symphony orchestra sound as if they have been tacked on as an afterthought. Instead of encouraging their students to be rhythmically inventive, music colleges demand an almost Pharisaical observance of the printed note, which quickly stifles any individual creativity. As a result, musicians come to regard music as a sort of rhythmic arithmetic, which is quite incompatible with the ability to swing. Unlike jazz musicians, who "feel" the beat, orchestral players require a conductor to marshal their efforts. Left to themselves they are incapable of taking those small rhythmic liberties which determine whether the music swings or not.

Within the Quota also failed for these reasons, despite the fact that superficially it was influenced by jazz in a simpler and more direct way. The ballet is organized like a vaudeville show. Each character encountered by the immigrant is the subject of a new dance. These maintain a steady meter in keeping with the very obvious jazz influences throughout. These sections work well enough individually. Cole Porter manages to use the regular pulse of the dances to develop interesting counter-rhythms. The dance of the cowboy, for instance, employs a very slow counter-melody in three time over the fast 2/2 of the basic rhythm, and the dance of the "jazz baby," which is an extended and very modern-sounding blues also uses constantly shifting syncopations which fall between the beats throughout. The music is often harmonically daring, but the dissonances used are integral to the chords and not merely notes placed against the melody for effect. He also manages to get beyond the simple thirty-two-bar form of Broadway song, and develop longer melodic lines consistent with the action. The biggest problems arise in the rather melodramatic whole tone sections between the dances, which describe the attempts to reform the young Swede

127

and sound like poor take-offs of Paul Dukas' "Sorcerer's Apprentice." This determined attempt to fuse jazz with "serious" music also failed in the end. On the one hand, Cole Porter lacked the skill and technique to write music which could fully express the dramatic possibilities of the story. On the other the performance was dogged by the same rhythmic inhibitions which spoil all attempts by the classical world to imitate jazz.

Milhaud never attempted to incorporate jazz into his work again. Describing his second trip to America, in 1926, he wrote:

> I once again disappointed American journalists by declaring that jazz no longer interested me. It had become officially recognized by all. The Winn school of popular music had even published three books entitled *How to Play Jazz and Blues*, in which syncopation was analyzed, even dissected.... Even in Harlem, the charm was broken for me! The snobs, lovers of the exotic and people avidly curious about black music had penetrated even the most out of the way corners. It is on account of that that I shall have no more to do with it.

It is almost impossible to believe that Milhaud can have deserted jazz merely for reasons of pique at the very moment when the first brilliant recordings by Louis Armstrong were appearing. His remarks prove that he was equally guilty of the kind of inverted snobbery he was attacking. In any case, he should have had no difficulty in distinguishing between the intrinsic merits of the music and the stupidity of some of its devotees. Perhaps Milhaud's attitude was a gesture of recognition that it was precisely because jazz was more than just a popular fad that its satisfactory integration with his own musical traditions was so difficult.

Ironically, the great French composer, Maurice Ravel, began a serious study of jazz in 1924, around the time that Milhaud, Auric and Cocteau were losing interest in it. One of those who helped him was Leo Vauchant. "I used to visit him every week from 1924 to 1928," Vauchant said, "except for a lapse of a few months from the end of 1927, when he made a tour of the States. But he came back and we took up where we had left off." This conscientious approach was typical of Ravel's character. At forty-nine, he was a fully mature musician who was not in the least interested in striking musical poses. He once wrote, "Sincerity is of no value unless one's conscience helps to make it apparent. This conscience compels us to turn ourselves into good craftsmen. My objective, therefore, is technical perfection. I can strive increasingly to this end, since I am certain of never being able to attain it. The important thing is to get nearer to it all the time. Art, no doubt, has other effects, but the artist, in my opinion, should have no other aim."

128

This attitude explains his determination to understand all forms of music to which his lively intelligence was attracted. "We developed some rules loosely speaking," recalls Vauchant, "things that one should avoid – playing the kind of jerky syncopation that was fashionable, instead of keeping it loose. So he got that. We'd already gone through the chromatic thing – E to E flat (E♭) to D to D flat (D♭), and so on. I was analyzing all of it. What I played was not the result of an analysis. I analyzed it after to see how I could explain it, and I found there were some things that almost made a rule."

Presumably, it is no coincidence that this was the time during which Ravel wrote the Sonata for Piano and Violin. The second, blues movement of this is the first serious attempt by Ravel to incorporate jazz in his work. Ravel's opera, *L'Enfant et les Sortilèges*, is usually given as the first example of the use of jazz, but the dance of the Wedgewood Teapot and the Chinese Teacup properly belongs to an earlier period and shows more ragtime influences than jazz.

The blues of the violin sonata was almost certainly inspired by his visit to the United States in 1928. During his visit, he wrote in *Contemporary Music*:

To my mind, the blues is one of your greatest musical assets, truly American despite earlier contributory influences from Africa and Spain. Musicians have come to ask me how I came to write "blues," as the second movement of my recently completed "Sonata for Violin and Piano." Here again, the same process, to which I have already alluded is in evidence, for, while I adopted this particular form of your music, I venture to say that, nevertheless, it is French music, Ravel's music, that I have written. Indeed, these popular forms are but the materials of construction, and the work of art appears only on mature conception where no detail has been left to chance. Moreover, minute stylization in the manipulation of those materials is altogether essential. To understand more fully what I mean by the process to which I refer, it would be sufficient to have these same "blues" treated by some of your own musicians and by musicians of European countries other than France, when you would certainly find the resulting compositions to be widely divergent, most of them bearing the national characteristics of their respective composers, despite the unique nationality of their initial material, the American "blues." Think of the striking and essential differences to be noted in the "jazz" and "rags" of Milhaud, Stravinsky, Casella, Hindemith and so on. The individualities of those composers are stronger than the materials appropriated. They mould popular forms to meet the requirements of their own individual art. Again, nothing left to chance; again, minute stylization of the materials employed, while the styles become as numerous as the composers themselves.

These remarks reveal all the important distinctions between Ravel's use of jazz and that of other composers. His attitude is dominated by an almost compulsive artistic integrity that drives him to study and analyze influences, and to assimilate them so thoroughly that his own individuality is nowhere threatened by the materials appropriated. This is what he means by "moulding popular forms to meet the requirements of individual art." Anything else would be pastiche, of which Ravel was artistically and temperamentally incapable.

His way of "leaving nothing to chance" was to seek the help and advice of Leo Vauchant, probably the best European jazz musician of the day. He recalls:

> Ravel got to understand a lot of what jazz was all about. If you see his piano concerto, people say there's a lot of Gershwin in it. No. There are a lot of jazz ideas in it – not Gershwin. . . . He wasn't a student of Gershwin. He was a student of what we were doing and of what was going on at the time. . . . He was such a marvelous man! People would drop by the house, and he'd always introduce me as his colleague. I wish I had a tape of that!

In some ways, the blues movements of the G-major sonata make the most obvious use of jazz of all Ravel's works. It opens with plucked chords on the violin, as if in delightful imitation of a banjo accompaniment. The piano takes this up, adding the occasional dissonance of an augmented fifth or a flattened ninth in a way which anticipates the style of Bill Evans more than forty years later. While the violin floats off into a haunting theme hovering around the beat, without ever quite departing from it, the taut, astringent accompaniment contrasts beautifully with the almost luxuriant sentiment of the melody. This tune is repeated and then gives way to a second theme introduced in a new key by the piano. After only a brief statement, the first theme returns with gathering intensity. The accompaniment is more harshly percussive and harmonically dense. Suddenly, Ravel changes key and mood yet again, and introduces a sprightly and very syncopated little tune before returning to the original theme, while the piano hammers away in a rising crescendo of flattened thirds and sevenths.

By 1930, when Ravel was working on his two piano concertos, Afro-American influences are much less obvious. It seems as if he has assimilated jazz so thoroughly that he has finally succeeded in making it "the materials of construction" in a larger musical purpose entirely his

130

own. Some of the features of the Violin Sonata reappear in the later works. The G-major "Concerto for the Left Hand," for instance, employs the same floating melodic technique over a firm, march-like rhythm in the allegro whose jazziness is emphasized by the use of wood-blocks. Also, the first movement of this concerto features a bluesy little tune which slides across the beat as it is reechoed by the various instruments of the orchestra. There is considerable use of syncopation throughout, and the last movement is full of the traditional smears and glissandi of jazz. Even so, Ravel's concern with the "minute stylization of materials employed" was beginning to produce music in which the jazz influences are so subtly merged with his own musical ideas that they are disappearing. The price of his success was the failure to preserve jazz in any recognizable form.

Even Ravel's dedicated approach ultimately failed to produce a satisfactory integration. Once again, the problems were mainly rhythmic. It was not that Ravel was indifferent to dance rhythms. On the contrary, his music is full of dance references. He often developed rhythmic subtleties within traditional meters in the same way as jazz does. Even so, his use of these techniques still fails to come anywhere near jazz. The irregular accents in the "Concerto for the Left Hand" are often cited as an example, but they are much closer to West Indian folk music than jazz. Even when the important theme, which appears at number twenty-eight of the score, is set against a regular pulse, the beat is more like that of a military band. Significantly, he nowhere uses the percussion as a means of contributing to the rhythm, but only as a way of marking time.

Perhaps Ravel himself was aware of his rhythmic limitations. Leo Vauchant recalls an interesting incident concerning the *Bolero*, probably the most famous of all the composer's dance pieces. It was written in 1928 while he and Vauchant were still having their weekly meetings. Vauchant recalls:

I played that piece before anybody else did. I had him change the key from D to C. I told him, "The trombone and the bassoon are not going to make those E flats above top C, eleven of which are consecutive." So he said, "How about a tone lower?" So he put it down a tone. Then he said, "The trouble is, the way you play it, I can't write it." And I said, "I know. It's even incongruous for me to play it this way because the other instruments don't. If I were you, I would let the other guys interpret it the way they feel it. Don't write in the slurs and so on – let them phrase it." So now everybody's playing it the way he wrote it with no expression marks at all!

Ironically, for a man who, despite the best intentions, never successfully combined jazz with his own music, Ravel has had a considerable influence on jazz. One reason for this is that he composed mainly for the piano. The relatively small scale of his works, and their spare but arresting harmonies, make them an excellent source of study for jazz musicians. Although at one time Ravel was considered to be a revolutionary, he was a musical conservative, concerned with developing diatonic harmony. He seems to have been worried by the harsh, atonal experiments of Schönberg and Von Webern. Accordingly, his music is adventurous but never arbitrary. His modern interpretation of conventional harmony – particularly his use of unresolved sevenths and ninths – was just what was required for improvised music which was already looking for harmonies which gave the maximum amount of melodic and rhythmic mobility. Generally speaking, it was the piano players who pointed the way ahead in jazz, not only because they were usually the best musicians, but also because they were familiar with the harmonic developments occurring in contemporary European music. Composers such as Ravel and Debussy, who wrote mainly for the piano, were particularly important in this respect. Their influence is obvious in piano players as diverse as George Gershwin, Duke Ellington, Art Tatum and Nat King Cole.

It is therefore quite wrong to suggest that Ravel was influenced by Gershwin. On the contrary, when the two men met at a party in New York in 1928, it was Gershwin who asked Ravel for lessons, not the other way around. Ravel's refusal, on the grounds that Gershwin might then start writing bad Ravel, was not the reply of a man likely to be influenced in this way. Moreover, the use of major sevenths and ninths common to both men had been as much a characteristic of Ravel's early works, such as *Jeux d'Eau* (1901), *Schéhérazade* (1903) and *Miroirs* (1904–1905), as of later ones. It is far more likely that, apart from writing dozens of songs which became jazz standards, Gershwin's main contribution to jazz was to have studied the works of Ravel and Debussy, thus acting as an important link between the worlds of popular and serious music.

The interest of important European composers in jazz, even if they never really understood it, conferred a special status which the new music could not have acquired any other way. Away from home, jazz became respectable. As a result, even those who did not share the rather self-conscious avant-gardism of French intellectuals in 1925 were forced to take it seriously. Jazz, particularly in its Parisian setting, had taken on a new intellectual significance. Aaron Copland recalls:

I had come directly from Brooklyn, where I had spent all the years of my life, so that ragtime and jazz were sort of everyday things in the area where I lived.

When I went to Paris, it really took on a different significance there. It seemed much more exotic and interesting musically, whereas at home, we took it more or less for granted." Copland studied with Nadia Boulanger between 1921 and 1924. His time in the "Boulangerie" was doubly profitable. "My purpose in going to Paris was to find out how the French were able to get away from the great German tradition and write their own recognizable kind of French music, because that's exactly what I wanted to do in my work – to reflect the America I'd grown up in, which, certainly in terms of serious music, had not done too well as far as creating a specifically American atmosphere. Well, being in Paris and listening to jazz there rather than here made me very aware of its highly American quality. It seemed more special."[7]

To this extent, snobbery, inverted or otherwise, played an important part in the history of jazz. If some of the works of Auric, Milhaud and Copland, inspired by the often ludicrous misconceptions of Jean Cocteau and his set, were not very good, they certainly opened up a new area of critical debate and provided a stimulating new viewpoint from which to examine European music.

JAZZ
INTERPRETED

"WHAT A DULL and dreary trade is that of the critic," wrote Diderot. "It is so difficult to create a thing, even a mediocre thing; it is so easy to detect mediocrity." This remark by the great French *philosophe* tells us more about the age in which he lived than about criticism. His comment about mediocrity is only true in a time which is sure of its cultural bearings. The eighteenth century is famous for having developed a neo-classical ethic which was widely and confidently accepted among all educated people.

There can hardly be a greater contrast to our own times. Today all the arts are almost infinitely fragmented into innumerable schools, each with their respective philosophies. Art is increasingly a vehicle for theoretical abstraction. The point has now been reached where some consider that music is not sound at all, but silence, and painting threatens to become as much theory about pictures as something to look at. This tendency has been disastrously encouraged by the spread of all kinds of media, which shows all the signs of lowering, rather than raising, the general level of artistic consciousness.

The most important result of this breakdown of agreed artistic standards is that the loss of confidence it implies begets an urgent need for critics. A world afflicted by *musique concrète* and conceptual art needs critics to interpret such ineffable mysteries. Mass communications and a decline in the power of patronage have made the artist more than ever dependent on the public, to whom art must therefore be explained. As a result, artists and critics seem to have reached a tacit understanding whereby the latter act as cultural brokers, trading in the fact that the public, despite its protests, loves to be shocked only slightly less than the artist needs to be loved. In return for acceptance of his role as intellectual arbiter, the critic sells the artist's work, as well as his bohemian image, to a public which is increasingly credulous and confused.

The purpose of this preamble is to describe a situation which was already developing in the twenties, and one in which jazz could never have any lasting place. Certainly in the twenties and thirties jazz was the complete opposite of art for art's sake. True, there was a brief period when primitivism was admired, encouraged by Gauguin's experiences in the South Seas and by the interest of Picasso and the cubists in West African art. But the musical establishment remained obstinately conservative, and sought new departures only in intellectual directions. Jazz, on the other hand, appealed directly to the emotions and was in any case played by untrained, usually black, performers. Whatever individual composers and musicians may have thought of it, critics whose role was to intellectualize music were militantly hostile. Some of their denunciations were almost hysterical. André Saurès, writing in *La Revue Musicale* for March, 1931, described jazz as the music of animals whose "outlandish excesses made it worse than monotonous." In his view, apes had been given free rein and therefore displayed the most obscene characteristics. He concludes, "These savages must be suppressed."

Questions of race and cultural impoverishment disposed of, critics gave equally short shrift to the technicalities of jazz. Lucien Rebatet, writing in *Radio Magazine* in 1930, seemed positively to relish the fact that,

> We will soon be taking the opportunity of expounding our ideas about jazz, whose revolutionary effects we have heard so much about, and which, in the person of the Negro Armstrong, its most famous exponent, reveals only a naive and impoverished anarchy allied to a puerile cult of dissonance.

The composer Ferroud even went so far as to say that collective improvisation was mathematically impossible.

> An improvisation by four performers not only presupposes extraordinary intuition, but asks us to believe that each performer has in his head a sort of logarithmic table of musical combinations and can guess what his partners are about to do. But we will belabor such an absurdity no further. Jazz cannot be improvised, such a thing would be impossible, even had the performer received from Prometheus that fire which he sought to steal from Olympus.

This reference to Olympus was precisely in line with all that cultural elitism which had lingered on in European art long after the various disputes between the classical and romantic schools had ceased to interest anyone but historians. The classical tradition planted the idea of a universal standard of excellence that European art had inherited, and by virtue of which it could not be surpassed. Perhaps there was some excuse for this in the 1920s when mass communication was only beginning to be a possibility, but there is no doubt that Europeans had constructed a conception of art in general, and music in particular, entirely based on the creations of their own artists. Consequently, there has been almost no interest in the musical achievements of other races. For a moment it seemed that Jean Cocteau had understood this when he bravely wrote in *Le Coq et l'Arlequin*: "In order to appreciate certain works one must know how to put oneself in a completely new state of mind and so not judge them by other standards." For a time it even seemed as if he and his circle had grasped that jazz was an enlargement of music and not an attack on it. Unfortunately, his dilettantish mind found fresh preoccupations just when his original prophecies were being realized. To the end of his days, Cocteau could scarcely distinguish between Duke Ellington and Guy Lombardo.

Once Cocteau, Milhaud and their set had abandoned jazz, the last hope that the establishment would recognize its value was gone. In 1927, Darius Milhaud wrote in his *Etudes*: "The influence of jazz has already passed by, like a salutary storm after which the sky is purer, the weather more reliable . . . little by little, renascent classicism is replacing the broken throbbings of syncopation."

With such powerful patronage withdrawn, the critics, for whom the natural vitality and inspiration of jazz had always been obscured by its lack of cultural pedigree, were free to intensify their attacks. They were right to do so. As the guardians of what music *ought* to be, as the keepers of a musical tradition in which improvisation was dead, and whose rules had to be painfully acquired in academies which stifled the kind of spontaneous attitudes which are the essence of jazz, it was quite understandable that they should regard it as subversive. Most of them secretly agreed with the virulent sentiments expressed by André Suarès, who wrote: "Jazz is just half a dozen clichés . . . (it) is music of the guts and of all those who carry their sensibility between their legs." With attitudes so hermetically sealed against cultural contamination, change clearly had to come from without.

☆ CRITICS

The history of jazz in France is more properly described as the history of jazz criticism. Admittedly, the French had produced four soloists of world class by 1930: trumpet player Philippe Brun, trombonist Leo

138

Vauchant, guitarist Django Reinhardt, and saxophone player Alix Combelle. But of these, Reinhardt was a gypsy, Brun and Vauchant found the jazz scene in Paris so limiting that they took commercial work in England and America respectively, and only Combelle remained in France. However good other individual musicians, such as the violinists Michel Warlop and Stephane Grapelly, pianists Stephen Mougin and Alain Romans and saxophone players Noel Chiboust and Andre Ekyan, may have been, France produced few good jazz orchestras, none of which lasted more than a few months at a time. In fact, French appreciation of jazz generally lagged behind that of the Belgians, Dutch and British. Nevertheless, most people, if asked which European country they thought had the liveliest jazz scene, would probably say France. This was partly because relaxed immigration policies and a romantic attachment among Americans for Paris encouraged a large number of jazz musicians to leave home. It was also because, even though France may not have been a country where jazz history was made, it was certainly the place where it was first written about. The man who, single-handedly, was responsible for this was Hugues Panassié.

Panassié's phenomenal role in the history of early jazz was directly inspired by his furious opposition to the kind of cultural elitism which the musical establishment betrayed in its attitude to Afro-American music. He quite rightly recognized that music is as much something for the emotions as for the intellect and hated the sterile academicism of most music criticism. His extreme youth, his small knowledge of music and his complete lack of experience in criticism were positive assets in his fiery, cantankerous war against what he saw as obscurantism and prejudice. No one who had been brought up in the ways of the establishment would have dared to match the arrogance of his opening salvo: "Inspiration without culture can produce beautiful works; culture without inspiration is incapable of doing so." As examples of creators of inspiring work he cited a bunch of uneducated American blacks, many of whom could not read a note of music. His perception and temerity can be gauged by the fact that the majority of jazz fans, who, at that time, admired the white American players like Red Nichols and Jimmy Dorsey, were only slightly less enraged by his comments than the serious music lovers. If Panassié was mercurial, quixotic, sentimental, prejudiced, childish and arrogant, these qualities, allied to his considerable insight into Afro-American music, were just what was needed to take on the whole cultural establishment single-handedly. It was not only childish, but unhistorical for later critics like André Hodeir to reproach Panassié for his lack of critical precision in drowning black musicians in a flood of hyperbole, instead of applying musical science to the business of explaining their qualities. It was imagination, not science, which was required to appreciate something as alien and barbaric as black jazz appeared to be in the mid-twenties. It was no coincidence that only a man as unschooled in both music and criticism as Panassié seemed capable of that kind of intuition.

Predictably, Panassié was met not only with ridicule, but, worst of all, indifference. He was impelled almost from the start to write about it in a spirit of bitter frustration at the rejection of his ideas by people whom he saw as arrogantly claiming to be his critical superiors. To make matters worse, he could not at first find the arguments to support his intuitions, which therefore seemed naive and ridiculous to the sophisticated musical establishment. Writing in *Twelve Years of Jazz*,[1] he describes his determination to reveal the true significance of jazz to the French public, who until then believed that Jack Hylton, Paul Whiteman, Ted Lewis and Fred Waring's Pennsylvanians were the leading exponents of the new music. After a general swipe at critics who, even when confronted by the genuine article, took no trouble to understand it and dismissed it out of hand, he recalls: "What finally decided me was a certain debate about jazz, a lamentable affair which took place in a cinema in the Boulevard Raspail. I had brought along certain Louis Armstrong records which met with complete incomprehension from the public. Such stupid arguments were put forward against jazz that I left incensed with rage, promising myself to do everything possible to publicize the real thing." This seems to have taken place around 1929.

From early 1930, Panassié abandoned his attempts to play the alto saxophone, on which he was an indifferent performer, and began instead to produce books and articles whose impassioned rhetoric and peppery sarcasm were to leave an indelible mark on the whole history of jazz.

Panassié's position in early jazz criticism was so dominant that he is often thought to have been the first as well as the best writer on the subject. In fact, by 1930 there was already a considerable body of jazz literature. The Belgian critic Robert Goffin had published a survey of the current scene entitled *Aux Frontières du Jazz*, and a Frenchman named André Schaeffner had also written a book entitled *Jazz* which dealt mainly with the origins of the music. In addition, Spike Hughes, writing in the British *Melody Maker*, Joost Van Praag and Henk Niesen in Holland, and John Hammond in America were all publishing perceptive articles analyzing and explaining jazz. In France, between 1929 and 1930, a paper called *Revue du Jazz* flourished briefly as a

140

source of record reviews and short analytical articles, most of which were written by interested musicians like Philippe Brun, Stephane Mougin, Michel Emer and Gregor. Gregor was soon to become better known as the leader of the Gregorians which, with Ray Ventura's orchestra, was the only French band to include a substantial jazz element in its repertoire. The *Revue du Jazz* had little influence, since almost the only people who read it were those who also wrote for it. Panassié's writings at this time were limited to a few record reviews in this paper and one longer article entitled "Hot Jazz," which he persuaded the distinguished critic Emile Vuillermoz to publish in his prestigious magazine *L'Edition Musicale Vivante.* As he notes rather smugly in *Twelve Years of Jazz*, "This was the first time, as far as I know, that information about authentic jazz musicians was given to the French public."

This apparently innocent remark reveals an important clue to understanding Panassié's character. John Hammond was intimately acquainted with the American scene, and knew more about black jazz than everybody else put together. Joost Van Praag had had more critical experience, Spike Hughes was an infinitely better musician, but Panassié was endowed with a quality much more important than all these – ambition. Whereas Hammond and the rest were content to evaluate the relative merits of Don Redman and Benny Carter, to promote the virtues of unknown black bands such as Claude Hopkins' over superior claims made for white orchestras like the Casa Loma, and even to tackle such tricky questions as the definition of swing, Panassié was stalking much bigger game. His concern was nothing less than an assault on the great citadel of culture. Enraged by the critics' contempt for jazz, he was determined to invest the ivory towers of music criticism and, by a powerful mixture of rhetoric, counter-argument and invective, raze them to the ground. Jazz had struck him with all the force of St. Paul's revelations on the road to Damascus. The musical establishment's indifference to it was not only an insult to his personal pride, it was a denial of fundamental truth. Increasingly, he came to regard the critics with the sort of loathing that seventeenth-century Puritans reserved for Anglican bishops. Critics, like bishops, were guardians of formality, superstition and various forms of cultural hocus-pocus which stifled natural creativity and divorced art from the public. As the years passed, Panassié's career became more and more like a Puritan Crusade and his books like successive articles in a sort of critical Grand Remonstrance.

This sense of mission, and the rage and rejection he felt at the condescending way it was received, went so deep with Panassié that it haunted his writings for the first twenty years of his career. *Jazz*

Jack Hylton and his
band: TOP LEFT at
Orly c. 1930; TOP
RIGHT at Waterloo
Station in London with
Philippe Brun playing
the cornet (right); and
at the Rex Cinema in
Paris in *Sing You
Sinners*. OPPOSITE
Paris, 1931.

JACK HYLTON
AND
HIS BAND
OUTSIDE THE OPERA HOUSE.
PARIS · · · PRIOR TO THEIR
APPEARANCE THERE - 16th FEB. 1931

LEFT Philippe Brun
playing in a Paris
nightclub in 1938.

FAR LEFT The brass section of
Hylton's band in 1929: (left to
right) Lew Davis, Leo Vauchant,
Philippe Brun and unknown.

ABOVE Bobby Martin's Band
with Hugues Panassié – (from
right to left) Kaiser Marshall,
Thelma Martin, Hugues Panassié,
Bobby Martin, Bob Macrae,
Ram Ramirez and three
unknowns.

LEFT A publicity poster for
Philippe Brun in the late 1930s.

Louis Armstrong in Europe, 1934:
ABOVE & TOP LEFT on stage in Turin;
CENTER LEFT the Armstrong band
waiting for a train in Brussels –
(back row, left to right) Louis, Valet,
Herman Chittison, railwayman,
Oliver Tines, Leslie Thompson,
Peter Ducongé, Cass McCord, Jack
Hamilton, (front row) Harry Tyree,
Rocco (bass), Maceo Jefferson,
Lionel Guimarez; BOTTOM LEFT a
reception for Louis in Marseilles.

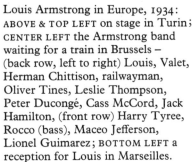

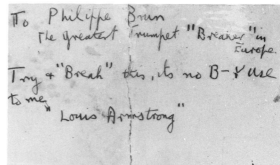

Signed photographs
from Louis Armstrong
to Noel Chaboust and
Philippe Brun and the
inscription on the back
of Brun's photograph.

147

Panorama,[2] published in 1950, shows that his resentment was still white hot. Even the introduction reads like a manifesto. He points out that jazz is now fifty years old. He reminds us that France has not only experienced visits by its two greatest names, Louis Armstrong and Duke Ellington, but that it has even produced its own jazz genius in Django Reinhardt. He recalls that no less a person than Stravinsky has recently been so inspired by jazz, that he has written a special work for jazz orchestra.

> Given all this, what is the position occupied by jazz in France today? It is more or less the same as ten or fifteen years ago. One could almost say that all that has been done has been in vain. Open the reviews and magazines; almost every one of them have their regular music column. There are interminable debates about the most mediocre new works given in concert, about the way in which Monsieur A or Monsieur B holds the baton, about concerts of new recordings which are given from time to time on the radio. But may I be blasted by the atomic bomb if there is the smallest mention of jazz. Even if jazz records are produced, and concerts take place, what is that to the music critics! They are supremely indifferent. Why this lack of concern? This ignorance? This incompetent opinion? For how much longer are those who are paid to know better going to ignore the most important new music of this century? Is it contempt for 'Negro music,' the music of savages? If it is in the name of our culture that we deploy such arguments, question, but for the arrogant and stupid use which we make of it.

If these, admittedly unusual, polemical talents were all that Panassié had to offer, he would have rated scarcely more than a footnote in jazz history. As it was, he was well aware that vituperation was not enough. If his initial reaction to the critics' contempt for jazz was one of moral indignation, the fact that their prejudices were so impregnably defended by the elaborate theories of the European tradition soon forced him to look for scientific counter-arguments with which to attack them on their own ground. Some of these arguments were not original, and are to be found tucked away in articles in the *Revue du Jazz* by musicians like Stephane Mougin and Michel Emer; others were first expressed by Robert Goffin in *Aux Frontières du Jazz*. There was also the incalculable influence of the American jazz clarinetist Milton "Mezz" Mezzrow which dominated his early thinking. But what distinguished Panassié from all other interested parties was his determination to uproot his opponents and to replace random comments with a full-scale musical ethic, a meticulously worked-out system so closely argued that it would finally force the cultural establishment to admit the error of its ways.

His tragedy was that even though most of his intuitions were right, he failed in the end for lack of technical skill. He was never quite musician enough to furnish the musical proof of what were otherwise mere speculations. His search for the essence of jazz – for those elements without which jazz would not exist – was never satisfactorily completed. This had to await the publication of *Jazz : Its Evolution and Essence*, a brilliant study by the musician André Hodier, who was one of Panassié's severest critics. The fact that, in this respect at least, Panassié had to play Giordano Bruno to Hodeir's Galileo must have been all the more galling.

In 1934, Panassié published *Hot Jazz*,[3] his first great treatise on the subject. The first chapter begins by stressing that jazz is a performer's music and that the composer's melody is merely taken as a harmonic framework for the ideas of the soloist. The performer in jazz is the equivalent of the composer in classical music. But even this is not enough, since even in classical music the performers "sometimes elaborate on the text set before them." Nor is the essence of jazz to be found in rhythm, however essential that may be. A continuous rhythm is like the foundations of a house without which the house cannot stand, but which is nevertheless different from it. More important still is what the musician does with this steady beat. The "essential element of jazz found in no other music . . . is 'Swing.' All true jazz must have swing; where there is no swing there can be no authentic jazz." This is what separates jazz from other forms of dance music with a continuous "lilt." "In jazz, swing is to be found not only in the rhythmic line but in the melodic line; with waltzes and tangos we can establish only a rhythmic fluctuation. In jazz swing is a dynamic element."

This, according to Panassié, is the only proper yardstick by which jazz should be judged. Jack Hylton's band has all the outward appearance of a jazz orchestra, "but there isn't any swing. Consequently, no one can properly say that Hylton's music is jazz. . . ." Paul Whiteman fares better since he "once had a band which could really swing," but his later commercial renderings are nothing more than "empty, pompous performances nicknamed symphonic jazz." In short, Panassié is emphatic: an orchestra which does not swing does not play *bad* jazz; it does not play jazz at all.

These comments show remarkable insight. In 1934, the concept of swing was only beginning to be understood even among the black musicians themselves. The late twenties represented the end of one era

149

and the start of another. This was the time when the influence of the pioneers was yielding to a younger generation of more sophisticated musicians. Their superior musicianship was an important factor in the development of swing. It was only in 1933 that the first Benny Moten recordings appeared featuring the extraordinary combination of Count Basie's piano and Walter Page's string bass. From these sessions came "Toby," "Moten Swing" and "Prince of Wales," which are among the most distinguished recordings in the history of big band jazz. Panassié himself wrote, "What is extraordinary in these records is the swing produced by all sections of the orchestra, in particular the rhythm section directed by the piano player, Bill Basie. 'Moten Swing' . . . possesses such swing that it is difficult to find a record which can be rated as highly in this respect." Duke Ellington's band was still in a process of consolidation following the leader's latest brilliant attempts to enlarge the form of his work with pieces like "Creole Rhapsody" and "Echoes of the Jungle." Although capable of considerable drive and excitement, swing was still a secondary consideration for him. And despite the fact that Fletcher Henderson's 1934 recordings of "Big John Special," "Wrappin' It Up," "Shanghai Shuffle" and "Rag Cutter's Swing" are probably his finest from the point of view of swing, this was really a swan song for the band, demoralized by Coleman Hawkins' departure for Europe and its leader's growing disinterest in holding it together. Other bands, like those of Chick Webb, Jimmy Lunceford and Cab Calloway, were less well known. It is, therefore, striking to find a European, and a non-musician at that, pointing out so early in the history of jazz that, "In jazz, syncopation – which is constantly present – is not accentuated. It is not an effect designed to impress the listener; it imparts, instead, a specific character to the music. From this comes that special quality we call 'swing.' "[4] He goes on to quote Stephane Mougin's comment in *Jazz-Tango-Dancing* for October, 1933: "To be natural is everything. Where there is a feeling of effort, or work . . . there is nothing natural and, consequently, no swing." Panassié adds approvingly, "Mougin's phrase is revealing. No musician has swing unless his playing is entirely easy. It is the principle of 'take it easy.' "

Once this idea of swing had been elaborated, it opened up the Great Divide between European and Afro-American music. This was the issue on which some of the fiercest battles were to be fought. Panassié took up the attack with obvious relish.

You condemn jazz . . . because the rhythm is said to be monotonous, because it is dance music; and you forget that two centuries ago in your classical music, all the best composers produced improvisations which were sometimes judged by their contemporaries to be more beautiful than their written works – that these same musicians wrote a lot of dance music – that music without a steady pulse was the exception rather than the rule.

And we ask you on whose authority do you place dance music below other forms of music? Better still, we assert that music conjures up the dance just as the dance demands music, and that if you scorn music with a regular beat, it is because your atrophied musical sense has robbed you of that rhythm which the blacks have retained.[5]

Panassié loses no opportunity to belabor the point, and his critics. Writing in *The Real Jazz*[6] he follows up an emotive description of swing: "The point when good dancers abandon themselves . . . the moment when the sensitive listener experiences an irresistible urge to mark time and call out an occasional 'yes, yes' . . ." with the inevitable tilt at classical musicians:

How far away are we, in such moments, from the too intellectual conception of music, which is the product of a century atrophied by a poorly digested civilization; how far from the "intentions" of composers who lack spontaneity, from the systematic research into an overcharged music to which one listens with bewilderment or a yawn, and which does not give for an instant his impression of expansion, of "joie de vivre" which a sane and natural music should not fail to give.

So far – and for those days Panassié had gone a very long way indeed – so good. Unfortunately, it was still not quite far enough. If swing was the essence of jazz, what was the essence of swing? He no sooner broaches the subject than he abandons it in despair. At the beginning of *Hot Jazz*, he writes: "When I try to define and explain swing, I find myself up against insurmountable difficulties." Even though all are agreed when swing is present, "so far no one has been able to give a precise definition." Panassié also fails to do so. The best he can attempt is a "vague idea" of swing, which weakly proposes that "swing is a sort of 'swinging' of the rhythm and melody which makes for great power." After correctly pointing out that swing is an individual attribute which differs not only from instrument to instrument, but in each musician, he gives up completely: "The moment one thinks one has at last succeeded in formulating a definition of swing, which fits all the characteristics of a musician's performance, one will discover – by hearing another performer play with a swing achieved by dramatically opposed methods – that one is on the wrong track."

This failure to clinch the argument is the source of most of Panassié's later errors. Instead of devoting the same admirable logic to the fundamentals of swing which he had shown in his search for the essence of jazz, the best he can do is waver between tautology – "swing is swing" – and metaphysics: "Swing is a gift – either you have it deep within yourself, or you don't have it at all. . . . Neither long study nor hard work will get you anywhere in jazz if you do not naturally know how to play with a swing. You can't learn swing."[7]

It was not until 1956, when André Hodeir published *Jazz : Its Evolution and Essence*, that this question was properly resolved. Hodier defines the essence of jazz as a tension-relaxation duality. He correctly points out that among the first jazz players, the element of tension – the hot quality in their playing – was much stronger than the element of relaxation. "Hot language may be said to outweigh swing in a proportion of nine to one."[8] By 1935, these two elements were roughly balanced; some of the earlier violence was modified in favor of more intense swing. From then on, the careers of Teddy Wilson, Count Basie, and particularly Lester Young, established that to swing was more important than to play hot. In particular, Hodeir emphasizes that swing – getting the note in the right place – is a technical matter which the kind of crude violence, so much admired by the critics of the late twenties and early thirties, seriously inhibited.

This very neatly exposes the anomalies at the heart of Panassié's thinking. For him, to play hot was not only a virtue in itself, it was a positive contribution to swing. He conceded that straight interpretations can swing, at least in theory, but insisted that "there are degrees of swing and almost always hot interpretations have greater swing than other performances." Not content with this, he goes on to make hot playing the first commandment in jazz. Accordingly, a hot player is preferable even to another musician who is more melodically inspired.

It is a question of the very essence of music itself. Whether we like it or not (if this rule is not followed), hot interpretation will cease to be hot and will cease to produce the masterpieces it has so far given us if we do not take into account these mysterious laws governing intervals. That is why we must rule out those musicians, however inspired, who do not conform to these instinctive laws. Let them spend their talents in some other branch of music instead of perverting the hot style. Here I am not quibbling; I am denouncing a clear and ever-present danger.[9]

152

This obsession with hot playing is the source of Panassié's disastrous conservatism. As a result, he was quite unable to reconcile his ideas with the admittedly rapid evolution of jazz. His study of that evolution is therefore littered with anachronisms. After reluctantly admitting that jazz, like any other music, must evolve, he is relieved to find that:

> The basic nature of jazz has not been damaged by evolution, because the essential element, swing, or, if you prefer it, the natural pulsation of the black race (it is a question of words) is still present. *For Nat King Cole or Lionel Hampton swing, as much as the New Orleans interpretations.*[10]

It need hardly be said that no musician of the twenties, except for Louis Armstrong, approached the phenomenal swing generated later by the Count Basie or Lionel Hampton bands. Musical technique was firmly associated in Panassié's mind with the sterile training which classical players received in their conservatoires. Since such training was inimical to jazz, musical technique, so far as Panassié is concerned, comes close to being an instrument of that sterility. He found it difficult, therefore, to grasp the fact that jazz in the late thirties had more swing because the musicians were more polished and technically proficient. Swing was always inherent in the black race, as their dancing, indisputably proves, but instrumental technique was still something that took time to acquire.

In short, the logic of Panassié's thinking points straight to Arcadia. He seems to have seen the New Orleans era of jazz as an ideal, archaic period, a golden age before the advent of commercialism, peopled by beings of primordial simplicity for whom music was not merely desirable but indispensible. The spread of radio was naturally incompatible with this romantic image. Panassié laments:

> The Negro public had until then a passionate love of their blues, and their own fine orchestras slowly lost their natural taste for their own virile and strong music as a result of hearing numerous ridiculous Broadway tunes sung by languorous and saccharine white singers over the radio. The youth was especially corrupted, for it had not been immersed in the atmosphere of the blues and true jazz for several years, and was consequently more quickly contaminated.

This completely ignored the vital contribution Broadway songs made to the jazz repertoire and the fact that the wide dissemination of jazz by black radio stations inspired the young musicians and kept their elders in touch with the latest trends. It is presumably this to which Panassié most strongly objects, since his peaceful Arcadian idyll is disturbed by threats of progress which disturb the scene like an intimation of mortality. In *The Real Jazz* he announces:

> At the risk of stirring up many prejudices, one cannot refrain from saying that there is no reason why civilization should necessarily imply progress as far as music is concerned. Those who have such preconceptions show that they have misunderstood the true nature of music. For music is above all a cry from the heart, the natural spontaneous song expressing what a man carries within himself. A man who ignores all musical theories, but who is endowed with extraordinary creative gifts, and who sings alone in the desert, can be more sublime, can be a greater musician, than the author of the most complicated symphonies and quartets if the latter is less inspired. The role played by culture in music is secondary. Inspiration without culture can produce beautiful works; culture without inspiration is incapable of doing so.
>
> We must go further and say that in music, primitive man generally has greater talent than civilized man. An excess of culture atrophies inspiration, and men crammed with culture tend too much to play tricks, to replace inspiration by lush technique, under which we find music stripped of real vitality.[11]

In 1930, this badly needed to be said, given the complacency of the musical establishment. Panassié was quite right to contrast scathingly the creative role of the hot jazz player with that of the musician in a symphony orchestra who "functions only as a transmitter," and has "nothing to do with the creative process." His comments about the stifling atmosphere of music academies remain substantially true today, particularly in Europe. Ironically, he was even right about the threat which evolution posed to the long-term future of jazz. Innovations in jazz today, which are nowhere more obvious than in the abandoning of swing, have fundamentally and perhaps fatally tampered with the essence of the music. But the preceding remarks were published twenty-five years before the first signs of a jazz avant-garde. If by 1942 jazz had absorbed a much higher level of musical technique, it had greatly benefited from it.

Almost all Panassié's worst errors proceeded from this blind conservatism. It is as if he wishes to deny the very idea of progress.

> As if continuous progress which is inevitable in science, was equally certain in music! If this were true Mozart would be fundamentally superior

154

to Bach, Wagner to Mozart, Debussy to Wagner, and the smallest offerings of Honegger to Debussy and so on.[12]

Yet in this diatribe designed to dismiss the innovations of Charlie Parker in the forties he yet again sets the kind of trap for himself from which he never escapes. He correctly stressed that jazz, "like all other primitive music" with an oral rather than a written tradition, is music which is "perpetually in motion . . . which will never fall for an instant into the funereal sleep of so many *chefs d'oeuvre* which often give the impression of being imprisoned in a pickled jar."[13] Yet he cannot face the consequences which inevitably follow. His die-hard conservatism prevented him from seeing that Charlie Parker's music, however technically brilliant, was firmly rooted in the blues, and that his innovations carried the harmonic and rhythmic possibilities implicit in earlier jazz to an audacious but quite logical conclusion. Panassié's cultural pigeons had finally come home to roost. His initial enthusiasm for jazz had been rooted in amateurism and naivety, and it was precisely these qualities which helped rather than hindered him to appreciate its significance. But this was also what stopped him from keeping pace with its progress.

For all his faults, it would be difficult to overestimate Panassié's importance. His enormous contribution to the understanding of jazz can best be measured by comparing him with others working in the same field. The closest to him in background and outlook was the Belgian critic Robert Goffin. Goffin's book *Aux Frontières du Jazz* was published in 1930, four years before *Hot Jazz*. It was the first long study of jazz that combined a survey of the current scene with an attempt to analyze it. Like Panassié, Goffin believed that jazz brought something totally new into the world of music. He too applauds it as a sort of proletarian revolt against elitism.

> The hot style . . . is the only intelligent, spontaneous, original one, putting the executant on the same level as the composer . . . melodic jazz [by which he means Jack Hylton, Paul Whiteman and other jazz "symphonists"] differs little from classical music. Hot jazz alone brings a modification in a way similar to modern art, which Epstein has recently defined as a new state of intelligence. Jimmy Dorsey or Louis Armstrong are to Puccini or Debussy as Cendrars or Aragon are to Victor de Laprade or to Lamartine.[14]

For all this, *Aux Frontières du Jazz* falls a long way short of *Hot Jazz*. Panassié correctly discerned that swing was the essence of jazz, even if

155

he could not properly define it. Similar attempts by Goffin were less successful. Having decided that jazz should be hot rather than melodic, he goes on to tell us that Jimmy Dorsey, Frankie Trumbauer and, incredibly, *Boyd Senter* have the monopoly among hot saxophone players! He never understands that an improvisation is not hot unless it swings. To the end, he confuses swing and improvisation.

> It is useful to state that what one calls hot in a piece of jazz is the character of a passage by one or more musicians who abandon the melodic theme in order to play an improvisation which develops within the framework of the piece and incorporates itself in it.[15]

In fact, he never got over his initial discovery of collective improvisation. In *Jazz : From Congo to Swing*, published in 1946, he is still obsessed with the virtues of the Original Dixieland Jazz Band.

> In one fell swoop the Original Dixieland Jazz Band reached the summit of all beauty, the highest emotional level, and this without any compromise with commercialism. . . . The Dixieland band didn't possess swing because they didn't need it. They had something better. They were right in the pulsating heart of jazz where improvisation was at its purest.[16]

More important still, Goffin had very little of Panassié's understanding of the black contribution to jazz. He concedes that: "The blacks have an unbridled spontaneity which the whites lack, a prodigious sense of rhythm and a need for personal expression which is demonstrated by an indifference to, even an absolute ignorance of music."[17] But he then proposes a list of the most promising musicians of 1930 which does not include one black name. This is all the more surprising since, unlike Panassié, he had already visited America and had even spent time in Harlem. He mentions visiting the Savoy, the Lennox Avenue Club, Roseland, the Nest Club and Connie's Inn. Unfortunately, the descriptions which follow display the fatal weakness for the exotic of those who liked to go slumming in Harlem. Observation gives way to fantasy and purple prose. "All the dance halls tremble with the same fever and are subjected to the assault of dazzling rhythms." Dancers are lost in an "artificial horizon which they have created for their nocturnal needs." Beautiful olive-skinned black women have "cow eyes" and mouths "painted like wounds." Musicians are possessed by "voluptuous demons." It is as if, for all his enthusiasm, he still cannot quite believe that black people actually inhabit the world he knows.

A few years ago, hot jazz won a certain favor expressed in the kind of

156

reverence which musicians professed for blacks. So much so, that little by little the colored orchestras were the only hot yardstick for Americans, to the point that any young white who wanted to achieve anything had to submit to the influence of Armstrong, Jimmy Harrison and a few others. . . . One was even able to hope that at that time the white school was going to give a new interpretation of hot jazz, which would be really its own. But alas, it was overwhelmed by the Harlem bands, and all that remained of their efforts was a brave attempt which for some had been a source of hope.[18]

Not surprisingly, therefore, all Goffin's heros are white. Louis Armstrong and the pianist Earl Hines are the only black musicians to receive unqualified praise. Instead, he prefers white players like Jimmy Dorsey (". . . in the opinion of many incontestably the best alto player in the world"), Red Nichols ("all trumpet playing from 1923 to 1928 has been influenced by him") and above all Larry Shields who "did for the clarinet what Louis Armstrong did for the trumpet" and Nick La Rocca who, according to Goffin, surpassed even Bix Beiderbecke. In *Jazz : From Congo to Swing* he wrote: "I can justifiably assert that Bix's records may well be forgotten before those of the Original Dixieland Jazz Band. I hope that this is not blasphemy, but I listened studiously to most of Bix's recordings the other day, and with two or three exceptions they are not worth listening to . . ." Even if he cannot deny the influence of black musicians he seems almost to regret it.

In fairness to Goffin, it should be said that Panassié nearly falls into the same trap too. *Hot Jazz* displays an almost hysterical enthusiasm for the Chicago school of white players who, of course, were themselves exclusively influenced by authentic New Orleans musicians. At one point, Panassié describes Frank Teschemacher as "a hundred times better than all other practitioners [of the clarinet] – blacks as well as whites. . . ." Not content with this, he adds: "Teschemacher had an astonishingly rich melodic invention, which occasionally is strangely reminiscent of Bach's melodic lines." In fact, he considers white Chicago jazz to be of such general importance that he devotes a whole chapter of *Hot Jazz* to the subject. (In later books, however, he comes to realize that his enthusiasm was misplaced. He admits that the success of Gene Krupa, Pee Wee Russell and Jack Teagarden, as well as Teschemacher, lay in their ability to copy the black players.)

If Panassié wrote better books about jazz than other Europeans, this was almost certainly because he was better advised. American attachment to Paris ensured the presence there of a large number of both black and white musicians. Panassié seems to have had a journalist's instinct for asking the right question of the right person. He was lucky even in his first contacts with jazz. When, following his polio attack in 1927, it was decided to buy him an alto saxophone, his father, quite by chance, found one of the best French jazz musicians to give him lessons. It was Christian Wagner who almost immediately introduced him to such classics of white jazz as Bix Beiderbecke's "Singing the Blues" and "I'm Coming, Virginia." According to Panassié, under Christian Wagner's guidance, he made rapid progress in the understanding of hot music. "Wagner was a good teacher, and all that he taught me on the saxophone helped me to get a feeling for the records."[19] Thanks to this, Panassié was one of the first to recognize the superiority of Bix to the more famous Red Nichols. One thing led to another. Again through Wagner he met Philippe Brun and Stephane Mougin, two of the best French jazz players, and Danny Polo, a talented American saxophone player. Both Brun and Mougin were to be of great help in broadening his knowledge and understanding, and during one of Wagner's absences from Paris, he even took a saxophone lesson with Danny Polo.

Panassié lost no time in profiting from his new contacts. One afternoon in the winter of 1928 he went to the Hotel Washington to hear a band which included Philippe Brun and Maurice Chaillou:

> The first time Philippe Brun and Maurice Chaillou sat down apart from the rest of the group. I approached them and complimented them. Then I was unable to refrain from asking Philippe Brun the great question of the day: "Whom do you prefer, Bix Beiderbecke or Red Nichols?" (For even though I preferred Bix, I still thought Red Nichols was a great musician.) The response was unequivocal: "Bix, a thousand times! There is no comparison! Red Nichols is of no importance!"
>
> After a pause he said: "Do you know the recordings by Louis Armstrong? He sounds a bit crazy, but I find it fantastic!" Philippe Brun then went on to recommend "China Boy" by Red McKenzie and Eddie Condon's Chicagoans as "one of the best records ever made."[20]

Thereafter, Philippe Brun became an increasingly reliable source of information. When Panassié first heard records of Duke Ellington, he was put off by the exaggerated growl and wah-wah effects.

> I showed these records to Philippe, saying they were no good. "No good!" he shouted. "But that's Duke Ellington, one of the best orchestras there is. Play them to me." He jumped up and down with delight at hearing these three recordings. ("Flaming Youth," "Doing the Voom Voom," and "The Mooche.") "Since you don't like them will you sell them to me?"

158

Imprudent Philippe! Having seen his reactions, I took good care to hang on to them. That's how it happened that, simply with a few gestures, he had led me to discover elements of unsuspected beauty in these records.

It was Stephane Mougin who put Panassié in touch with the man who was to become his greatest influence, and was the initial source of introduction to most of the American musicians who later arrived in Paris. In March, 1929 the American clarinetist Mezz Mezzrow arrived to play with a band at L'Ermitage Muscovite in the Rue Caumartin. Within half an hour of hearing the news, Panassié was climbing the stairs of L'Ermitage, and almost as quickly had secured Mezzrow's agreement to give him saxophone lessons.

Mezzrow's own description of the event sheds amusing light on Panassié's character.

> I like this kid's enthusiasm, so I went over to see him one day, lugging my records and my horns along. I found him living in a great big house where he had a special study lined with shelves and shelves of records. Then he got straight on my version of "My Blue Heaven." I played the second harmony sax part along with him, and that got him steamed up some. Then I let him hear those records, and all excited he ran into the foyer and shouted for his whole family to come down and listen. The question he asked made me ashamed to admit that I came from the good old USA. "Why Milton," he wanted to know, "haven't I heard any of these terrific records before? I never saw them in any of the record companies' catalogs before." That was when I realized companies in those days were keeping this wonderful music from the world. The records the great colored jazz artists were always listed under a separate heading as "race records." To a naive guy like a Frenchman . . . that listing might have suggested horse races, car races – almost anything but jazz.[21]

This meeting was the beginning of a relationship which transcended friendship, and became a sort of partnership. There is no doubt that it was Mezzrow's influence which turned Panassié more and more towards blacks as the only real source of jazz. This was a debt Panassié never failed to acknowledge. He wrote in *Twelve Years of Jazz*:

> I must insist on this: Mezzrow heard everything, understood everything before anybody else. You think you have properly appreciated an orchestra, a record; with one word, one gesture, he knocks down everything you were going to say and makes you feel how profoundly wrong you were: he had straight away put his finger on something essential which you had missed.

159

He is completely free from cliche and prejudice; this man who is prodigiously intelligent, always judges things with absolute spontaneity.

Mezzrow is equally complimentary about Panassié. He wrote:

> That youngster sure kept himself busy in the years that followed – writing a book called *Le Jazz Hot*, starting a jazz monthly review in Paris by the same name (it soon had dozens of rivals, in almost as many languages, all through Europe), and launching the Hot Clubs of France, which got to be a world-wide movement; then he supervised jazz recordings on both sides of the Atlantic, ran jazz programs on the radio, and wrote a second book that was published in this country as *The Real Jazz*. Practically every jazz critic that I know about today – Timmy Rosenkratz, Harry Lim, Roger Kaye, Nesuhi Ertegun, John Hammond, Charles Edward Smith, Frederick Ramsay, Charles Delaunay, Walter Schaap and even Leonard Feather – was discovered, or helped along, or in some way influenced by Hugues. . . . Ever since that cat latched on to jazz, he's been a one-man mass movement.[22]

Meeting Mezzrow and becoming his firm friend was a unique piece of good fortune. Mezzrow was undoubtedly a man of great intelligence. More important, he was a white man who could relate to his own kind on that level, but who could pass for black among black musicians. He lived and played almost exclusively in the black world, and had the insights which only that could provide.

Even so, it would be a mistake to conclude that Panassié made a reputation out of borrowing other people's ideas. He nearly always over-stated his case, and was prone to sometimes disastrously high-flown sentiments. He could be a vicious and even petty-minded opponent if he felt slighted, as his quarrel with Jacques Canetti proved.[23] But for all that he had the good sense to seek information from those people who knew the answers – the musicians. The fact that Philippe Brun, Stephane Mougin, Leo Vauchant, Michel Emer, André Ekyan, as well as Mezzrow and so many other Americans, helped him as much as they did proves that they must have felt he had something to offer.

As a result, he was more often right than wrong. The English composer Constant Lambert published a highly original critique of music in 1934 called *Music Ho!* in which he makes some very flattering remarks about jazz. For all his musical training – or, more probably, because of it – his comments are sometimes ill-judged by comparison with Panassié's. Although he starts promisingly enough with the statement that:

160

. . . although Tin Pan Alley has become a commercialized Wailing Wall, the only jazz music of technical importance is that small section which is genuinely Negroid. The "hot" Negro records still have a genuine, and not merely galvanic, energy, while the blues have a certain austerity that places them far above the sweet nothings of George Gershwin.

But even if Lambert is delighted by Duke Ellington, who "is a real composer, the first jazz composer, and the first Negro composer of distinction," he quickly blows the gaffe. Almost at once he is falling into the old European preoccupation with form. There follows the amazing statement that:

> His [Ellington's] works – apart from a few minor details – are not left to the caprice or ear of the instrumentalists; they are scored and written out, and though, in the course of time, variants may creep in . . . the first American records of his music may be taken definitively, like a full score, and are the only jazz worth studying for their form as well as their texture.

This is putting his foot in his mouth. But he nearly swallows it when he goes on to announce: "I know of nothing in Ravel so dextrous in treatment as the varied solos in the middle of 'Hot and Bothered,' and nothing in Stravinsky more dynamic than the final section." In fact, the middle of "Hot and Bothered" is nothing more than a string of improvised solos which, by definition, have nothing to do with form, which is anyway much less evident here than in most other Ellington pieces. It is also based on "Tiger Rag," surely one of the most well-worn tunes of the day. The ending, which is supposed to dwarf Stravinsky, is the simplest possible riff played by the brass, while the saxophones scurry through the tune.

However, it is important not to deny Constant Lambert's considerable understanding of jazz. Despite his hang-ups about musical structure, he heard and understood things in jazz that almost all other classical musicians missed. His comments on rhythm are particularly interesting:

> In the best Negro jazz bands the irregular cross-accents are given so much more weight than the underlying pulse, that the rhythmic arabesques almost completely obscure the metrical framework . . . paradoxically enough this "bar line" music often achieves a rhythmic freedom that recalls the music of Elizabethan times and earlier, when the bar line was a mere technical convenience.

He also adds, almost in parenthesis:

Actually, had not the course of English music been interrupted, first by Handel, and then, more gravely, by Mendelssohn, we should probably have found English music very much more eccentric and more full of "conceits" than the tradition of jazz. As it is, certain jazz songs show a more apt feeling for the cadence of English speech than any music since the seventeenth century.

This is first-rate stuff, almost reminiscent of the thinking of A. M. Jones, until one realizes that even he has failed to grasp that jazz swings precisely because the bar lines are meticulously observed. Once they are removed, the "rhythmic arabesques" cease to mean anything at all. His rather scathing references to improvisation also suggest that he did not understand that all the distinctive qualities of the jazz musician – his unique instrumental sound, his rhythmic freedom as well as his melodic invention – are all part and parcel of the improvising abilities he disdains. This is what makes a nonsense of Lambert's earlier comment:

> Improvisation is all very well in its way, so long as its expressive and formal limitations are realized. At first sight it might seem that improvisation would lead to a greater freedom in music, but in actual practice it proves a considerable restriction – at least in music based on the European harmonic system.

Of course it all depends on who is free to do what. It goes without saying that solos based on a thirty-two bar chord sequence will have more formal limitations than a symphony or even a sonata. In making this comparison, Lambert is judging jazz by the standards of European classical music in exactly the way which Panassié warns us against. Having accepted this limitation, it still seems that the only freedom which is restricted is that of the artist-composer to impose his unalterable will on future generations of musicians.

☆ REVIEWERS

The supremely important fact about European jazz is that it arrived by means of the gramophone record. Records alone account for the fact that Europeans were way ahead of Americans in appreciating the artistic significance of Negro music. At the same time though, the fact that jazz, for most Europeans, was a recorded and not a live experience, en-

162

couraged certain important peculiarities in their attitude towards it, and unavoidably governed every aspect of the way they tried to play it.

European enthusiasm for jazz has always involved an almost unworkable combination of culturally incompatible attitudes. Black society in America in the twenties was at best semi-literate, and therefore preserved some of the aural features of a tribal society. Great jazz reflected something of the freedom and spontaneity which this kind of culture encourages. The fact that nothing is written down means that although artistic conventions exist, they are formalized in a way which paradoxically encourages individuality rather than restricts it. In Western white society, on the other hand, recorded scholarship and the inevitable intellectual establishments which derive from it make it more, not less, difficult and daunting for the ordinary person to exercise his creative talents. The doctrine of an artistic elite not only deprives the common man of the opportunity to create, but even of belief in his own creative abilities. The very act of writing things down and then printing numerous copies for others to read separates thought from action and the artist from his audience. By contrast, black music depends on an interplay between players and their audience which European "art" music does not. Even today, many of the basic techniques of jazz are employed by most ordinary black Americans in church every Sunday.

There was no danger, however, that Europeans, no matter how well disposed towards jazz, were about to forsake their own cultural sacristy for the Amen Corner. Inevitably, almost their first reaction to the increasing import of jazz records was to *write* about them, as if on the principle "How do I know what I feel until I see what I write?" Articles about jazz had been appearing in various magazines since 1920, beginning with Robert Goffin's article in *Disque Verte* in June that year. But the really important event was the establishing of the *Melody Maker* in England in 1926. A study of the record reviews provides a fascinating survey of European cultural attitudes applied to jazz, and of the almost insuperable difficulties Europeans had in accepting the new music.

Records are said to be one of the earliest instruments of the electronic epoch, which is turning the old world of print into a new era of communication. Certainly in 1925, they must have seemed a rather shocking intrusion into that decorous world where manuscripts and musical scores symbolized artistic achievement. But in fact the gramophone record was probably less a radical detour on the road to McLuhan's Global Village than a logical development of the collection and storing of information which began with the invention of printing.

163

Far from heralding a return to a more spontaneous improvised music, the first years of recordings did almost as much to obscure the real nature of jazz as to promote it. Records, even of improvised music, can be referred to in the same way as books, and this was precisely how Europeans used them. Rather than being dazed with culture shock, they rapidly adapted this new instrument of the electronic age to traditional usages. Fans learned solos from discs in much the same way as if they had read them from printed scores. Even if records meant that musicians were *listening* to music instead of merely reading it, they were still using their ears for reference rather than inspiration. The original inspiration of black jazz was almost buried alive under the weight of European custom and practice. If the popularity of American music in Europe was an impressive demonstration of the Global Village in action, the villagers were tuned in to the fact of recording more than to the idea of improvised music.

But whatever other objections there are to the predictions of Harold Innes and Marshall McLuhan, they were probably right that the invention of printing progressively deprived Western civilization of the use of its ears – an unusually severe handicap as far as appreciating jazz was concerned. J. C. Carothers, writing in *Psychiatry* in November, 1959 on "Culture, Psychiatry and the Written Word," points out:

Rural Africans live largely in a world of sound – a world loaded with direct, personal significance – whereas the Western European lives much more in a visual world which is, on the whole, indifferent to him . . . sounds are, in a sense, dynamic things, or at least are always indicators of dynamic things – of movements, events, activities, for which men, when largely unprotected from the hazards of life in the bush or the veldt, must be ever on the alert. Sounds lose much of this significance in Western Europe where man often develops – must develop – a remarkable ability to disregard them. Whereas, for Europeans in general, "seeing is believing"; for rural Africans, reality seems to reside far more in what is heard than in what is seen.

Within a relatively short period of time, we therefore found ourselves in a situation where only what is written down is art. In these terms, jazz was a non-starter. Equally, literacy creates the need for education, which in turn favors those who can afford it. Most Western intellectuals are therefore essentially middle-class moralists, who find art interesting only in so far as it reveals or reflects their values. Jazz, particularly at its "nigger end," was socially as well as artistically beyond the pale. The first seven or eight years of jazz history are a

164

record of the frantic attempts by white jazz fans to purge the music of its black influences and clean it up for middle-class consumption.

Indeed, as late as April, 1931, the *Melody Maker* published a piece entitled "Keep it Clean" which deplored the "retrograde" tendency by musicians to imitate the "piquant barbarity of the Negro" and laments that even "so refined a white combination as the Five Pennies" is "relapsing into dirt" by imitating the "husky tone of the colored man's voice." The author concludes by urging that British musicians should take a stand and "should only borrow from [the Negro] when it is not to the prejudice of their own duty, viz: the refinement of dance music by means of the positive and more highly developed musical qualities which they have inherited."

This holier than thou attitude is difficult to forgive, considering its considerable practical limitations. Musical literacy converted music into a kind of mathematics and thereby enlarged its harmonic possibilities. At the same time, however, by insisting on the "true" pitch of every note, it robbed music of its expressive vocal qualities, and the limitations of written notation imposed crippling rhythmic restraints. This is why almost all white jazz of the twenties completely fails to capture the robust, earthy quality of black music, and sounds more sentimental than swinging. Even though white musicians quite quickly came to grips with the problems of improvising, they did so in a meticulously analytical way which robbed the music of much of its spontaneity and emotional intensity. It was as if Europeans had to intellectualize jazz before they could understand it.

In April, 1929, the *Melody Maker* published an article by Al Davidson, MA, which perfectly illustrates the point. "What started as dance music is rapidly proving that, owing to its progress, it will have to be recognized in the near future as something serving a far greater purpose than merely an accompaniment for dancing . . . modern rhythmic music has arrived at a stage where, at its best, it is worthy of being considered as a form of music which is by no means valueless even when adjudged with the highest artistic standards in mind." Breathing an almost audible sigh of relief that jazz has finally found its way into a safe, familiar cultural haven, Mr. Davidson proceeds to dissect Paul Whiteman's recording of "Sweet Sue" as if addressing a course at the Royal College of Music.

> Probably you will have already noted from Ex. 2 that the extraneous matter consists of a series of secondary sevenths in their first inversion (alternately known as chords of the added sixth).

165

You will notice that each note of these chords is at a distance of a tone from its adjacent notes. This is an ingenious way of producing the effect of the whole tone scale. Although the melody line cannot be looked upon theoretically as part of the whole tone scale, since the notes of which it is comprised are all diatonic to the scale in which the movement is written (C-major), the notes which form the harmony are not all diatonic, and the false relation between the diatonic and the non-diatonic notes (i.e., between Eb of the second chord in bar one and the Eb of the third chord in the same bar) combined with the consecutive fifths in the bass and the consecutive tones between the top and third of the four parts, produce the strangely rugged effect without any inflection of the diatonic melody notes.

Bix Beiderbecke's famous solo chorus got the same remorseless treatment the following month. Davidson wrote:

> The lead-in quavers before bar one are composed of the same notes as the melody proper, i.e., Eb and F, and form a useful bit of stock-in-trade.
>
> The C in bar two is the major thirteenth of the dominant chord and is of course an appoggiatura to Bb (understood) of the fourth beat.
>
> The C's of bar three are appoggiatura notes to the essential Bb.
>
> The Cb of bars four and five is the flattened major third of the tonic chord. The mental effect is, I think, that of Bb, which is the appoggiatura note to Cb. This is characteristic of present-day hot dance music, and I believe Red Nichols did much to popularize the expression.

Not all such analyses were as didactic as this. In October, 1931, the *Melody Maker* published an interesting article by Spike Hughes on Babe Rusin's chorus on "Just a Crazy Song." The piece contains plenty of technical detail for those who like that sort of thing, but wherever possible it is used to explain *melodic* ideas.

> The first bar of the second section (bar nine) is nothing more than a short phrase on the chord of F with an added sixth. The next bar, however, introduces an emphasized seventh into the chord; not, let it be noted, Eb, which would demand a change to Bb to be perfectly logical, but Eb, a major seventh. This Eb resolves to a D in the orthodox manner, but it also gives, curiously enough, the suggestion of the melody, but, as it were, a bar too early. . . . Bars twelve and thirteen run together in a very attractive

166

way, so smoothly in fact, that the change of harmony to G⁷ is hardly noticeable. The twelfth bar is another way of playing the well known phrase:

which must have been used in a thousand and one Negro blues. . . . An
old friend from the twelfth bar reappears in the twenty-second bar.
Again, by tying the last quaver (D) over into the next bar, continuity of
phrasing is preserved.

A less gifted player might well have played the passage thus:

– which makes the phrase awkward and the following bar (twenty-three)
not a little ordinary. The line of this bar is interesting for on the chord of
C⁷, it introduces the ninth (D) and a diminished chord of the last half of
the bar, before finally coming to rest on C⁷.

Spike Hughes seems to want us to understand the harmonic ingenuity
should be used in the interests of melodic ideas and not as an end in
itself. He notes that Babe Rusin's chorus is "almost ideally suited as a
study of hot playing," because "it departs less from the melody than
some of Jimmy Dorsey's choruses and Armstrong's famous 'Tiger
Rag.' . . . Compare these choruses with Babe Rusin's and you will find
that Babe's is clarity itself when it comes to recognizing the melody. His
method is instructive; he sets out to paraphrase the original tune and
gradually develop it as he gets to know it better." He goes on to advise
students of hot music to keep the melody clearly in mind when improvising, adding that "some of the most effective choruses are nothing
more than simple paraphrasing of the melody. When the melody is not
particularly active, then it is time to indulge in a few fireworks. Be
sparing with the arpeggio business; use your knowledge of passing notes
and play around the chord."

As far as it goes, this kind of advice is both sensible and illuminating.
Unfortunately, it does not, and can never, go far enough. The jazz
musician, by definition, is engaged in a sort of musical odyssey – a
search to find himself. For obscure psychological reasons which are
hard to define, an intellectual approach to music makes this harder to
achieve. Analysis seems to objectify musical experience in a way which

is at odds with the more intuitive, even sub-conscious reflexes of the jazz musician. Indeed, contrary to popular belief, conceptual attitudes generally create more, not less, fashionable conformities, a fact which probably explains why in the second half of the twentieth century it is easier than ever before to confuse uniformity with excellence.

The fact that even musicians as perceptive as Spike Hughes were not yet able to see jazz in anything but a European context shows the extent to which these musical habits died hard. It took Europeans nearly ten years to realize that such attitudes to jazz harmed its vitality and halted its swing. Consequently, jazz before 1930 did not mean Louis Armstrong, but Ben Bernie, Vincent Lopez, Paul Whiteman and other specialists in "symphonic" jazz. This music faithfully reflected the European obsession with harmony and its relative neglect of rhythm. Complicated arrangements were the hallmark of good jazz among jazz "symphonists," who vied with each other in devising a thousand ways to cast the fox trot in the form of a symphony. In so doing they congratulated themselves on the fact that their efforts had raised the music from its crude, amorphous origins towards a more acceptable place in the European Pantheon. It was taken for granted that black bands were crude and unmusical. Their broad instrumental tone and heavy vibrato recalled the worst excesses of the Original Dixieland Jazz Band.

In January, 1927, the *Melody Maker* reviewed two sides by Jelly Roll Morton's Red Hot Peppers, recorded in Chicago the previous September.

A band of which I have not hitherto heard called Jelly Roll Morton and His Red Hot Peppers is introduced to us in "The Chant" and "Blackbottom Stomp," both hot charleston numbers. No one can say that the musicians are not wonderful performers. Nevertheless, we are treated to an exhibition of blues and jazz, not as it should be today, but as it was six years ago. The fact that this is about the best record to have come across for charleston dancing, owing to the hot rhythm behind it, certainly does not excuse the fact that it is crude in organization and poor amusement to listen to.

A third side, "Sidewalk Blues," received similar treatment in the April edition: "There is nothing much out of the ordinary rut in any one [of the HMV recordings issued that month] except "Sidewalk Blues" by Jelly Roll Morton's Red Hot Peppers, the extraordinary point about which is that it was ever issued at all, as it is hopelessly old-fashioned in style, even if the musicians can play their instruments, and recalls the Original Dixieland Jazz Band."

168

Some black bands of the time might have justified such harsh criticisms, but to describe these sides in this way was a colossal blunder which precisely illustrates the problems. Europeans had in appreciating jazz. "Blackbottom Stomp," for example, is beautifully recorded, its exuberance and vitality perfectly captured with exceptionally natural acoustics. It has all the Morton ingredients: built-in breaks, stop-time phrases, rhythmically lively themes, frequent contrasts of sustained whole note phrases with bouncily syncopated eighth-note patter, and a brilliant stomping trio. Gunther Schuller, writing in *Early Jazz*, adds: "But beyond this, it offers a special dividend, perhaps unique in diatonic music, classical or otherwise. The first part, with its three separate themes, is in B♭, and yet no B♭ chord (with the single exception of a passing tone second inversion) ever appears; it is avoided and delayed until the ninety-sixth bar of the piece. This gives the whole first part a curiously suspended and unresolved feeling and imparts a unique forward momentum. . . ."

The disastrous reception of these wonderful Morton recordings was all the more ironic in that European writers were never tired of complaining that black jazz lacked form. For all that, they never noticed that Jelly Roll, who was obviously bored by the theme-solo-theme format of most jazz, was concerned instead to create the maximum variety in his music, using several themes in contrasting keys, and experimenting with instrumental texture in a way which was less dramatic than Ellington but, at least in 1926, was highly effective. In short, despite Duke's greater reputation, it was Morton – not Ellington – who was the first composer in jazz, perhaps even its first intellectual, a fact which probably explains their undying enmity. As Gunther Schuller pointed out in *Early Jazz*, "Through an effective balance between repetition, near repetition and variation, Morton was able to achieve sophisticated forms which often came close to the Rondo form, and occasionally even surpassed it in complexity."

Reading the record reviews of the time in papers like the *Melody Maker*, it is not hard to see how the confusion arose. In November, 1927, the paper reviewed "Down Our Alley Blues" by Duke Ellington and "Whiteman Stomp" by Fletcher Henderson.

"Down Our Alley Blues" [is] played by Duke Ellington and His Washingtonians, a colored unit in which the expected faults of coon bands – a noticeable crudeness and a somewhat poor tone – are by no means so apparent as usual. The *orchestration* [my italics] of this number is clever.
But when it comes to really good nigger style, I'm afraid that Massa

Ellington will have to give pride of place to . . . Fletcher Henderson and His Orchestra, who have excelled themselves for this company [Columbia]. Their orchestration of "Whiteman Stomp" is a masterpiece. It contains stuff worthy of any symphony. The performance is unusually musicianly (some extraordinary technique is displayed) and the rhythmic ingenuity in syncopation for which the colored races are renowned has not been lost in any way.

Significantly, Don Redman's arrangement of this Fats Waller number was so complicated that even Paul Whiteman's band could not play it at first. So, although there is indeed some ingenious writing in the piece, particularly in the use of 3/8 and 3/4 figures for the reeds, the record is ultimately a failure because it is pretentious. White reviewers presumably liked it because it reflected the same flashy, meretricious style of orchestras like Paul Whiteman's and, later, the Casa Loma. The preoccupation of these bands with complex harmony and elaborate displays of technique constantly got in the way of the rhythmic drive which was the sustaining force of black bands like the Red Peppers. Swing encourages the distillation of a melodic idea to its essence; its distinguishing feature is understatement. By contrast, the gimmicks and symphonic pretensions of white bands dated themselves, and so the success of each succeeding fad was short-lived. No sooner was some new symphonic brand of jazz on the market than the moss was already seen creeping up its limbs.

A comparison of Don Redman's arrangement of "The Chant" for Fletcher Henderson with the Red Hot Peppers' version perfectly illustrates the point. Redman's training at the Chicago and Boston conservatoires infected him with a weakness for white orchestral practices, and his early work for Henderson shows a disastrous tendency to try to outdo Paul Whiteman. Henderson's recording of "The Chant" is therefore dull and gimmicky by comparison with Morton's. Although it was written by Mel Stitzel, "The Chant" contains all the elements which Morton fashioned so brilliantly in his own compositions: a multi-thematic form, sudden and unusual harmonic shifts – there is even a suggestion of a bitonality in the introduction, whose call and response alternates between D and D♭ – and riff-like melodies which Morton works up to an exhilarating climax. Except for a decidedly old-fashioned trombone solo, the whole piece rocks relentlessly along. No white musician at that time could have matched the relaxed, unhurried phrasing of the syncopated figures in the introductory strain. The bass player, John Lindsay, plays two rather than four beats to the bar, but he

170

has obviously reached the point of changing to a smoother, four-beat style, and in fact does so behind Jelly Roll's piano solo. George Mitchell's tone and attack on the trumpet are excellent throughout, but Omer Simeon in particular turns in some searing, bluesy clarinet solos, whose emphasis on the flattened fifth subtly suggests the bitonality of the introduction. White reviewers heard none of this. To them, this kind of torrid playing recalled the painful memory of the Original Dixieland Jazz Band, and they dismissed it as so much old hat, quite unaware that this was where jazz was inexorably heading.

It would be easy to explain the neglect of those outstanding records as pure prejudice. And it is certainly true that the whole gamut of reactionary racial nostrums and taboos prevented both black and white jazz musicians of the 1920s from confronting each other as equals. Jelly Roll Morton was, therefore, "coon" music, brash and unsubtle almost by definition. But even the most irrational prejudice has its roots in some tradition. Behind the racism, there lay less obvious but much more compelling reasons why the white cultural establishment of 1927 should prefer the fragile, tinselly sweetness of Red Nichols to the drive and excitement of Jelly Roll Morton. In the first place, European music was traditionally concerned with harmony rather than rhythm. Accordingly, black bands were admired for the complexity of their arrangements rather than for their rhythmic drive.

Unfortunately, though jazz was already developing an ever lighter but more powerful swing, jazz critics showed very little understanding of this essential fact. Instead, they were more concerned to prove that Ellington, who was a composer, was therefore superior to Louis Armstrong, who was only a virtuoso soloist. Before Armstrong appeared on the scene, there may have been some excuse for not knowing what was happening. Poor technique and worse instruments often hampered the rhythmic drive of black bands in the early twenties. But after Louis' first recordings with Earl Hines had appeared in early 1928, there could be no possible doubt that swing was the way jazz was going. It was to preoccupy both black and white musicians for almost forty years.

The other equally important reason why whites were so slow to grasp the significance of swing was the fact that acoustic recordings rendered bass and drums almost inaudible. Consequently, tubas, saxophones and, later, bass saxophones became popular in the twenties because they were easier to record. However, only the string bass combines the mellow tone and subtle attack which swing requires, and the history of swing is largely the story of the emergence of that instrument as the key element in the jazz rhythm section. Ironically, when electronic recording

171

restored the balance between the rhythm section and front-line instruments, it was the older New Orleans pioneers like John Lindsay, Pops Foster and Welman Brand, who had developed the use of the bass fiddle in jazz before the First World War, who reemerged from the shadows to set the light but driving beat which was to be the basis of swing for the next fifteen years.[24]

These factors were the governing influences in the development of jazz in the middle twenties. Chicago was still the geographical center where the best music was concentrated. New Orleans was too far off the beaten track, and New York had not yet come into its own. Consequently, only a small minority of the best white musicians ever heard live black jazz, and records were the main means of communication. The fact that black bands tended to be badly recorded, even by acoustic recording standards, encouraged belief in their inferior musicianship. Moreover, back music, which was more concerned with swing than with fancy arrangements or a pretty sound, was bound to suffer disastrously from recordings which reduced the rhythm section to little more than a dull thump in the background. So even good white players often failed to appreciate the real significance of black music. "I didn't like the sound they produced," recalls saxophonist Gene Prendergast. "Black orchestras had inferior instruments. I remember McKinney's Cotton Pickers had a particular intonation problem . . . such bands often didn't play in tune those days. . . . They had drive but they had no influence on the music field at that time."

Such attitudes were reflected in the fact that jazz recordings were dominated by East Coast white musicians like Red Nichols, Miff Mole, Jimmy Dorsey and Arthur Schutt. Nichols and his colleagues were based in New York, which was the center of the recording industry, and to that extent they had less contact with the South Side of Chicago, with its huge concentration of black people, where the new sounds were evolving. Their music was polished, professional, tuneful, even occasionally ingenious, but it never had the drive and excitement of the real thing. "None of it was jazz," recalls pianist Jack Russin. "Red Nichols wasn't jazz. . . . Even Bix wasn't jazz. It was just pretty music, but it had no real drive." Saxophone player Bud Freeman confirms this:

You see, New York was way behind Chicago as far as jazz was concerned. I remember when I got the offer to go with Ben Pollack in 1928. That meant leaving Chicago and going to New York and I ran into Don Redman who was arranging for the Fletcher Henderson band and who was a good friend. And he said, "Bud, you're not going to like New York – they

172

don't swing there." I said, "You mean everybody? Black and white!" He said, "I mean they don't swing period." It wasn't until Louis went there in 1924 that they heard that kind of swing.

Inevitably, change came only when the handful of white players who had been brought up with the music of Chicago's South Side clubs began to make their own records. Bass saxophonist Spencer Clark, who worked for both Lud Gluskin and Ray Ventura in France in the late twenties, remembers distinctly that "the first four-beat music I heard was the recordings by the Mezzrow-Condon group from Chicago, with Jim Lanigan on bass. They made four sides for Okeh – "Liza," "China Boy," "Nobody's Sweetheart" and something else I can't recall. . . . This was music which was really trying to swing. . . . They got it from the music they heard over on Chicago's South Side."

The various Mezzrow-Condon groups did indeed exercise considerable influence in jazz as founders of what later came to be called Dixieland. But listening to these records today, it is clear that while they certainly introduced an uncompromisingly hot sound into white jazz, the music was more raucous than swinging. The real innovators were two other white musicians who almost single-handedly changed the face of jazz by their skilful adaptations of the New Orleans jazz they heard in Chicago. The first was bass player Steve Brown, who was from Louisiana and the brother of band leader Tom Brown. After appearing with his brother's band in Chicago in 1915, Steve Brown later formed the New Orleans Rhythm Kings, the first white group to be directly influenced by King Oliver and Jelly Roll Morton. By 1926, Steve had developed a fast, driving four-beat style of string bass playing which transformed the polite society bands of Jean Goldkette and Paul Whiteman with whom he was then playing. According to Gene Prendergast, the effect was sensational. "I was in the Greystone Ballroom in 1926 when Steve Brown joined Goldkette. I remember the first rehearsal when he took a chorus. . . . It was unheard of. It was so good, everybody cheered when he got through. Nobody could believe it."

The other great stylist whose influence persisted at least until the 1940s was the drummer Dave Tough. "Dave was way ahead," recalls Bud Freeman. "In fact, Dave started what the modern drummers do today. Dave was very much influenced by Baby Dodds and then he surpassed that. . . . I never heard a drummer as good as Dave." Leo Vauchant, who worked with Dave Tough in Paris in 1928 and 1929, agrees. "Tough was way ahead of all the other drummers. He wasn't the first to play four to the bar. I was. I was doing it in 1918 when I was

173

listening to that Mitchell band. But Dave was the first to complement the soloist's rhythmic ideas. He kept a marvelous beat and he had this wonderful ear so he'd pick up the rhythmic ideas in a solo and complement them on the drums." It is clear from this that he had distilled his early experiences in Chicago listening to King Oliver and Jelly Roll Morton to produce the supple, sensitive but irresistible pulse on which good jazz depended until the avant-garde revolt of the 1960s. Black drummers like Sid Catlett, Chick Webb and Joe Jones were probably doing the same thing, but the fact that Tough was white and that he had therefore worked with men like Benny Goodman, Bunny Berigan and Tommy Dorsey, who all recorded extensively, greatly increased his influence and importance.

If the history of jazz, particularly in Europe, was governed first and foremost by records, reviews in the various jazz papers and magazines were scarcely less important. The *Melody Maker* was the first and most important English language paper to devote extensive coverage to jazz, and its influence in Europe was correspondingly great. From 1926 until 1929, the paper faithfully reflected the attitudes and opinions of all white jazz enthusiasts everywhere. Bix Beiderbecke, Joe Ventura, Eddie Lang, Adrian Rollini and Arthur Schutt "were the finest players of this type of music." The California Ramblers produced records which were "as hot as they can make 'em – even in America!" Red Nichols' recording of "China Boy" was "the best hot record ever made." Arthur Schutt was "probably without exception the finest of all the many great pianists devoting their talents to modern rhythmic music." Reading through the reviews, it is difficult to believe that Red Nichols Miff Mole, Arthur Schutt, Adrian Rollini, Frankie Trumbauer and the various members of the California Ramblers had not got the hot record market sown up.

But in April, 1931, an event of unusual significance occurred when Spike Hughes, writing as "Mike," replaced Dan Ingman as hot record reviewer. Hughes was not only an excellent writer and musician, but a bass player. Reviewers and musicians were already becoming more aware of the importance of the rhythm instruments in jazz as recording techniques improved. In October, 1929, the *Melody Maker* noted in its comments about Miff Mole's version of "That's a Plenty" and "I've Got a Feeling I'm Falling" that:

The great strides made in American recording which permit of both bass and drums being used exactly as they are when a band plays ordinarily in public have given Stan King (drums) great chances which he does not fail

174

to take. Not only does he supply a rhythm which is as rock-solid as it is delightfully lilting – and this is most important in this record because, remember, there is no bass instrument, and the whole foundation of the rhythm has to be carried by piano and drums. . . . Note that Stan plays four beats to the bar on his pedal most of the time!

Hughes' appointment decisively confirmed this trend. Only a month after he joined the paper, he wrote an article about the role of the bass in jazz, significantly entitled "Latest Development in Style." The article sets out to describe the new rhythmic freedom which was developing in America. It begins with the revolutionary comment that "there is no such thing as hot bass playing – some play with more swing than others, that is all." It is hard to overestimate the importance of this remark at a time when musicians and critics alike still believed that playing hot and playing with swing were one and the same.[25] He then goes on to discuss various rhythmic figures, adding that bass players should cooperate at all times with the drummer and quoting various side drum effects used by Stan King. The rhythmic figures he quotes are less interesting than his encouragement of bass players to make greater use of both their ears and their imaginations, as shown by the example of Welman Braud with Duke Ellington. He writes:

> There are two ways of enhancing the value of four-in-a-bar rhythms. For example, a phrase as in Ex. 9 –

> may be played –

> or split up into the arpeggio of the chord as in Ex. 11 –

Both of these methods, played with plenty of attack, give some scope to the player's individual talents. If you have a good gramophone, you will find a lot to intrigue you in Duke Ellington's records, who makes a definite feature of a strong bass rhythm.

Thereafter, "Mike" never missed an opportunity to stress the importance of swing, to point out the contribution made to it by bass and drums, and to persuade listeners to play records in order to become better acquainted with this fact. In August, 1931, he reviewed "Panama" by Luis Russell's band.

> That the whole record is full of the most astounding rhythm goes without saying. Luis Russell's telegraphic address is "Rhythm, Harlem." The drummer, Paul Barbavih [sic], takes the honors in this respect. . . .
>
> George Foster (Pops) plays his usual formidable bass.
>
> I am sorry if this is a rather roundabout method of reviewing this record, but I am recording the first impressions.
>
> On first hearing all one notices is the rhythm.

After flattering references to J. C. Higginbottom and Henry Allen, he concludes, "The famous 'Mike' Monthly Tin of Pineapple Chunks, however, is awarded to the drummer with the picturesque name [Paul Barbarin]."

Again, in January, 1932, he wrote a similar review of Duke Ellington's "Stevedore Stomp."

> As is usually the case when Ellington calls a number a stomp, there is a minimum of ensemble playing and a maximum of solo work.
>
> The monthly award for endurance goes without protest to Brand, the bass player.
>
> This man is terrific. What a contrast he affords to our solid English two-in-a-bar and when-do-we-eat players!
>
> So important is he that I am almost tempted to say Brand is accompanied by various solos.

Even more significant were his comments on Claude Hopkins' recording of "How'm I Doin'?" in November of the same year. He wrote:

> The real honors of this record go without a doubt to the rhythm section, whose delicate swing is the most thrilling thing in years.
>
> Listen to the sound of the rhythm behind the vocal passages; now go home and come to me when you hear anything like it in any English band and I will start to take English dance music seriously.

It is when I start listening to details like this, and this is not a particularly outstanding record in any other way, that I realize how far we, in this country, have to travel before we are fit to look a band like this in the face and say, "We play dance music too."

Spike was confirmed in such opinions by his meeting with the American writer and jazz connoisseur John Hammond in the summer of 1931. Hammond was not only a good journalist with a real sympathy and understanding of black music, he knew all the best players in New York personally. This unique combination of good taste and encyclopedic knowledge made him one of the most important critical influences in jazz history. In February, 1932, he became American correspondent for the *Melody Maker*, which had at last become dissatisfied with Herb Weil's indifference to black music. Hammond, by contrast, was uncomprisingly pro-black. He later wrote:

> In the years since, I have often been accused of chauvinism because of my preference for Negro musicians. I suppose I must have seemed so to English readers, but I was being honest. I could not, and still cannot, compare the often stiff feeling of white jazz rhythm sections to the unbuttoned freedom and swing of a superb Negro section. As any musician will tell you, great improvisation depends on, takes off from, is inspired by the drive of proper rhythmic support. I said so again and again in print, prompting some people to call me "nigger lover" or to think I must be black.[26]

It is presumably, therefore, no coincidence that by September, 1931, "Mike" was asserting that blacks were not merely the equals of white musicians, but that they left them standing. He wrote, "It is to the colored bands that we refer for precision, rhythm and ideas rather than those of their white colleagues." Reviewing the year's output of records in December, he enlarged on this adding:

> There can of course be no question that the Negro spiritual is a direct forebear of hot music. The music of a revival meeting is in effect nothing more than a series of vocal extemporizations on, and rhythmic developments of, any theme chosen by the preacher on the spur of the moment.
> The foregoing remarks upon the Negro spiritual and its connection with modern dance music are not intended as mere statements of already well-known facts, but only to explain and account for the indisputably superior position occupied today by the colored as opposed to the white band. . . .
> Thus it is we find the Negro back in the position which is his by right. Thus it is that we find among the highest paid and most sought after bands

in the States the names of Duke Ellington, Fletcher Henderson (what a comeback he has made!), Luis Russell, Mills' Blue Rhythm, Chick Webb, McKinney's Cotton Pickers and, of course, Louis Armstrong.

Within weeks of Hammond joining the *Melody Maker* his columns and those by Spike Hughes read as if they were designed as much for each other as for the ordinary record-buying public. In March, 1932, John Hammond kicked off with a very unflattering review of the currently famous white jazz orchestra, the Casa Loma:

> Well, the Casa Loma finally came to New York again a couple of weeks ago at a most unfortunate place known as Roseland, where folks, downtrodden by day, can relieve themselves of the gold crisis complex.
>
> But to their great misfortune there was another band there, that of Claude Hopkins, a colored combination. First one would listen to the brilliant, over-arranged orchestrations of the white band and think that here was something almost worth hearing. But as soon as the Hopkins crew began one felt a swing and rhythmic urge totally lacking in the other famous aggregation.

Only a month later "Mike" reviewed "Black Jazz," by the same band in almost identical terms, comparing it with "You Rascal You" by Fletcher Henderson. He wrote, "After the slickness and excessive polish of the Casa Loma band, it is almost like a breath of fresh air to hear genuine unpretentious playing like this Connie's Inn record of 'You Rascal You.'"

Both continued to insist on the supremacy of black musicians throughout 1932. In September, John Hammond wrote:

> It is about time we got over terms such as hot music, corny, commercial, etc., all of them expressions of the white man. Either music is sincere or it isn't. If it is the latter, we can overlook it completely without bothering to characterize it. The reason I so greatly prefer the Negro's dance music must be obvious by now; he knows only how to play from the heart. 'Tis the white man, with his patent lack of sincerity, who has given jazz the malodorous name it possesses.

"Mike" responded in kind the following month.

> John Hammond so aptly summed up his reasons for preferring Negro to all other dance music in his "American Notes" last month, that in reply to the multitude of letters which I receive accusing me of undue bias in favor of Negro music, I can only say, "Them's my sentiments too!"
>
> I do not want to give the impression, however, that I consider all Negro

bands and music automatically the last word. . . . I have heard downright bad Negro bands in my time that have played out of tune and technically all wrong, but always with that sincerity and conviction that give a hundred times the thrill of the most suave and polished society bands, just as in Vienna two bad fiddles and a zither playing a Strauss waltz have enchanted me more than ever the London Symphony Orchestra could playing the same piece.

At last Europeans were getting the point that however desirable good tuning and intonation may be, the overriding consideration was that the music must swing. It would be hard to exaggerate the importance of writers like Hughes, Hammond and later Panassié in altering European attitudes to jazz. In 1928 and 1929, Paul Whiteman and Jean Goldkettle were riding high and the barbarous influences of the Original Dixieland Jazz Band were only a distant, if painful, memory. "Nigger" music seemed to have been tamed and *Melody Maker* reviewers were slightly reluctantly admitting that records like "Take It Easy" and "Jubilee Stomp" by Duke Ellington's Wonder Orchestra "exhibit a much more up-to-date style as well as better balance, tone and ensemble than the usual run of colored bands. There is some very surprising technique displayed by the various solo instruments. . . ." It is all rather like Dr. Johnson's dog: it was not merely surprising that the black musician could play well, but even that he could play at all. The February, 1930 review of Earl Hines' piano solo "57 Varieties" refers to "amazing technique," "fecundity of ideas" and "a great swing," and then goes on to sigh over Hines' tendency to relapse into "nigger style." The reviewer concludes with the amazingly patronizing remark that "the record gives the impression of a thin veneer of the more sedate style usually associated with the best dance musicians of a less dusky hue, through which, nevertheless, the colored man's individuality forcefully presents itself."

The history of jazz has always moved extremely fast; Spike Hughes and John Hammond were almost alone in being able to keep pace with events. Looking back today, it is difficult not to feel sorry for reviewers so imminently about to be overtaken by events. Suddenly, only a year or so after jazz writers had been congratulating themselves on getting jazz sewn up in a neat, "legitimate" musical package, there was a new uncertainty in the air. Something – nobody knew quite what – was up. Not only were the blacks showing signs of unsuspected musicianship, but there was a fresh and alarming authority about their music. The tight cultural ship of which jazz critics had so recently boasted seemed about to founder. Then, almost before they knew it, the classical mould in which Europeans had tried to cast their jazz was literally blown apart by Louis Armstrong's arrival in England in July, 1932.

Armstrong's live appearances confirmed that everything was suddenly and shockingly different from what had been supposed even by those who had studied jazz carefully. For years, European jazz enthusiasts, separated from black music by their own musical prejudices, by huge cultural and racial differences, by indifferent recordings and by the Atlantic ocean, had groped their way with great difficulty towards an understanding of the music. The lack of contact with live jazz was a crippling disadvantage. Inevitably, records encouraged imitation – not originality. In July, 1932, English trumpet player Nat Gonella described the almost agonizing efforts he made to imitate Louis Armstrong. "I failed miserably to produce anything remotely resembling the sound which came out of my gramophone. I tried playing with the records. But Louis' range was infinitely greater than mine, and as he always wandered up to his dizzy top register, every few bars, I had to suffer the ignominy of playing the very high ones an octave down." After weeks of struggling with his range, Gonella began to be able to play with high D's and E's, only to discover: "Even though I could play the same notes in exactly the same time values (or absence of them!), I was still very much aware that the effect I produced was nothing like that which came out of the gramophone." He therefore set himself to alter his tone. With great effort he slowed down his vibrato. Then, by using a wider bore trumpet and progressively larger mouthpieces, he broadened his sound. Having learned most of Louis' solos, note for note, he finally produced a passable Armstrong imitation. He concludes, "My copying tactics, as I have tried to show, have improved me immeasurably as a dance player. If my playing (even when I do originate) is inevitably flavored with Louis Armstrong, I am quite content. Short of being a musical genius (which I certainly am not), to my mind the next best thing is to model oneself on the lines of someone who is."

It's interesting that despite such infinitely laborious studies of Louis Armstrong records, no one had yet been able precisely to put their finger on what was the genius of the "world's greatest trumpet player." In January, 1930, the *Melody Maker* published the text of a BBC broadcast by a certain Major Stone. Stone acknowledges Louis world stature, but his tributes are still rather vague. He states, "Take Louis Armstrong's performance on the trumpet; he seems to have an extraordinary knack of expressing himself. He just tells you the whole story in his own manner, not in orthodox language, but in colloquialisms which he has made inimitably his own."

180

Louis' vocals, no less than his trumpet playing, earn equally lavish but imprecise praise. In May, 1930, the *Melody Maker* wrote of Louis' vocal on "After You've Gone," "To say this is great is absurdly inadequate. In breathless recitative style that is all his own, he sings some totally incomprehensible words. Not that one worries . . . it's the rhythm he gets into it which is so marvelous." Again, of Armstrong's version of "I Can't Give You Anything but Love" in November of the same year: "It's positively thrilling in its intensity. As usual, the diction is terrible – one can hardly understand a word he says, but what rhythm! What phrases! What style! And what feeling! Any dance musician who doesn't get a kick out of this should take up tiddlywinks. . . ."

The first blast of Louis' trumpet on the stage of the London Palladium blew away the last remaining clouds of mystery. Suspicion darkened into horrified certainty. Armstrong's music confirmed the idea of John Hammond and Spike Hughes that, regardless of everything else, jazz must swing. For the first time Europeans were face to face with jazz. Used to recordings, the audience was almost overwhelmed by the reality of the performance. Spike Hughes rushed triumphantly into print. He wrote in the *Melody Maker*:

His personal appearance at the Palladium – to which this journal has already made ample and well-informed reference – is more than a tonic for the overworked critic; it brings to light many points which have hitherto, on the gramophone, been matters for conjecture. . . .

The technique of mechanical sound reproduction being what it is, one must necessarily be left in the dark on listening to gramophone records as to the true nature of Armstrong's playing.

For the benefit of those who were unable to see the "Great Fun Man" of music, let me say that Armstrong is all, and a hundred per cent more, that he impresses you as being when recorded. . . . Until the evening of July 28, 1932, I had never realized the extreme economy of means by which Armstrong achieves his effects, and the light and shade he uses to build his climaxes.

This instinctive building of climaxes reveals the true artist; never in my experience have I known Armstrong to defer or anticipate the last note of a number or allow a bar to go on for too long. You know that when he has finished playing there could never have been a second's more music and that the last word on the subject has been said.

But the bricks used in this colossal edifice of sound are of the simplest. Each brick, be it ever so humble, is the extreme concentration of rhythm. . . .

Armstrong will put so much into a minim (half-note in the USA) that it will set the rhythm going for the next two bars or even longer.

This was the point. It has become a cliche that black people have a natural rhythm sense. But Louis' abilities transcended this. His incomparable sense of swing derived from an uncanny ability to place notes in a way which was both logical and unexpected at the same time. It was this which gave his melodic ideas their uniquely economical quality. It was this *rhythmic* sense which enabled him to say more with one note than a lesser artist could with a dozen. His playing, therefore, was the absolute antithesis of musical verbosity. Every note of an Armstrong solo is placed so as to produce the maximum drive. In a word, it was dynamic. His placing of those notes shows so much understanding of dynamic tension that the very gaps between them produce an irresistible forward thrust.

For most people, conditioned to believe that any personal exhibition during a musical performance was a gross affront to the composer's artistic purpose, Louis Armstrong's live appearances were nothing short of outrageous. The Belgian critic Robert Goffin was at the London Palladium for Louis' opening.

> The tempest of "Rocking Chair" breaks loose and Louis plays, conducting with his eyes and sudden jerks of his hands, capers and contortions of his whole body, as though he wanted to terrify the three saxophones who find themselves called upon for a hot ensemble. . . .
>
> In action, Armstrong is like a boxer; the bell goes and he attacks at once. His face drips like a heavyweight's, steam rises from his lips; he holds the trumpet in a handkerchief, passes into a kind of excruciating catalepsy and emerges. Armstrong, the skyscraper rockets aloft into the stratosphere, blows like one possessed and foams at the mouth; the notes rise in a wailing and the whole right side of his neck swells as though it must burst; then summoning up all the air in his body for another effort, he inflates his throat until it looks like a goiter.[27]

This was more than even most musicians could take. Some, like Reginald King, were incensed ("Louis Armstrong's show offends against all reasonable definitions of good taste and I regard it as an insult to any musician"), or nauseated, like Percy Bush ("A disgusting and abortive exhibition likely to nauseate all decent men"). A rather larger group acknowledged his talent but seemed concerned to protect the public from direct exposure which might shock them. Gerald Moore, for instance, remarked that while he was "a colossal artist," he was "not for the general public for whom his enormously advanced work cannot

182

possibly have any appeal." Ray Noble agreed that he was "the supreme artist" but objected that he "exercises insufficient restraint upon the style which is bound to prejudice certain uninitiated people against him." Joe Crossman admitted that Armstrong's position as the initiator of "half the good things in dance music" was unassailable but confessed that "his actual presence gave me, in a sense, a shock, and I much regret to have to admit to finding something of the barbaric in his violent style and mannerisms." He concluded that it was better to "employ his records than hear the man in the flesh."

It was worse for the general public, who were even less prepared than the critics and musicians for the flamboyant exhortatory style of live black performance, and clearly believed they were in the presence of a dangerous lunatic. The drummer Bert Marshall, who was visiting London from Paris at this time, also heard Armstrong during his 1932 visit.

> He was playing one of those music-halls in Chelsea. And Pete du Congé and some of the boys who were playing with him said to me, "Bert, go behind the pit and catch what the audience are saying!" So when I came back they said, "How did it go?" and I said, "Well, it sounds good to me, but if I tell you what the people are saying, I don't want you to kick my ass right out of here." They were saying, "That man's mad! All that scooby-doo-de-dat! He should be locked up!"

Nat Gonella confirmed this impression. "The business for Armstrong's first visit to the Palladium was said to be a record for the theater at that time. . . . Every performance would be full at Louis' opening, but by the time he had finished, it would be half empty, and I was there every night."[28] Philippe Brun, who was playing lead trumpet for Jack Hylton at the time, remembers even more extreme reactions than this.

> They had to lower the curtain because he used to get tomatoes thrown at him. I swear it! Manchester, Leeds, Blackpool, even London. When he came the first time, it was like that. He laughed, like he laughed at everything. But inside, he was sad. He told me, "They don't understand. . . . They don't like me. I wonder why? In America they like me."

The answer, of course, was that Louis Armstrong was simply ten to fifteen years ahead of his time. To that extent, one can hardly blame the reactions his performances provoked. It was as if there were no precise musical definitions for the extraordinary emotional responses which Louis' playing aroused. By an absolutely unique combination of musical genius and unextinguishable personality, he had shattered all those restricting elements which European musical attitudes had grafted on to jazz in order to ensure its status as "Art." Ironically, he replaced this with something infinitely more artistic. Meanwhile though, intellectuals, even those who liked jazz, adrift from their cultural moorings, found themselves hopelessly at sea with a music which bypassed all their treasured cultural attitudes and addressed itself directly to the emotions. This was music which positively screamed for an unequivocal gut reaction. You loved it or you hated it; you *participated* or you sat there shivering with shock. But whether you liked it or not, from now on, the logic of events was inescapable for anyone who had ears to hear it. Swing was the essence of jazz and Louis Armstrong was its personification. Records like "I Can't Give You Anything but Love," "Dallas Blues," "I'm a Ding Dong Daddy," "Muggles" and "Basin Street Blues" had already prepared the way for acceptance of other great black artists – Earl Hines, Henry "Red" Allen, J. C. Higginbottom, Coleman Hawkins and many more were being listened to with a new appreciation. Louis Armstrong's live appearances in London meant that Europeans would never listen to those records the same way again.

HIGH
SOCIETY

N OCTOBER, 1931, the *Melody Maker* announced in its "News from France" column that the popularity of American music was on the wane. Instead, there was a new demand for French popular songs. The reason given was that "the era marked by a surfeit of rich, money-spending tourists is a thing of the past." This report, hidden away at the back of the paper, conceals the truth about the early popularity of jazz in Europe. Apart from a tiny group of dedicated fans, jazz was merely the fashionable background for the antics of a rich, predominently American, international set. Once the Depression set in, it reduced their need for entertainment proportionately.

The war not only changed America's isolationist attitudes, it altered the face of the Western world by introducing a new age of international travel and communication. Tens of thousands of American soldiers "discovered" the Europe their grandparents had been forced to leave. For many, the experience was a revelation. So, once peace came, the old idea of the "Grand Tour" suddenly became democratized and accessible to a new phenomenon, the tourist. Europe, and France in particular, seemed to offer enticing possibilities of new experiences agreeably different from those of puritanical America. The United States' obsession with the evils of alcohol, for instance, besides launching the greatest crime wave in the country's history and creating a lasting contempt for its laws, also unleashed a flood of tourists hungry for places where the world's finest wines and brandies were a natural addition to the daily diet.

Paris in particular enjoyed an almost legendary reputation among Americans. It was said to be *the* intellectual center, as well as the source of the world's best and cheapest food and drink. Paris, it seemed, catered for everybody. Artists and writers were drawn to the city's extraordinary intellectual life; the rich came to enjoy the leisurely, stylish pace of the world's most fashionable capital, and the not-so-rich were encouraged by talk of the good life in cheap surroundings. It was a city of bewildering contrasts where fact seemed to outrun even the wildest fantasies of moral, middle-class America: a place where Russian princes drove taxis or waited at table, where major-domos dressed up like South American dictators and maître d's treated you with almost royal condescension. Despite the old-world elegance, the refinement and good taste, it was all so exotic, so funky. To young Americans brough up on plain fare and the Protestant ethic, it must have been hard to take it all in. All that good conversation and fine food, for example – food whose spicy sauces and rich sweetmeats sometimes revisited the American digestive systems with such urgent reminders of mortality. Food and talk seemed to be inextricably mingled. Ideas in aspic! Great thoughts flambés! Overcome with it all, you staggered back to your hotel. There you crouched to empty the consequences of your rash enthusiasm for "good conversation" into a hole in the floor, while the plumbing coiled around the walls like so many yards of giant colon, a grim, galvanized reminder of your own intestinal functions. The clean-cut American morality, through which the odor of Listerine habitually wafted, found it all shockingly irresistible. Ignoring Mom's warnings, Americans like the young composer Virgil Thomson flocked to Paris in their thousands to "get screwed, sharpen their wits and eat like a king for nothing."[1]

At its richer and less adventurous end, however, American respect for European refinement was hedged about with caution. A taste was stimulating, but too much could result in a nasty attack of cultural DTs. Those who could afford it therefore sought protection from contact which might prove too close for comfort. Les Ambassadeurs, Chez Florence, Le Boeuf sur le Toit, Zelli's, the Casino de Paris, the Perroquet, the Embassy and Chez Victor were some of the expensive and fashionable restaurants and nightclubs which thrived on the need to import just the right amount of European decor into the American's desire for home from home. Jazz in particular was the indispensable background of their enjoyment of the Old World. Musical establishments vied with each other in presenting bands like Paul Whiteman, Fred Waring, Irving Aaronson, Abe Lyman and Ted Lewis. It was irrevelant that their music was a safe, sometimes ludicrous pastiche of the real thing. The point was that jazz managed to be both fashionable and slightly shocking at the same time. Its novelty, the outrage it caused to the Daughters of the Revolution, its vulgarity, all made it the ideal accompaniment to an age which hid its uncertainties behind an affectation of thoughtless hedonism.

☆ THE IN CROWD

The fact that the twenties were known as the "jazz age" undoubtedly reflected a variety of modern attitudes much more than love of the music. Since most jazz in Europe was shaped and conditioned by these attitudes, it is important to understand them. In 1920 the world seemed to be standing at a watershed. America, and even Europe, was moving into a new age of communication and mass production, and all those obscure psychological laws which link technological progress with a relaxation of social conventions had begun to operate. At the same time, the horrors of the war, and the final ghastly victory, encouraged those who could afford it to forget it all in an orgy of frivolity and pleasure seeking. Society lived for kicks, and tried to do so as publicly as possible.

The Honorable David Herbert was a member of the international set which made its headquarters in Paris in the twenties: "Although life in Paris was elegant it was slightly vulgar too.... It was really the beginning of Café Society. It was a society which thrived on publicity and an image and clowning around. They wanted to be in all the papers, they wanted to be well known internationally."[2] Significantly, many of these gatherings were the most lavish costume parties. Costumes were designed by some of the leading couturiers, took months to prepare and often cost as much as a thousand dollars. There was something fiercely competitive in the desire to be noticed, to be talked about. Consequently, no expense was spared in the creation of an outfit which guaranteed its wearer a sensational entrance. "They'd cost thousands of francs," recalled David Herbert. "You always tried to arrive last. It was always a great secret what you were to wear. It was a sort of race in reverse. ... Really, the whole Paris thing was parties. We went to exhibitions and things, but the parties were the thing."

All this theatricality and dressing up was probably symptomatic of the times. Past realities were too appalling to contemplate. At the same time, a new, automated world was accelerating towards an unknown future. Accordingly, the rich and fashionable retreated from these uncertainties into a private world of make-believe, a land of Cockayne where almost the only absurdity was to take things too seriously. Life was a masque and high society was its stage.

The theatrical designer, Oliver Messel, was a frequent guest at such affairs.

At one time there were costume parties of one kind or another almost every night. . . . I remember there was the marvelous party Nicky de Ginsburg gave with Elsa Maxwell which was a Fête Champêtre. It was absolutely beautiful, in this lovely house he had in the Bois. And Christian Bérat had done some lovely designs for the house. He made it all into a sort of toy theater – almost the whole house draped in blue with the windows all festooned. . . . And Lady Mendl was going to make an entrance stripped to the waist on a white horse. . . . And there were haystacks and all these marvelous fantasies in the garden. Melchoir and Lida sang and there were flashlights popping in all directions. I went dressed as the hind legs of a cow. Perhaps it was the front legs, I'm not sure. I remember making the cow's face decorated with garlands of flowers, with eyes that blinked and huge long eyelashes.

The only way for Americans to get invitations to essential parties was to give them. The problem was how: how to balance the mysterious equations of the European social scene; how to cut through the onion layers of hangers-on to find that inner sanctum, that select congregation of the right people? For many, the answer was Elsa Maxwell. "Anyone who had any money in those days gave her money to give a party," recalls the singer Elizabeth Welch. "This was how she launched the Americans that came to Europe. If I wanted to meet you and I had the money, I got hold of Elsa and she arranged all the big people to be there. She got all that Café Society, and they were nicely mixed from royalty on down, and so I would meet you."

Elsa possessed three essential assets for the social-climber: driving ambition, a sense of humor and an indestructably thick skin. David Herbert knew her well. "Elsa's great thing was this enormous gaiety. Indefatigably, she was the life and soul of every party. She looked like a seal – the ugliest woman I ever saw in my life. But she had a marvelous hearty laugh. . . . You couldn't snub Elsa. If she'd allowed herself to be hurt, she'd have been in her grave." According to Valentine Lawford, "She'd produce a cable from someone like Mr. Attlee for all to admire and it would say, 'I'm terribly sorry, I can't come to your party.' Or she would ring up and say, 'Do come tonight. Douglas Fairbanks is coming and the Duke of so and so. . . .' And you'd go there and there'd be nobody there except yourself and Old Mrs. Hearst – who was very nice."

The activities of hostesses like Elsa Maxwell and her parties added a new American flavor to the European scene. In particular, Americans imported a taste for novelty into the decorous old-worldliness of French and English society. The twenties were a time when it was chic to be

189

modern, and jazz, which was one of the most obvious expressions of being up to the minute, benefited accordingly. It was a concern which had nothing to do with music. Leo Vauchant frequently played for the international set. "These parties – they had no idea! They would have booked anybody. They would have booked Lawrence Welk. If you were playing at the Ambassadeurs, they assumed you were the hit of the day and they hired you." Such people's social priorities were also quite contrary to the spirit of jazz. They wanted background music which would not intrude on the more important business of the good life with its gossip and intrigue. "If you didn't want to dance, you'd sit around and talk and so the music had to be fairly discreet," recalls fashion photographer Horst. "It was schmaltz in a way. It wasn't like disco-teque stuff at all. It was 'Dancing with Tears in Your Eyes' and all that. Even the fast things were not played full blast – that was very bad form."

Society's insistence on the minimum musical interference with its enjoyment had one unforeseeably happy result: indirectly, at least, it helped to increase the reputation and earnings of the Quintet of the Hot Club of France. Although this famous group was fronted by the remarkable violinist, Stephane Grappelly, the band was really built around the extraordinary talents of the guitarist Django Reinhardt. Despite the loss of the use of two fingers of his left hand, Reinhardt's solo style displayed a speed, attack and melodic invention which were unheard of in the early 1930s. In addition, his accompanying of singers and other musicians showed a poignant sensitivity and an intuitive understanding of harmony which was unsurpassed in jazz at that time.

Society, of course, was quite indifferent to this. What mattered was that the Quintet, made up of three guitars, bass and violin, played quietly. As a result they were not only regularly employed in chic places like Bricktop's and Chez Florence, but also at many exclusive private parties. Unwittingly, the rich and fashionable danced the nights away to some of the most extraordinary improvised music to be heard in either Europe or America. Louis Vola played bass with the Quintet during its early years.

Barbara Hutton didn't know Django. She knew the band because we often played the cabarets. I was engaged to provide the band for her marriage. So I got the singer Adelaide Hall and the Quintet. She was delighted. . . . I did a lot of parties like that. It was good because we didn't need a piano or drums. That gave a light sound and it was that which the rich people wanted – not too much noise. Also, I used to set easy tempos. And people used to say, "It's funny – with this band I find I can dance."

☆ NIGHT LIFE

The same people who prided themselves on their lavish parties also patronized innumerable restaurants and nightclubs. In keeping with the spirit of the times, Paris in particular became a place where the best entertainment was available almost twenty-four hours a day. The business of life was pleasure and it was therefore right and proper that the rich and fashionable should apply themselves to this end with almost professional dedication. There was practically no time of the day or night which did not have its allotted social activity. In a world where to see and be seen by the right people was all important, where one's standing was determined by the company one kept, "keeping up with the Jones's" became a sort of endurance test requiring almost Olympic stamina.

In this age of the TV dinner it is hard to imagine a time when dining out was just the beginning of the evening. After dinner at the Ambassadeurs or the Embassy, where one danced to Fred Waring, Irving Aaronson or Paul Whiteman, society moved on to an almost infinite variety of nightclubs whose entertainment was carefully calculated to match the lateness of the hour. Such clubs provided employment for dozens of American musicians, some of whom were good jazz players.

One of the most famous of these was run by Ada Smith, an American Negress known affectionately as Bricktop. She recalls:

They'd come to Chez Florence first, and they never came to there before 11.30 or midnight. Then maybe around one o'clock they started coming on to Bricktop's, and then, they wound up way late in the morning in a place called the Casanova.... The Casanova was a Russian place – Russian music and dancing. Chez Florence had five Negro men, usually Opal Cooper and Sammy Richardson's group, playing for dancing and entertaining. And Bricktop's was just Bricktop's. That's when they said, "Well, I don't care where I go, before I go I gotta go and say hello and good morning to Brick." And everyone arrived. Corned beef hash. Creamed chicken on toast. No great menus, no great food. Just club sandwich and champagne. We had a piano – and some of them were awfully bad – and Mabel Mercer who sang. But no one was paying any attention. Everyone knew everyone. Cole [Porter] would arrive and would be playing the score from his next show. Tallulah Bankhead would arrive and be on with her act naturally. . . . Those places like Chez Florence, Casanova, Scheherezade, which were the chic elegant places. I mean they were only big enough

191

for *the* crowd, *the* people that *belonged*. And they were there every night. You see, people didn't go out once or twice a week in those days. They were out every night. The dance floor was only as big as a dime. But they didn't care about that. They came to meet each other. They would just arrive and someone would say (as if I didn't know), "Brick, this is the Marquis of this, the Count so and so, and so and so."

For those who made it, it was exciting to discover that despite all their money and titles these people were so interestingly ordinary. Bricktop was astute enough to grasp that the only way to make a royal duke feel different was to treat him as though he were not. It was a discovery which made her famous.

> That's what they liked more than anything else. Do you know why the Prince of Wales fell in love with Mrs. Simpson? Because she didn't tell him "Yes" all the time. She'd disagree with him: "No Boy, that's not right...." It was something he'd never had in his life. That's the way I was with them. I have always had good manners but never been subservient to anyone. Never, never, never. Whatever their title was, I guess they just saw a little red-headed girl who didn't give a damn. They were just people as far as she was concerned. Which they were. . . . It was a pleasure to be with them, I can tell you.

It was no accident that Bricktop, who had worked the speakeasies of Chicago and New York, was an integral part of this scene. High Society was unassailable precisely because its rules of access were so indefinable. Admission was no longer a straightforward matter of class. It was as if society recognized that its select coterie would be all the healthier for the addition of a certain mongrel element. It was not enough even to be rich and famous. For the first time, there was a distinctly low-rent side to being up to date. You had to contribute, to sustain that mood which was so amusing and modern, which the new American age had introduced.

Bricktop was therefore just what such a society was looking for. She has always been a lady of unusual wit and intelligence. In the very early twenties she was working with Florence Mills and Cora Green at Chicago's famous Panama Club at 35th and State Street. Although not a jazz or blues singer, she was part of that black musical world whose stars were King Oliver and Jelly Roll Morton. "I met Jelly Roll back in 1916–17 in Los Angeles," she recalls. "He was a temperamental boy. He couldn't make up his mind whether he wanted to be a pimp or a piano player, so I told him to be both." Bricktop was famous for never being

192

surprised by anything. Her cool, ironic view of the world, her supreme self-confidence, her tough, hustler's past in the speakeasies, combined with a remarkable talent for handling people, assured her a unique place in a society which was already acquiring a taste for black entertainers.

I arrived in Paris on May 11, 1924. This girl Florence Jones who was working in this little place the Grand Duc had left. And her husband told the manager, "Why don't you send to New York and get a little girl named Bricktop." I was about half the size I am now. He said, "She's no great singer or anything but she's got a terrific personality." So the manager said, "Won't she be competition for your wife?" And Palmer Jones said, "My wife needs competition – her head's got too big already. And this little red-headed girl will really give her personal competition."

So that's how I got to Paris. I arrived and I sat around for months and months and months. I got paid, but people would come looking for Florence or one of the other Negro entertainers – there were about half a dozen in Paris at that time. And I'd say, "They're down the street, down the street."

One night a man came in and was standing at the bar having a drink, because that was the only way you could get a drink, at the bar. And this man said to me, "Are you colored?" I said, "Well, certainly I am colored." He said, "Don't you know there's another Negro girl singing here in Paris?" I said, "I know. It's only Florence." He said, "What's your name?" I said, "My name's Bricktop." He said, "I think you're awfully good. Do you know my wife?" I said, "I don't even know you." He said, "My wife is Fanny Ward."

Well, at that time, Fanny Ward and Elsa Maxwell were running neck and neck, who was the biggest hostess in town. He said, "I'm going to bring my wife here to see you." So he brought her in a couple of nights later. And she said, "Can you stand success?" I said, "Nothing excites me" – I was a fresh little kid you know. She said, "Florence got excited." I said, "I'm not Florence – I'm Bricktop." She said, "I'm going to pack this place overnight." And overnight they packed it. Fanny Ward and Jack Dean, her husband. They were one of the first facelifts. Jack had his lifted first. Then later Fanny had her face lifted. But they packed the place until they had to come back home. Then the place sort of fell down.

And then the Left Bank started coming in. All the artists and painters from Montparnasse – like Mainbocher, and Ernest Hemingway and Bob McAlman. And one night Scott Fitzgerald and Zelda. Well, that became a love match for Scott and Zelda and Bricktop. And you know Scott was a very mischievous boy, but a beautiful wonderful person. . . . And then one morning a few months later there was one man in the place who was having a bottle of wine and corned beef hash. And as he was going out a colored musician came in and was hugging him. So later, I said, "Buddy, who was that man?" And he said, "Cole Porter." So I said, "Oh, my goodness gracious! I was just singing a song of his." Well, he came back the next evening and he asked, "Little girl, can you dance?" He didn't ask me about the singing – he knew I couldn't sing. I said "Yes."

Well, the charleston had never been introduced you know in Europe. It had just been introduced in New York – this was about 1925. So he said, "Let me see you do it." Well, as they later wrote in the French papers, "Mistinguett does not have the most beautiful feet and legs in the world. They belong to the little mulatto who works up in Montmartre. Bricktop is her name."

So I did the charleston for him, and he just looked and said, "That's some legs. They talk! They really talk!" He said, "I'm gonna bring some friends in to see you." And he brought in Elsa Maxwell.

Then a man arrived late one night – Amos Lawrence was his name. He said to me, "Brick, I want you to come to my house." I forget the night – it was sometime the next week. He said, "I think His Royal Highness is going to be there." Well, I had never met the Prince of Wales, so I went to this man's party, and the Prince of Wales arrived with the Marquis de Polignac. And they sent for me – he was over in another salon. It was a big place. So I went over. And he didn't want to learn the charleston. He already knew the charleston. But he wanted to know, could I teach him the black bottom? That was the dance that followed the charleston. So I said I would and I showed him some steps – he was a great dancer you know. So Mrs. Bates, who was a distant cousin of the Royal Family, said, "The Prince wants to have a private lesson tomorrow. Can you do it?" I said, "Certainly."

So the next day, I took the great Hutch [Leslie Hutchinson], who was playing piano for me, to play my charleston party for me. And Mr. Bates said, "Brick, the Prince wants to give a party tonight. Where could he give it?" And Hutch walked over and said very politely, "Brick, if the Prince gave his party tonight in that place you're going to open next week – that's it!" And so I told him – and it was!

The House of Windsor had appreciated Afro-American music since at least the 1850s when Juba, "King of Dancers," had appeared before Queen Victoria. Since then, Bert Williams, who had introduced the Royal Family to the cakewalk before the First World War, and Will Marion Cook, whose band performed spirituals and even blues for

194

The Ray Ventura Band
in Paris, 1928 – ABOVE
Noel Chiboust is third
violinist from left and
Ventura is in the center
– and LEFT the band in
the mid-1930s.

Gregor and the
Gregorians in 1930: –
ABOVE Gregor (extreme
left), Stephane Grapelly
(fifth from right) and
Philippe Brun (extreme
right); and RIGHT at
the Olympia in Paris
in the same year.

ABOVE The Eddie South
Band in 1937: (from
left to right) Tommy
Benford, Isidore
Langlois, Eddie South,
unknown, and Dave
Martin.

LEFT Louis Cole in the
early 1930s.

Mabel Mercer in the
early 1920s – these
photographs were
probably taken in
London.

The Fred Adison Band: OVERLEAF in the early 1930s; BELOW LEFT in the late 1930s; and LEFT a montage of the publicity that surrounded them in Europe – note that Ray Noble followed them in Holland.

RIGHT The Coquatrix
Orchestra – Noel
Chibouste is in the
center and Alex
Combelle is at the
extreme right.

BELOW Waring's
Pennsylvanians: Leo
Vauchant is in the back
row, second from left.

LEFT The Rosotti Orchestra in Algiers, 1932 – Noel Chiboust is second from right.

BELOW LEFT Browning and Starr in *Joie de Vivre*, Paris, 1936.

BELOW Cabaret in a Paris night club – the drummer (left) is Billy Taylor and Harry Cooper (right) is on trumpet.

LEFT Philippe Brun's Band in Paris, 1938.

STUDIO PIAZ

MICHEL WARLOP

SWING

OPPOSITE Michel Warlop in the mid-1930s.

LEFT The Lud Gluskin Orchestra in 1930 – Gluskin is the center front and Leo Vauchant is in the front row second from the left.

BELOW The Jack Butler Band in the late 1930s.

RIGHT Bricktop with Salvador Dali (left) and other guests at her club in the early 1940s.

Bricktop and Mabel Mercer together in Paris night spots on two occasions; BOTTOM Bricktop center, and BELOW Bricktop is on the right.

Scenes from Frisco
Bingham's nightclubs:
ABOVE Mistinguett and
friends; BELOW CENTRE
the trumpet player
(right) is Alphonso Cox;
ABOVE RIGHT Frisco
with the Marquis de
Polignac and Count de
Rochefoucauld; BELOW
RIGHT the band
rehearsing in the
deserted club – the
piano player is believed
to be Dan Parrish; and
BELOW LEFT
anonymous revellers.

ABOVE & RIGHT Frisco Bingham, nightclub host, and TOP LEFT visiting the chateau owned by one of his regular patrons, the Marquis de Polignac (left). TOP CENTER Two other regular patrons, the Prince of Wales and Mrs. Simpson, and TOP RIGHT Louis Armstrong pays Frisco's a visit.

BOTTOM LEFT Mistinguett stands out from the crowd in Frisco's; BOTTOM RIGHT Arthur Rubinstein was another regular visitor seen here seated (right) and BELOW on the left.

More revellers in the
club.

ABOVE LEFT Jam session, and LEFT the ultimate gay young things at Frisco's.

TOP RIGHT & ABOVE Two of Emile Savitry's photographs of the high life in Paris.

BELOW LEFT The photographer Horst (center) poses for Cecil Beaton with the Hon. David Herbert and an unknown friend.

BELOW RIGHT Horst's photograph of Princess Jean-Louis de Faucigny-Lucinge dressed as the Empress of Austria at "Le Bal des Valses" which was given by Baron Nicolas de Ginzburg.

ABOVE Bricktop (front right), Julius Monk (extreme right), Mabel Mercer (second from left) and friends in the famous club Bouef sur le Toit.

RIGHT Dancing in the Paris Lido – André Ekyan is the saxophonist on the left.

TOP Freddy Taylor in Paris, *c.* 1935.

ABOVE Willie Lewis in 1935.

RIGHT The Bobby Martin Band in 1937 – the singer is Bobby's wife, Thelma.

them in 1919, were just two of many who had brought black art and entertainment to Buckingham Palace. The Prince of Wales' liking for jazz was in a time-honored tradition.

The fact that he liked to play the drums also enhanced the popularity and importance of jazz. It set the royal seal of approval on what was otherwise only a social affectation. Many of the stories about the Prince's drumming are no doubt exaggerated, but he certainly seems to have sat in with enough bands to prove that his interest was genuine. In 1925, Leo Vauchant was working at L'Abbaye Thélème with a group which included Roger Fishback on saxophone and a Dutch piano player named Freddy Van Root.

> The Prince of Wales used to come in – and get stoned! Then he wanted to play drums. He'd come in a party of maybe four – and they'd get pretty looped. So if he wanted to play we'd let him. He just kept time. He was with us or he wasn't. But mostly he was. We never had much conversation – except maybe if he was to give us a little tip. He'd just come up to the band and say, "I'd like to sit in you know." And we'd say "OK." And we'd play a tune and the people would applaud and then we'd play the same tune again.

Claude Hopkins, who led the band which accompanied the *Revue Negre* with Josephine Baker, also played with the Prince.

> Bud Fisher, the cartoonist for Mutt and Jeff, and the Prince of Wales were very dear friends. And they'd come to this club. I can't remember the name of it, but they were there almost every night. We'd take both of them out feet first every night – dead drunk. I had some pictures of Bricktop, the Prince and myself. The Prince liked to drum and he'd get up on the stand and play. He wasn't very good. He could just about hold the time but not very well. He wasn't too bad if you kept the tempo down. There might have been worse drummers! But he was very popular you know. And then he'd give us a couple of hundred franc notes for letting him sit in for a couple of numbers. I don't know if he was taking drum lessons. He must have been because he knew how to hold the sticks and he could do a roll.

Alain Romans was working at Victor Berrusino's Club in Le Touquet in 1929. "I took Dave Tough with me after he split up with the group at the Abbaye when his wife went off with Jack O'Brien. And we used to open the place up an hour before time and Dave Tough used to play drums just for the Prince of Wales." Bud Freeman, who also worked briefly at the Abbaye asked Dave what he thought of the royal drummer.

Dave was playing at this Argentinian place in the Place Pigalle. It seemed to me to be the most cosmopolitan restaurant of its time. The Prince of Wales, later to become King of England, used to sit in with the band on drums. F. Scott Fitzgerald frequented the place, and he and Dave wrote limericks together. Fujita, the famous Japanese artist, was there with bangs and earrings doing the charleston. I remember asking Dave what he thought of the Prince of Wales' drumming and he said, "He might make a good King."[3]

Despite such royal sanction, society's adoption of jazz was little more than a sophisticated form of tokenism, a fashionable authentication of the "modern" attitudes of the rich. The jazz of the nightclubs was still carefully modulated so as to lull the customers' sensibilities. The result was a sort of musical candy floss into which not even the level of alcohol or the lateness of the hour could inject any drive of excitement. According to Bill Dillard, who played lead trumpet with Lucky Millinder's band on their visit to Monte Carlo and Paris in 1933, Willie Lewis' orchestra sounded ten years behind the times compared to New York standards. Visiting musicians who might have improved things by sitting in were discouraged, and jam sessions, those supreme musical championships where new sounds and styles were perfected, were invariably outlawed. According to Bricktop:

> Those kinds of musicians never hung out at my place – or most others either. They didn't belong in there in the first place. Secondly, it was too small to have a lot of musicians hanging round. They had their girls that they picked up in the street, and I didn't want them girls in Bricktops. I just didn't want them around. Any of those places would have had a fit if Fats Waller had walked in hollering and carrying on. No, they didn't hang out at Bricktop's. We didn't have no jam sessions and all that messy stuff.

Such behavior was permitted only by very special request. Trombonist Herb Flemming's Plantation Orchestra, including Ed Swayzee on trumpet and the nineteen-year-old Jack Mays on piano, was playing at the Abbaye Thélème in the fall of 1930. Flemming recalls:

> At the Abbaye we worked from midnight till 4 AM. There was a tango band opposite us and we would play fifteen minutes in each hour with the tango band doing the rest. . . . So one evening, one of the waiters comes over and hands us a thousand franc note and says: "An American gentleman wants some lively American music!" We were just playing the usual stuff, but we changed right quick. A thousand francs! So we hadn't played more than eight bars when the waiter comes over and hands me another thousand

franc note and says "The lady with him wants you to play slow and soft." It turned out that he was Samuel K. Martin, the millionaire, and she was Mary Jane, one of Ziegfeld's top dancers who had recently been in *Whoopee* with Eddie Cantor. Anyway, they kept on sending me thousand franc notes until the place closed up. So the guitar player took off and the bass player went home too. Jack Mays and I stayed on. And Martin comes up to me and says, "You fellers through now?" I said, "Yes." But he's all set to get us to go someplace else and play some more. So we end up in a club called the Music Box, where we find Georges the owner is about to close too. I said, "This is Mr. Martin. He says he wants more champagne." So Georges says, "Well, I'll have to send for it." "Sure," says Martin, "get all the champagne you can get!" So when Georges saw all that money, he got so much champagne it popped up out of the ground, and we stayed there playing till ten o'clock in the morning. Finally, the drink gave out and Martin passed out! When we split the money, we had something like twenty thousand francs apiece.

It is clear that people neither knew nor cared what they were listening to. Heard but scarcely heeded, the music was little more than audible wallpaper for people who were only interested in jazz to the extent that it was part of being fashionably turned on. Musicians were servants, purveyors of rhythm whose function was to serve up entertainment in any way their employers thought fit. Bert Marshall was working as drummer and vocalist with Freddy Johnson's band at Bricktop's in the early 1930s. "Sometimes we'd get into some pretty odd situations. . . . I don't mind singing a song for tips. But there are some things I will not do. One night there was this rich American woman. After everyone had gone home, she paid the band to take their clothes off. Strip down! And the boys did it because they knew she was loaded. Well I wasn't having any of that. I went home. The others made about ten pounds each just for taking their clothes off and playing."

Such circumstances were not conducive to playing interesting music of any kind, and certainly not jazz. Consequently, as the twenties wore on, almost the only American visitors who were disappointed with their trip to Europe were the young white jazz musicians. Dave Tough, Babe Rusin and his brother Jack, Bud Freeman, Jack Purvis, Mezz Mezzrow, Mugsy Spanier, Jimmy Dorsey and Bunny Berigan were just some of the better known white jazz musicians who heard fabulous tales of life in Europe and worked their way across on the transatlantic liners or joined society bands to see for themselves. With the possible exception of Dave Tough, who came looking for European culture, they

220

found the musical scene unbearably restricted. Jack Rusin commented: "No one who wanted to play jazz had any reason to come to France – except to see France of course." "Berlin wasn't too bad," conceded Jack O'Brien. "We laid 'em in the aisles there. But Paris! It was just damn society music. We could never stretch out." Bud Freeman's trip to Paris lasted exactly eleven days.

> I left Ben Pollack to join George Carhart's band, which was working the "Isle de France" – its second voyage. I was with the top band in the country; it was insane to leave! But I wanted to see Paris. . . . The band on the boat had Babe Rusin, who was only a kid of eighteen, and Jack Purvis. It was just a jam band, but good. So I went for eleven days and heard this terrible music – not because the musicians played it badly, but because it was just music for acts and cabaret. And I said to myself, "Oh God, I've got to get back to music," although it was great to see Dave.

Attempts to play a more robust type of music were ruthlessly punished. In 1929, bass saxophone player Spencer Clark was working with a group which included the first great white jazz drummer Dave Tough. "Dave had a very strong beat and laid it down four to the bar. We were playing the tea dances at the Negresco Hotel in Nice. We played sugar, nice and slow but with a good steady beat. Dave was really driving the band along, the gigolos were swinging the old ladies around and everybody was tapping their feet. Less than half-way through the number the manager came down and fired us on the spot. We were out on the street, drums and all, in less than half an hour." Jack O'Brien, who played piano with Tough at the Abbaye Thélème in the same year, confirms the story and adds that when Dave applied to replace Ted Gobal as the drummer with Lud Gluskin's band, he was rejected. "Gluskin thought he was no good. He was playing at the Perroquet at the time, a very expensive nightclub above the Casino de Paris. He knew he'd never hold the job if he hired Dave. He was making money keeping the international set happy."

Given the public's alarm at music which swung, and the cautious venality of restauranteurs who sternly policed any enthusiasm their musicians might have for hot music, authentic jazz had no chance of survival. The general public had never heard of Fletcher Henderson; jazz to them meant Jack Hylton or, worse still, one of his numerous imitators. If such bands were musically competent, their orchestral precision only emphasized the lack of rhythmic interest. Deprived of the drive and swing which would have sustained Ellington or Henderson versions of the same tunes, such orchestras had a stricken, lifeless quality.

Dripping with sentiment, their sugar-sweet melodies unfolding like bolts of wet wool, their records make depressing listening today.

Contact with European tastes even stayed the vitality of black bands like Sam Wooding's, which included such excellent jazz players as Tommy Ladnier, Gene Sedric, Doc Cheatham, Freddy Johnson and Al Wynn. Hugues Panassié heard them at the Embassy Club on the Champs-Elysées in the fall of 1929.

> I found the first hour almost unbearable. The orchestra played nothing but sweet rubbish. "Yet again, these damned proprietors and this damned public taste!" I groaned to myself. In the end, I scribbled, "Please play hot!" on a scrap of paper and asked a waiter to take this message up to the band. It was Doc Cheatham who got the note. He looked at it for a moment in amazement, as if not believing his eyes, given the tastes of the white public, then he looked up and glanced around the room to see where the unexpected message had come from. As soon as I saw him looking in my direction, I raised my arm. He gave a big smile and waved back; all the other musicians did the same when they realized what had happened.
>
> And the orchestra began to play hot – terrifically hot. Cheatham took elegant solos. It was the first time I had heard a black orchestra in the flesh rather than on record and I was amazed by their dynamism, which was so much greater than white bands.

The audience must have been bewildered by this sudden display. Normally, the jazz which was played in places like the Ambassadeurs and the Embassy was carefully diluted for the public's consumption and made every possible concession to the European musical tradition. To make quite sure that their public would not get lost in unfamiliar territory, band leaders appropriated that most familiar of all cultural landmarks, the conductor. Musically, this served no purpose at all. The interpretive use of "accelerandi" and "retardandi" in classical music requires a conductor. But when a jazz musician departs from the beat, he leaves it where it is. A band swings only when the rhythmic pulse is shared by each individual player. It is something which is felt, not organized. Instead, the jazz band leader had a quite different role: his job was to conduct the audience not the orchestra – to ensure that they, not the musicians, knew what was happening.

One musician who made this surprising discovery was Bruno Coquatrix. Coquatrix caught up with jazz as a student in 1927. He formed his first professional orchestra from the disbanded remnants of Gregor's Gregorians. Almost at once he fell, by chance, into one of the top jobs in Parisian show business, at the Ambassadeurs. Fred Waring's

Pennsylvanians were unable to get an extension of their work permit and Coquatrix got the job at short notice.

> I knew nothing about the business. At that time, the thing was to have a baton as an orchestra leader. Of course, I didn't have one. At the last minute, we found two women who washed up in the kitchen. Apparently they sat and knitted in between doing the washing up. So one of them gave me a knitting needle and we stuck it through a champagne cork. Et voilà! Baton de chef d'orchestre! Anyway, the director of the Ambassadeurs said to me, "It's very simple. The orchestra know the tempo. You follow." I said, "Is that all I have to do?" He said, "That's all. The orchestra have absolutely no need of you. It's the public who need you. . . ."

Such ignorance, naivety and concern to keep the public happy at all costs combined to produce chaotic results. French orchestras suffered particularly badly since they could only absorb the alien influences of jazz from a handful of very imperfect recordings. As bands negotiated the rhythmic hazards of the latest American fox trot with gingerly deliberation, their "leaders" gesticulated out front like men desperately communicating semaphore to a foundering ship. Indeed, disaster was seldom far away. Many European leaders understood even less about conducting than about jazz. Confusion reigned, though only occasionally as chaotically as at Gregor's opening at Olympia in Paris in 1929. The saxophone player Noel Chiboust recalls:

> The show began at 2 PM, with a film which ran for about two hours. At a quarter to four, the lights went up and the orchestra was supposed to play for a quarter of an hour. They'd been rehearsing the arrangements and the cues for weeks. Gregor had almost all the best jazz players, but he was a dancer, not an orchestra leader. He got his hands so mixed up trying to bring the band in that the musicians understood nothing at all. . . . So the curtain went up and the music started and then almost immediately stopped again. And there was Pierre Allier on the left and André Ekyan on the right, both of whom thought they had to do something to save the situation. So Pierre Allier launched into "Nobody's Sweetheart" just as André Ekyan began to play "Dinah" – and they were not even at the same tempo! Everybody was lost in total chaos. The curtain came down and that was that! Début de Gregor à Paris!

In fact, French bands were lucky to survive at all at this time. Jazz had arrived for the tourists, and inevitably it was the American bands who got the jobs. Furthermore the French, uncharacteristically for a chauvinist race, ignored their own good musicians and insisted that all jazz players must be American, and preferably black. Only two French bands made any impression at all. The first was Gregor and His Gregorians. The other was Ray Ventura's Collegians. The contrasting history of these two orchestras is an instructive lesson in European attitudes to home-brewed jazz.

Gregor was an Armenian who had made a small reputation as an American-style dancer earlier in the twenties. His notably eccentric personality combined with a genius for publicity to make him a well-known, though not always popular figure. He was chauffeured around in the latest and most expensive cars, dressed extravagantly and went everywhere accompanied by two large Afghan hounds. Alain Romans recalls him:

> One day, Gregor advertised in the paper announcing that his famous dogs had been stolen and said that he was offering one thousand dollars reward. He invented it all of course. The dogs were locked up at home, while everybody rushed around looking for them. It was just a publicity stunt. Unfortunately for him though, one of his saxophone players knew what was going on. So he broke in where the dogs were being hidden, took them down to the police station and made Gregor "pay up."

Gregor combined his eccentric behavior with a genuine love of good jazz. Leo Vauchant toured with the Gregorians in South America in 1930.

> Gregor was not really a musician. He was a good dancer – rather in the style of Jack Buchanan or Harry Pilcer. He played a little violin – syncopated stuff – by ear, but he could tell a good player from a bad one and his band were all pros. They were some of the best. Alex Combelle, Philippe Brun, Stephane Mougin, Michel Emer, Stephane Grappelly. The arrangements were good too. I did some. Others were done by Mougin, Lucien Moravek and Michel Emer. The band had a good jazzy sound. At that time, it was better than Hylton.

In fact, Gregor seems to have loved jazz not wisely, but too well. His attempt to combine all the best French jazz talent in one band proved too difficult and costly to maintain. Even if it had not, the French were not inclined to be sympathetic to the grandiose claims he made for himself and his orchestra. Alain Romans was working in Le Touquet when the Gregorians were appearing at the nearby Casino de la Forêt. "Gregor would drive up each evening in a large open car wearing spats, a top hat and white gloves. He then marched up to the waiting orchestra preceded by a little boy with a trumpet who blew a fanfare and announced,

'Gregor! Le Roi du Jazz!' " Almost the only thing which French people understood about jazz was that it was American, and they resented being put upon in this way. Gregor finally took the band on a tour of South America where, true to form, they survived a couple of revolutions in six months, and managed not to be paid at least twice. Burdened with debt, the Gregorians broke up after less than two years.

Ray Ventura, by contrast, has enjoyed a long and profitable career in music, a success largely due to the way in which he was always prepared to compromise his early taste for jazz. Ventura first became aware of American music in 1918 when, as a young boy, he first met American soldiers stationed near his home at Auteuil. By 1927, he had organized an orchestra of college students which played every Tuesday in a fashionable club at 25 Rue de la Pompe. "It was, how shall I say, 'un endroit chic, à la mode.' I used to have American musicians who came there because they'd heard we were ahead of the professionals as far as jazz was concerned." When the band recorded "You'll Want Me Back Again" in 1928, Ventura added the Americans Spencer Clark and Danny Polo in order to add weight to what had started as an amateur orchestra.

The band continued to be popular throughout 1928 and 1929. Ventura called in professionals like Leo Vauchant and Philippe Brun from time to time to advise him on how to improve the group. The best American stock arrangements were bought for the band by the mother of Montaigu, the second trumpet player, who ran a maison de couture in New York. Meanwhile, Ventura went everywhere American musicians were to be heard. "There was a band run by a French saxophone player called Paul Gazon which played ten dances at Claridges Hotel," recalls Leo Vauchant. "Gazon had some good Americans with him – Gene Prendergast on saxophone, Ruell Kenyon on piano, and Eddie Ritten on trumpet. Ventura was there every day."

Even so, Ventura's attempts to play jazz seem to have been increasingly fraught with problems. He was unable to keep the few first-class players like Leo Vauchant and Philippe Brun who had first helped him, and the jazz talent of the band remained weak. The American saxophone player Russ Goudy toured with the Collegians in 1930 and 1931.

The band had no jazz content except for myself and a trumpet player named Ray Bender who copied Bix Beiderbecke solos but with none of the feeling. . . . Rhythm didn't seem to be a natural thing with Europeans. The musicians were too stiff. They had to learn every little syncopation by heart. Instead of improvising, they copied things from records note for

225

note. . . . Whenever Ventura let me solo I'd try very hard to get the rhythm section going, but it was almost impossible to get things swinging.

After 1930, jazz was becoming a luxury which Ventura was having to finance himself. Russ Goudy remembers that his salary came to more than the band was actually earning, something which not even a rich family like Ventura's could afford for long.

It was probably with some relief that Ventura realized that the Wall Street crash and the consequent decline in the numbers of American tourists was going to change things. "I realized that only a small minority of French people liked jazz. So I started to build up a large stage orchestra with a lot of showmanship. Before we did that, we had no real push with the French public. Then we started to do numbers like "Tu Vas Très Bien Madame la Marquise" which was a fantastic success. It's still popular today." Despite the band's trip to New York in 1929 where the musicians spent a great deal of time up in Harlem listening to great black orchestras like those of Fletcher Henderson, Don Redman and Chuck Webb, they played less and less jazz. There were no more attempts to feature important American jazz musicians, even though performers as great as Benny Carter and Coleman Hawkins were in Paris in the middle thirties. Ventura said: "Our show was more French. That's how we succeeded really. We had some part for jazz. I had a harmonica player called Max Geldray who was very good. We had Alix Combelle and the bass player Louis Vola. But we never had more than twenty to thirty per cent jazz in the repertoire. . . . I had to do it like that because of the French public." Ventura was not even interested in employing the great French guitarist Django Reinhardt.

Well, I had in my orchestra a guitar player, Louis Gasté, and it was difficult for me to throw out any basic musicians because they were good enough. . . . I don't think it would have made any difference to the band to have employed Django because I had such fantastic hits with "Tu Vas Bien" and many, many more. . . . It was the French songs which were the hits.

 EPILOGUE

THE NICE JAZZ FESTIVAL

THE DRUMS BEGIN SO QUIETLY you have to strain your ears to catch the beat. Slowly the volume increases, suggesting an approaching band. However, there is none of the Old-World formality of Remembrance Sunday or the Bastille Day parades here. This is small town America on the move. The beat is less that of a march than a shuffle, improperly insistent on the second and fourth beats as if the shades of the cake-walk had never quite departed.

A whistle blows once, twice, three times. A trombone tailgates and the band falls in with a rollicking calypso. The theme is one of comically exaggerated simplicity. Prodded along by the trombones, the trumpet section clambers laboriously upwards for four bars, before backing down the dominant chord as if relieved to regain its original starting point. There is a moment of tension in the bridge section, sustained by a long press-roll on the drums, while the clarinets trill derisively behind the brass. Cumbersome, slightly clownish, the piece nevertheless hides

227

a certain sly irony behind the kind of mock-heroics more often associated with a football game. Even so the calypso beat means that, however raucous, things are swinging too. The temptation to skip is overwhelming. "Jump for joy!" – for the Fourth of July, for County Fair, for the Orange Queen! It's Carnival Time.

The music dies away. Then, as if catching an echo, the trombones pick up the last phrase and repeat it, tentatively at first, then with gusto. Proudly they turn it over to the trumpets, who in turn pass it on to the saxes. Each section tries it out, adding personal touches, first in unison, then building up to a towering edifice of sound. The Thad Jones-Mel Lewis band version of "Oregon Grinder Swing" is fat and funky but with a rough edge to it that cuts through the warm, humid Mediterranean night like a chain saw through cheese. The 1977 Nice Jazz Festival is under way.

The festival is traditionally held in the Arènes des Cimiez, an ancient Roman amphitheatre. Its echoes of the past seem strangely appropriate to the purposes of a European jazz festival. Three separate stages operate simultaneously, and players from different groups sit in with each other to add interest and excitement. But the majority of the musicians are older generation mainstream players and, disappointingly, their shared musical background seems to limit rather than expand the repertoire. In a single crossing of the Arènes des Cimiez it is impossible to avoid at least one version of "Stomping at the Savoy" or "Don't Get Around Much Anymore." Players like Zoot Sims, Clark Terry, Count Basie, Teddy Wilson, Joe Newman and Milt Hinton have played together all their lives. Perhaps inevitably the resulting mixture is more tincture than transfusion.

On the far side of the arena, a group of the most famous swing musicians are assembling on the Garden Stage. They are to play some of the great charts which made the Basic band famous in the thirties and forties. Buddy Tate will be featured on Broadway, and Benny Carter on "Moten Swing." "Jumping at the Woodside" will divide the honors between Clark Terry and Joe Newman, while the Count himself will sit in for "One O'Clock Jump." Out front a forest of microphones are being rigged, tapes and cassettes checked, battery and sound levels established. Hunched over their Audiotronics, Sonys and National Panasonics, these people are shut off from the world by enormous headphones, locked into their private time machines and poised for blast-off – destination Kansas City. It is interesting to speculate on the ways in which such technology might have interfered with the history of jazz.

Certainly the memorex world of today has done little to encourage originality. The loudest applause is invariably reserved for the most accurate renderings of the original solos of thirty years ago. It seems the business of a jazz festival in this age of recording is not creation, but recreation.

"Hey, everybody! Let's have some fun." Clarence "Gatemouth" Brown profits from the silence to adjust his slide. A fiddle player from Kansas City who has learned the rudiments of blues guitar, he minimizes his technical problems by adjusting the slide rather than the key. He tries again, his voice pitched higher, more insistent. "Hey, everybody!" This is an unequivocal invitation to respond. A faint mutter is audible. Gatemouth is obviously encouraged. He leans closer to the microphone, leering at the audience. "Let's have some fun," he bawls. By now his listeners are shuffling uncomfortably. Europeans are accustomed to receive music in a spirit of passivity. Neighbors eye each other nervously, unsure whether it is more embarrassing to participate than remain aloof. But Gatemouth is not to be denied. He halts the proceedings to explain that this is a song by Louis Jordan, a very good friend of his, and he'd really like the audience to get with it.

"Let the Good Times Roll" is under way at last, to the faint, antiphonal mutterings of a disconcerted audience.

> Don't sit there mumbling and talking trash.
> If you wanna have a ball – go out and spend some cash.
> So let the good times roll. Oh, yeah!
> Don't care if you're young or old – let the good times roll.

British saxophone player Tony Coe is sitting in for the set. His solo begins earthily enough but, as it unfolds, it moves out towards the upper levels of the chords. Someone starts to boo. It is a sad comment which says a lot about the second-hand nature of European jazz appreciation. European attitudes are so conditioned by recordings that they ignore the fact that a recording stops history in its tracks. Classics of the moment become classics for all time, as unalterably fixed in wax as the historical figures in Madame Tussauds. Europeans were among the first to appreciate these moments, and rightly so. But they are only moments in a jazz continuum whose dynamic element has always been the cross-fertilization of ideas. The European collector catalogues his records and pidgeon-holes his ideas at the same time. In fact the jazz tradition is far richer than many of its most devoted admirers suspect.

229

Don't let nobody play me cheap.
I got fifty cents more than I'm gonna keep.
So let the good times roll. Let the good times roll!
Don't care if you're young or old – let the good times roll.

Gatemouth's words echo in a void of silence and respect.

On the Arena stage Clark Terry and Zoot Sims are swapping fours on a fast version of "Broadway." The audience, deferential as ever, is further awed by the presence of several television cameras. Applause is dutifully synchronized with the huge arc lights which are switched on at appropriate moments for applause. Late-comers approach their seats bent double like soldiers under a barrage, lest they should come within range of one of the cameras. The session has a tired, lifeless quality. Not even Clark Terry, playing trumpet and flugelhorn simultaneously, as if to prove how easy it is to master an additional left hand technique on odd afternoons off, can rescue it. It appears that after a week of "Stomping at the Savoy" and too much "Not Getting Around," they have finally ground to a halt themselves.

Today spice, if not life, is to be added by the guest appearance of clarinetist Tony Scott. Head entirely shaved except for a beard the color of won-ton soup, and wearing a black silk kimono decorated with orange leopards, he emerges from the bushes behind the stage, right in the middle of the number. His solo is short and badly amplified. The Parker influences in his playing only emphasize the fact that Pee Wee Russell left little room for maneuver by later generations of clarinet-ists. Scott retires to the bushes while Ray Bryant's driving, bluesy piano takes over. This too is badly amplified, perhaps as a concession to the television technicians who do not want too much feed-back for their own microphones. Meanwhile Tony Scott begins a bewildering series of exits and entrances looking for all the world like a Chinese pirate in search of the local pantomime.

It is 2:30 AM. Even so the little bar at the top of the Europa Hotel is hot and crowded. Billy Mitchell, Buddy Tate, Arnet Cobb, Al Grey and Joe Newman are twenty-five minutes into a version of Duke Ellington's "Take The A Train." The musicians are hitting their stride in flagrant contradiction of the 280 year aggregation of their ages. While others solo, those awaiting their turn chat to each other or call to their friends in the audience to exchange private jokes. The answering shouts of laughter never seem to disturb the soloists, who appear to take it all as a sign of encouragement rather than a source of distraction.

230

The scene is presided over by the hotel manager. His face wears a self-satisfied, almost proprietory expression. All day his portly, diminutive form was to be seen scuttling between the festival stages touting for musicians. Tonight he has assembled a first-class rhythm section, and some of the most indefatiguable jammers from the festival have come by to sit in. Business is booming, and he is settling back to reap the twin rewards of patronage and profit. The only interruption is the intermittant ringing of the telephone, as neighbors call up to protest about the noise – a sound which the chimes of the cash register nearly, but not quite, obscure.

It is Buddy Tate's turn to solo. His tone is lush and sonorous. He plays with the relaxation of a man whose grueling apprenticeship of one-nighters has taught him that this is the only way to survive them. Close your eyes and you can almost feel the floor of the Savoy Ballroom rocking under your feet as one of the great bands of the thirties drives the dancers out across the floor.

Billy Mitchell takes over. His solo begins with a phrase snatched from the last four bars of Buddy's solo. He repeats it, but each time with a different rhythmic emphasis. The short stabbing phrases gradually lengthen into a developing melodic line as he explores the harmonic possibilities of the tune. The others fall in behind him with a riff which fits snugly under the solo, catching the spirit, matching the mood, laying a firm foundation from which Billy builds towards the climax. "Go on Bill! OOOOOEEEE!" The audience, mainly musicians and their friends, boisterously parody the pitch and timing of his phrases in their shouts of encouragement.

Early the next afternoon a quite different event is taking place. Rodney Jones, who plays guitar with Dizzy Gillespie's group, is on the Arena Stage. He is incongruously flanked by Clarence "Gatemouth" Brown, a blues singer from Kansas City, and Bucky Pizzarelli, at one time with Benny Goodman and now a New York session player. For once the musical mixture looks like boiling over. It is as if some malevolent spirit had cast the past, present and future of the guitar in some sort of musical apocalypse.

Rodney is quick to profit from the confusion on stage. He launches triumphantly into one of his own things, delighted at the chance to play outside the restraints of Dizzy's tightly organized group. The eight bar theme and the twelve bar bridge into the solo are conventional enough. But he immediately doubles the time, leaving Freddy Kohlman, the veteran New Orleans drummer, trailing gallantly behind. This

231

music seems to live in the cracks between existing musical ideologies. It is not based on any obvious harmonic structure, but it is not entirely free of it either. Instead the melodic lines seem to circle round a tonal center, occasionally exploding outwards in a succession of whole tone runs. The frequent use of consecutive fourths and fifths appear to hover just out of range of final resolution and give the music an unnerving, spectral quality. There is no attempt to coax the listener into a shared emotional experience. You either inhabit Rodney's emotional plane or you do not.

"Give us some blues." The conservative element in the audience is close to mutiny. Bucky Pizzarelli is watching events with an amused smile. Gatemouth wears the sardonic look of a man who has heard better music produced by a kitten chasing a ping-pong ball across the strings of a grand piano. Wearily he declines a solo. "Give us some blues!" The musicians pick up on one of those timeless Kansas City riffs which span the thirty years between T-Bone Walker and Jimmy Hendrix. You give up the struggle to discover a new musical consciousness, and return to familiar territory with the relief of a sea-sick passenger regaining dry land.

We are sitting outside one of the American-style Pizza restaurants which now proliferate along the Corniche coast. Even the fastidious eating habits of the French are finally being eroded by the wave of tourists who crash annually on their coasts. Rodney Jones is thoughtfully picking the remains of a mushroom pizza from between his teeth. He seems fiercely determined not to allow any romantic notions about the past to color one's judgement of his music.

"I can dig the fact that those old guys have still got the guts to get up there and play – that they're still making music and keeping happy. But I wouldn't let that kind of sentimentality confuse the reality of where it's at musically. Those guys go off and play at those jam sessions because that way they feel needed. It makes them feel alive to put out all that energy. That's why they keep playing because when they stop, that's the end of them."

There is an almost perfect irony in the fact that the jazz history which Rodney is so determined to escape, is precisely repeating itself as he talks. Thirty-five years ago Dizzy Gillespie, with whom Rodney has played for nearly two years, was a brash young soloist trying to break out of the same sort of musical straight jacket. Although Gillespie's music can still approach those incredible adventures in harmony and rhythm with which he and Charlie Parker startled the world in the

232

forties, Rodney rudely describes his recent attempts to cash in on the disco craze as "Afro-playboy."

"It's the worst music I ever heard in my life. We added seven new numbers to the book this week alone. They're all 'disco' numbers. On the arrangement it says: 'Eight bars funk – not jazz.' " Rodney's rebelliousness recalls Dizzy's own.

It is after 1:30 AM. The manager of the Europa hotel is getting worried. Except for a small group of noisy and obviously drunk French locals, the bar is almost empty. The only American in the place is Rufus Reed, bass player with the Thad Jones-Mel Lewis orchestra. He is flanked by two beautiful girls who languidly compete for his favors. A record of the Mezzrow-Bechet quintet is being played loudly for the third time. The manager rushes to meet each new arrival, tremulously hopeful that it will turn out to be a musician arriving to jam. At each disappointment his expression becomes more crest-fallen. "Are you sure you have not got your trumpet with you?" he demands of a client who has rashly admitted he once played that instrument.

It seems that his commercial instincts have got the better of his artistic ones. Having built up a considerable trade with the late night jam sessions, he has tried to capitalize on it by quadrupling the price of the drinks. Dancer Jimmy Slyde has the definitive word on it.

"It's just bullshit – no argument. We jammed there the first night. Next time we went in the drinks had gone from five francs to twenty. So we just boycotted. I mean if you've got a hundred francs in your pocket and you want to have a little party, you want to be able to buy a few drinks without checking your American Express card first."

The manager's response is one of weary tolerance. It is only a small addition to his burden that ignorant foreigners should attack him when at the same time, the union and the performing rights people, to say nothing of the local authority, are sucking his blood. "Before I know it, half my takings are gone! And then there is always a little something for the musicians." It seems the trials of Saint Sebastien are slight compared to those of a French hotelier.

Before he can explain the advantages of an almost empty bar to one full of people drinking, his attention is diverted by the arrival of a group carrying instrument cases. Richie Perry, a young tenor saxophone player with Thad Jones has arrived to jam. The manager – a man triumphantly restored to his destiny – hustles a waiting French piano player and drummer to their places. Moments later they are off on "Au Privave," a fast Charlie Parker blues number. Richie is rolling almost

233

from the opening bars, playing with that slightly demonic quality which all disciples of John Coltrane affect. It is as if he wants to shatter the well-worn cadences of the blues forever and replace them with strange angular affinities of his own. The rhythm section is barely adequate even though a bass player has mysteriously appeared from somewhere. Unhampered, unconcerned even, Richie is in full flight. The irresistible urge to flex some hidden muscle in his subsconscious is on him.

Next it is "Now High the Moon." He hurtles through the changes, courting every risk, embracing every harmonic complication the song has to offer. This is music requiring fire in the belly and ice in the veins. The French party bang their glasses on the table in a drunken counter-point of their own. Their empty, spiteful chatter achieves an even more disagreeable level of vehemence. One couple stagger to their feet, breaking one brandy glass and spilling the contents of another. Clasped in an amorous wrestle, they sway about in front of the musicians shouting encouragement. The manager, a man you can always count on to balance propriety against even the most extravagant spending, inter-venes. Things have suddenly gone very quiet. The bass player who apparently doubles as bouncer, joins them. There is an agonizing moment of suspense. Then a punch is thrown – the expectant silence demands it. Men gather up their drinks, women their gowns and handbags. Every-one tucks themselves into their seats, seeking as much security against events as possible.

By this time it is impossible to sort out the two original contestants from the general scrummage. Someone has found time to put Sidney Bechet back on the turn-table. His soprano sax wails majestically over a crescendo of breaking glass and tumbling furniture. The fight sprawls out onto the landing. With commendable courage – no doubt inspired by the even more frightening effect of all this on tomorrow's trade – the manager has managed to force himself between the warring factions. At that moment a badly aimed punch smashes the glass door of the elevator. The sight of blood is enough to restore a moment of sanity. It is long enough to hustle the drunken Frenchman who started it all into the elevator. As it sinks from sight, the sounds of renewed struggle echo up the shaft like the voices of the damned. Rufus Reed shifts his large frame to a more relaxed position.

"Shit," he mutters. "To think they wanted me to bring my bass up here tonight."

234

 APPENDIX

INTERVIEWS

IN CONDUCTING THE RESEARCH for this book I was lucky to meet a number of jazz musicians who have not previously been interviewed. What follows is a selection of some of the more interesting of those interviews. The only exception to this is the section devoted to Django Reinhardt, who, although he does not strictly belong within the historical compass of this book, is too important musically and too good an example of all that I hold to be vital in jazz to be left out. Unfortunately Django is dead. For lack of a conventional interview I therefore decided to begin this section with a short piece about him, and then to make a montage of comments made by other musicians who worked with him.

☆ DJANGO REINHARDT

Django Reinhardt was a genius. There have been many European jazz players who could more than hold their own with their American counterparts. Reinhardt is the only one to have become a major influence in the United States as well as over here. He is indisputably the single most important guitarist in the history of jazz and would have to be included in any list of all-time greats. At the same time, Django's romantic origins in the gypsy world and his many eccentric qualities have greatly encouraged the spread of a Reinhardt mythology. Most reminiscences concentrate on the more fabulous aspects of his talent and the comical peculiarities of his character. This is how most people experienced him. Unfortunately the resulting legend is rather longer on anecdote than understanding.

Perhaps the tendency is to treat genius as something which is, by definition, beyond analysis – particularly genius as tightly wrapped in hagiographical detail as Django's. The trouble with this is that it is an easy way out of reaching any better understanding of his unique talents. These talents, I believe, can only be properly understood in their context. To this extent it is more important to consider Django as a gypsy than as a genius.

A lot has been written about the lively musical situations existing wherever there were large concentrations of black people in America, particularly in New Orleans and, later, in Kansas City. One of the best descriptions of this was given by the New Orleans guitarist Danny Barker:

One of my pleasantest memories as a kid growing up in New Orleans was how a bunch of us kids, playing, would suddenly hear sounds. It was like a phenomenon, like the Aurora Borealis, maybe. The sounds of men playing would be so clear, but we wouldn't be sure where they were coming from. So we'd start trotting, start running – "It's this way! It's that way!" And sometimes after running for a while you'd be nowhere near that music. But that music would come on you any time like that. The city was full of the sounds of music.

According to Barker there were more jobs than musicians.

There were countless places of employment that employed musicians, not including private affairs, balls, soirées, banquets, marriages, deaths, christenings, Catholic communions, confirmations, picnics at the lake-front, country hayrides and advertisements of business concerns. During the carnival season [Mardi Gras] any little insignificant affair was sure to have some kind of music and each section would engage their neighborhood favorite. It might be Joe Oliver who lived around the corner; or Cheeky Sherman on somebody's piano; or Sandpaper George; or Hudson on toilet pipe, now called bazooka; or Picou on kazoo, a kazoo inserted into an old E♭ clarinet, which he fingered as he blew. . . .

The point of this digression is that the gypsy world is in some ways similar. It was Dizzy Gillespie who defined the difference between black and white musicians less in terms of skin pigment than social environment. The example of European gypsies in the 1920s seems to prove his point. Both the Afro-American and gypsy races live within a culture but are not part of it. Their own cultural and social identities are thereby reinforced. It is therefore no coincidence that such societies display a taste for music at a very practical level. The world outside does not cater to their needs and so they provide their own entertainment. In the twenties and the thirties the gypsies were the last European ethnic group in which music still played an important part in ordinary daily life. In the same way as Danny Barker describes, every social event was inevitably accompanied by music. Musicianship was openly encouraged by the tradition that Romany men do not work. It was the function of men to gamble, drink wine, play music and dress in as much splendor as their estates permitted. Ordinary workaday people were referred to as "peasants." Accordingly, gypsies have often produced great music, notably Hungarian czardas and Spanish flamenco. This was the tradition which Django inherited. Added to his own remarkable gifts, it produced a musician of genius and explains how a European gypsy emerged from nowhere to become one of the most important soloists in jazz at a time when jazz was even more foreign to Europe than it is now.

Charles Delaunay, in his biography of Reinhardt, confirms the importance of these musical traditions in his development.

> While he was still very young, Django felt an irresistible attraction for music, and was to be seen at all the traditional festivals that unfailingly gave occasion for musical entertainment. He would leave his friends and steal off into a corner, straining to catch every sound, his whole being possessed by overpowering emotion. When he was only ten years old, he begged his mother to get him a guitar, but she thought this was only a child's whim and, moreover, had not the fifty francs that were needed. Not until he was twelve did he get the longed-for guitar. . . .

> Although he had not yet learned to play it, Django never left his guitar, not even to go to sleep. At night he would wake up and pluck a few notes whose sound was a source of constant wonder to him. During the day he would go and listen to musicians, eagerly watching their gestures and the positions of their fingers. He engraved these on his memory, and once he had returned to the caravan, did his best to copy them. In this way he learned to play by himself, mastering the guitar rapidly and with amazing accuracy. The musicians of the neighborhood were amazed when they heard him for the first time. No one could play so fast or with such confidence.

> He would play for hours on end, encouraged by the admiration of his elders; very soon he was taking part in the village festivals, even making so bold as to back up singers. Leaving his old comrades to their own devices, he began to seek out musicians instead.

Aside from the great musical traditions of his race and his own unique talents, Django was also lucky. The miracle of jazz was that it was able to live and grow within the framework of the commercial entertainment industry. Gypsies, unlike blacks, were completely beyond the pale both economically and socially. Their musical traditions, though strong, were therefore amateur. Jazz, however, is very much the music of professionals, and a professional elite at that. Reinhardt's good fortune was that he was not only supremely gifted but that time and circumstances enabled him to be adopted by the white world – a world which, miraculously, was still sensitive enough to value not only the strength, but also the delicacy of his musical qualities. Had the gypsy world been more economically dynamic there might well have been other Djangos in the same way that Roy Eldridge and Dizzy Gillespie grew out of Louis Armstrong, and Charlie Parker developed from Lester Young. As things were, the world is lucky to have known even one Django Reinhardt.

The most striking fact about Django's

genius was that it was "natural." To the end of his life Reinhardt received no formal education whatever and could scarcely sign his name. His whole approach to music was therefore intuitive. Saxophonist André Ekyan once remarked of him: "Of all the musicians I have known, Django is the one with whom I have exchanged the least number of musical ideas but with whom I get along best from a musical viewpoint." Other musicians who worked with him agree that Django's comments about music were limited to, "This I like," or, "That is not very good." Although his harmonic sense was so formidable that he is really better described as an orchestrator than a guitarist, this was a triumph of intuition rather than intellectual analysis. Charles Delaunay put it well when he wrote, "The joy of savoring, analyzing, or marshaling notes was not for him a problem to be resolved on paper, but an edifice in sound which builds up inside oneself. It was the very art of sound, not an arithmetical arrangement of black and white notes . . . a magnificent vision which he himself was the only one to experience, and which disappeared without trace." Although this meant that many of his numerous compositions were simply forgotten the day after he had composed them, even this was a small price to pay for the purity of his invention and his absolutely flawless good taste. Stephane Grappelly once wrote of him, "He liked great things. And I believe he experienced them in the way that they should be experienced. To see his expression in the glorious church of St. Eustache in Paris, hearing for the first time the Berlioz Requiem, was to see a person in ecstasy."

In the end this kind of musical innocence was to cause Django problems in the increasingly self-analytical world of the forties and fifties. Jazz was particularly affected by this. Bebop, for instance, was a largely intellectual reaction against the commercial restrictions of big band music. The younger American musicians led by Charlie Parker and Dizzy Gillespie were deliberately trying to make their music as different as possible. Django was temporamentally incapable of conceiving music in this way, and for a time this inability caused him trouble. Hubert Rostaing played clarinet and saxophone with him throughout the forties.

Django was a fantastic musician but he was a gypsy. His musical intelligence was more developed towards melody. Also his life-style – always disappearing in a caravan and touring around, doing the odd concert here and there – he couldn't have come to grips with a new style like that. . . . The attitude of the younger musicians later on towards him was shocking. They more or less rejected him as old-fashioned. It's a perfect example of how one should never pass judgments too quickly. . . . It's a bit like Armstrong. Armstrong was a monument to jazz, and he remained that without ever changing his style, which never became old-fashioned. Django was another musician who does not date.

Django's gypsy origins also make a moot point of the question of whether he would have benefited from a more academic training. It is possible that legitimate musical skills would have enabled him to crystallize and, above all, set down more of his ideas. He might well have gained wider recognition in this way. But it is more likely that his originality and spontaneity would have been impaired. He already possessed naturally most of what an academic musical education would have given him. His intuitive understanding of harmony was extraordinary. He said: "The harmonies – that's what I like in music. There you have the mother of music. That's why I like the music of J. S. Bach so much. All his music is built up from the bass." Almost all his music reflects this instinctive grasp of how music is made, so much so that even classical musicians were impressed. Constant Lambert wrote of him, "Django is without doubt the most interesting figure in the world of jazz since Duke Ellington, and like him, he is not so much an arranger as a composer." Given all this it seems even more pointless to suggest exposing him to the perils of twelve-tone serialism and atonality which were beginning to preoccupy music academies in the forties, than to expect him to respond to the intellectual discontents of bebop.

DJANGO REINHARDT

STEPHANE GRAPPELLY   The most amazing thing about Django was his harmony. You can learn that. But he instinctively had knowledge of harmony. Today you have Erroll Garner, who can play in any key because he can't read music and doesn't know the difference. Martial Solal is the same.

LOUIS VOLA   Django didn't read music. But he had ears like an elephant, you understand. I did things with him with a big orchestra where he had to play an arrangement which Paul Baron had done for a very good trumpet player called Aimé Barelli. Barelli got sick and Django did it instead. He listened to the orchestration twice and then played it as if he had known it all his life, though he had never heard it before.

ALBERTA HUNTER   He accompanied me many times . . . many times. I remember he used to make some notes on that guitar that I'd almost have to stop singing. He could always bring tears to my eyes.

GERARD LEVECQUE   What people don't know about Django as a guitarist is that he was really more of a harmonist's and an arranger's guitarist and a guitarist for big orchestras than he was a virtuoso – because as a virtuoso he only had two fingers to play with. That's why he had a rapport with Ellington. He liked Duke's music and also Duke could hear what Django was doing harmonically. Django was ahead of us harmonically. He understood the importance of things like "Harlem Airshaft" long before the rest of us.

HUBERT ROSTAING   I listened to all the great soloists and orchestras – Duke Ellington, Benny Goodman, Benny Carter and the rest. But the person who taught me the most was Django, even though there was something a bit gypsy about his playing. So I owe everything to Django first and foremost. Of course what helped me was that I had a certain musicianship already through studying – I already had a certain competence. I had been to the Conservatoire so I was not thrown by his extremely developed sense of harmony, because although music was still fairly straightforward in those days, he complicated it with his extraordinary harmonic sense. His solos prove it – sixths, added notes, passing notes.

GERARD LEVECQUE   I remember that when as a young clarinetist leaving the Conservatoire, I still remembered the classical things we used to play there and Django used to accompany me without ever having heard the piece before. It was incredible. He never knew how to read music, but he perfectly understood the music of Debussy because we used to play it on stage. And we used to play the *Norwegian Dances* of Grieg and "Carmen" from the Bizet opera – and he knew all those Bizet harmonies. Even if they were differently arranged he always found new things to do behind them. These were much more difficult harmonies than were found in the jazz of that time and, moreover, they were harmonies which were especially difficult to play with only two fingers. Not being able to use four fingers like everybody else, he had invented a whole new system for getting around the problem. In addition to this, his handicap meant that he couldn't play either very high up or low down the instrument – so he had to change all the inversions.

LOUIS VOLA He loved classical music – Debussy especially. That's why he wrote the "Bolero" – with three violins and a trombone. He took the brass section from Ray Ventura's band and four violins – among them Bragiotti, Michel Warlop and Stephane Grappelly. He loved great music – that really impressed him.... Every Sunday we had the *Opera Comique* in Paris, and every Sunday we used to go together and listen to the classical concerts they had between five and seven. I used to choose the program carefully: Debussy, Ravel, Paul Dukas. . . . We used to sit through those concerts and afterwards we'd sometimes not say a word for the rest of the day. We'd just smile at each other occasionally. Sometimes we'd play some jazz afterwards and he'd say, "I can't hear myself any more."

GERARD LEVECQUE After a while the Quintet ceased to interest him except as a means of earning money and the pleasure of playing. What he wanted was to make it as a writer of serious music. He wanted fifty violins and one hundred singers. He even wrote a symphony. It was going to be played by the orchestra at the Salle Pleyel with an introduction by Jean Cocteau. All the musicians were laid on of course. I wasn't going to conduct it because I was very young and I was scared of making a mess of it. I wasn't as yet a professional, so I got a

conductor who was. It was Django who asked me to get this man. Anyway, the day before the concert we went over to his place to collect the music and he'd disappeared. What we think happened was that he was a Hungarian and he had been seized by the Nazis and deported. There was never any news of him again. But the story has a sequel because the other day some people came to see me about a book they were doing about Django's music and they told me that someone had heard the piece played over the radio in either Hungary or Roumania. So what they think happened was that this guy was taken by the Germans and that after the war he was installed as head of an orchestra in either Hungary or Roumania and that that was how this manuscript survived.

The work was also played in France because in 1946 I joined Ray Ventura and at that time Django was approached to do the music for a film which has since been lost called *Le Village de la Colère*. And in this film he incorporated the best of his music for the Mass and the symphony. He asked André Hodeir to write it out for him and Hodeir, who is a great musician, wrote it out note for note. And I saw this film with Django – he asked me to go with him – and the music sounded great. Hodeir orchestrated it perfectly with a great respect for Django's ideas. With me, on the other hand, Django would literally dictate note for note from the guitar – first trumpet, second trumpet, third trumpet, second horn, etc. We put them down one after the other. It lasted about fifteen minutes in all. It was quite hard to play because it was composed by a guitarist with no real knowledge of violins or other instruments. Also it was very original. It was like the *Marriage of Figaro*. It wasn't normal run-of-the-mill stuff. His ideas were always outside the mainstream.

240

Django was always talking about the idea of writing a Mass. You have to understand that every year the gypsies go to St. Marie de la Mer, which is a little French port on the Mediterranean where there is a Saint – St. Sarah – a black statue which is the patron saint of all the gypsies. And Django, who considered himself superior to the rest of the world, wanted to write a special Mass for the gypsies. It was never finished. There was never more than a few bars of it. Anyway, since everyone had heard about this famous Mass of Django's, the Radio Diffusion Française asked to record it. So he came around to see me and said, "Look, we have to do something because the radio want to record this thing." So he sat down at the piano – he'd got to the point where he could pick out chords and so forth on the piano – and I wrote down what he dictated. You can see there's not a lot of it. The special directions about which organ stops to pull out were noted by the organist of the Sacré Coeur de Montmartre. There's only about a minute and a half of it and it's never been developed beyond that point. It's perfect classical writing – with a certain affinity with the music of J. S. Bach. This proves that Django, in addition to everything else, had the musical sensibility of eighteenth-century classical music. It could have been a whole completed work. But you know Django was lazy. He worked very little. He was always in bed. . . . There isn't enough of it. There's no indication which part of the Mass it is – the beginning, the middle or the end. For him it was just a Mass.

At the same time he was a prolific composer of tunes. To my knowledge he had written at least a hundred compositions. They were written down but very badly because Django didn't write music and they were all taken off records. Moreover he didn't belong to the Society of French Composers, because it was impossible to belong to it if you didn't write music. Unbelievable! So he belonged to the English equivalent instead. Also for membership of the French one there was a very important and difficult exam. So without these qualifications you couldn't get any royalties. It was a measure of his genius that his lack of education did not handicap him more.

ALAIN ROMANS There is a funny story I must tell you about Django from before the war. We were working at the time at Bricktop's. And one day an agent arrived from England to make a contract with Django and Grappelly. Django asked me to be there because he didn't speak English. Suddenly, in the middle of the discussion, Django, in order to show off that he knew how to read, reaches over and takes the contract from my hand and, in front of Stephane, puts his finger on a clause and says, "This I don't like." Stephane looked at it and began to laugh. I looked and began to laugh too. It was a clause stating that the expenses would be paid by the agency.

The other story about Django which is also true is that one time he was living in an hotel with his brother Joseph and cousin Camembert, both of whom he was working with. Camembert had that name because he liked to eat Camembert cheese all the time. Anyway, Django had this room – a beautiful room – and in the day all his friends would come and visit him. But another of Django's friends wanted that room for himself, and so every morning at about five o'clock this fellow would knock on Django's door and whisper in sepulchral tones: "Django, this is the voice of your grandfather telling you to leave this room." This went on for about a week until Django, who was terrified, couldn't stand it and moved out. The cousin immediately moved in and when Django heard about it he was furious. He believed it was some spirit you know.

GERARD LEVECQUE   He was scared of ghosts and everything supernatural. . . . It was quite natural – he'd never had any instruction or gone to school. His race is quite separate. They don't obey the rules like the rest. They steal chickens, they put their horses out to graze in other people's fields of corn. I sometimes think that his race is more rootless and out of context than any African that comes to Paris. They are right outside society. When they take the Metro they can't read the names of the stations. They have to ask if it's Châtelet or Les Halles. It's worse than being blind. Django got away with it by being a genius. But at the same time it handicapped him all his life.

HUBERT ROSTAING   At the same time his lack of formal education helped him keep a kind of innocence. Probably this was part of his extraordinary musical expressiveness. . . . He'd burst out laughing and slap his thighs when he'd taken a good chorus. There was no pretense in that – it was quite logical. He'd played well and he was happy like a child would be. There was a perfect logic to it.

GERARD LEVECQUE   He was always delighted with his own playing. He'd sit there saying, "Aren't I great? How well I'm playing now. Just listen to this!" He believed himself to be the greatest, and it was true.

HUBERT ROSTAING   Another thing about Django was that when he had money he was quite unapproachable. He played the Grand Seigneur and it suited him. He had a completely natural aura of distinction. When he had money he didn't want to work. He went out with very pretty women, he bought cars and anything else which took his fancy. He'd hardly bother to say "Good morning." He was impossible. Not in any way pretentiously, but because he was being a millionaire. I remember one time a contract came up to work in Belgium. He had two impresarios at the time and they were asking him how much he wanted for the job. When he was asked how much he said, "How much does Gary Cooper get? Because whatever he gets for a film, I want the same." You have to understand that this was wartime and Gary Cooper was an American film star and had no connection with Django at all. But he wasn't convinced. "Do you think I am worth less than Gary Cooper? So please find out what he gets because I want the same." It wasn't the money – it was symbolic for him.

LOUIS VOLA   He loved the cinema. His wife, my wife, he and I used to go to three or four cinemas a day. He used to get carried away by characters who impressed him in films. One day he said to me, "Come on, let's go out. I've got an urge to fight." So he dragged me out to some bistro in Montmartre where he started looking around for someone to fight with.

STEPHANE GRAPPELLY   One time Django and I were invited to the Elysée Palace by an important personality. We were invited to dinner and afterwards to perform. Django did not show up. After dinner the important personality is very polite but I can tell he is waiting, so I say I think I know where Django is, when, in fact, I don't know at all. The man calls his limousine and I go to Django's flat in Montmartre. His guitar is in the corner and I ask his wife where Django is. She says maybe he is at the Académie playing billiards. He was very good at billiards – very adroit. He spent his childhood doing that and being in the streets. His living room was the streets. So I go to the Académie and when he sees me he turns red, yellow, white. Despite his being almost twice as tall as me he was a little afraid. In the gypsy world age counts

242

although I am only two years older than he. Also, I could read – I was educated. He has two days' beard on his face and his slippers on. So I push him into the limousine and we go back to his apartment to clean him up a bit and to get his guitar. Django was like a chamelion. In one second he could change completely. He was embarrassed about everything, but his natural self came back. And when we arrived at the Elysée and the guard at the gate saluted the limousine, Django stuck his chin out and said: "Ah, they recognize me."

GERARD LEVECQUE He was a very imposing man. Despite his absurdities he had a natural nobility. When he came into a restaurant or was walking in the street, even without knowing it was Django, people would ask if this was some Oriental prince or an oil mogul or some such thing. Of course he was not as well known in France as he was in England or Germany. It happened all the time. He was always being invited by important people – and he was never a bit impressed by it. When he was invited to lunch by their Royal Highnesses of Belgium, Django ate the salad with his fingers – and it was great! The Queen Mother was a great music fan – the wife of Albert and the mother of Leopold. She was a very old lady, very made-up. There were major-domos all over the place, and Django ate his salad with his fingers – and did it with great elegance!

ALAIN ROMANS One day we were at a party playing for Baron Rothschild with Django and Grappelly. And on the piano there was a big silver box with cigars in it. And Django was sitting there playing away and, while still holding his guitar with his left hand, his other arm would reach out every now and then and grab a handful of these. And every time Stephane saw this hand shoot out he would rap it with his violin bow. And all of a sudden we hear a scream and a very old man covered in medals had come up to the piano and reached out to take a cigar. And Stephane, without looking, had cracked him across the knuckles, thinking it was Django!

LOUIS VOLA Django was like that because he didn't care. . . . I took him to Toulon once. And he was having trouble with his feet at the time – he couldn't walk very well. So he saw these military boots in the window of this store which sold things for the Navy. He tried them on and liked them and afterwards hardly wore anything else. When we did a gala for the Rothschild family where there were all kinds of ministers and fifty or so guests, he put his feet up on the antique furniture in these boots and tartan socks. He didn't notice things like that – he wasn't interested.

HUBERT ROSTAING He only played when he wanted to. The day he heard me play the blues and decided he wanted me in his band, we went off for a drink and he spent the whole evening talking to me. He didn't bother to go to work at all. And if he had a gig in a club, and there were friends of his working across the street, he'd much rather go over and play with them, because they were friends of his, than he would do his own gig. I remember that I was working in a club, and Django had got together an orchestra at the Boeuf sur le Toit. And he had asked me to lend him some arrangements for it, so I got him all fixed up. But even so he used to come around to us almost every evening because we were his friends, and he only liked to play with people he liked.

HUGUES PANASSIÉ It was not always easy to be sure of getting Django's services. He always agreed to come, but it would have been madness to expect him to get to the studio under his own steam. Most recordings took place in the morning between nine o'clock and midday. Since Django went to bed around seven o'clock in the morning, there was no question of waking him or, if he was awakened, of his feeling like getting up. I invariably sent someone around at eight o'clock in the morning. This person would wake him as gently as possible. Django would not wish to move. Whereupon my envoy would repair to the nearest café and return with a café crème and some croissants. Django, delighted, would sit up in bed to have his breakfast. This was a first success. Then he usually expressed a desire to listen to some music; his radio was tuned until something was found to his taste. At last, after a great deal of hesitation he agreed to get dressed. There was no question of hurrying him or all would have been lost. Finally, he arrived at the studio at a quarter to ten, having lost us a precious three-quarters of an hour – but his participation was so vital that this wasted time was more than compensated for.

ART LANIER Django Reinhardt! He was comical. You know, like they say, he was a gypsy. But like we would play Friday night, Saturday night. "OK. See you Monday." After about a week or ten days he'd come in. "Hello. How you been?" No one would say *Where* you been? Then he'd stay for two or three weeks. Then he'd pack up and say he was going. "I'll be gone for so long," and just go.

LOUIS VOLA One day at the Palm Beach Casino in Cannes during the tea dance, his brother Joseph said to me: "Django is ill." A little before the end of the session Joseph told me that he too had toothache, and that he was going back to the hotel to rest. He said, "I'll be back this evening." In between the tea dance and the evening set I went back to the hotel to rest too. While I was there I heard this noise while I was resting for half an hour or so – I heard this noise on the staircase. I paid no attention. Then I changed, washed and got ready for the evening and went to the Palm Beach. No Django or Joseph. So I set out in my car feeling like busting their heads and I went down to the railway station and what should I see but his wife and his mother on the sidewalk outside the station. And I said, "What are you doing?" "Oh," they said, "Django is crazy. He's across the street in that café playing billiards. He wants to go back to Paris." So I took the tickets off her and told her to tell him and Joseph that they had a very important gala at the Palm Beach in an hour and a half and that they'd better be there. So they showed up an hour and a half later as if nothing at all had happened. And from then on we had no more trouble till the end of our stay.

Django was very difficult to include in an orchestra because he was the type who didn't want to be working, working, working all the time. He was capricious, and if he wanted to go off fishing he'd just go. If he wanted to play in a bar with some of his friends he'd go and play with them, and Mabel Mercer, who was the singer at Bricktop's, would have to go out looking for him. Because often very good customers like President Roosevelt's son would come to Brick's just to hear him play. He was capricious. If he wanted to play he'd play and if he didn't he wouldn't. He could be very temperamental towards his other musicians too.

ALAIN ROMANS Django was not very easy to handle when he was working. . . . He instinctively found the right chords. But often musicians had a hard time with Django if they put in a wrong chord. He'd stand up and start shouting that the guy couldn't play and that he was no good. That was the bad side to Django – he could never admit that anyone could play a wrong chord.

HUBERT ROSTAING   When Django was playing with someone whose playing he didn't like he'd get annoyed. We made a record once called "L'Oeuil Noir." It was just like that. If there was a guitarist or a pianist who wasn't swinging or if someone's chords didn't suit him he'd start to give him *l'oeuil noir* – the black look. He'd get furious. He was not exactly unkind – it was a kind of impatience.

GERARD LEVECQUE   Django used to get very nervous on a gig. It was always a terrific effort for him to play in public. He sweated tremendously – he was never at ease. It required a big physical effort for him. And whatever problems there were with taking numbers at very fast tempos or with complicated chord sequences, there was never any rehearsal. We'd arrive, play something over for two or three minutes, and then he'd say "OK. That's it. Lets go." And we'd go on stage like that without rehearsal or anything. Normally there'd be a little introduction and then the number would finish whenever he felt like it. It was rather like Arab music if you like. It could last three, six, ten, twenty minutes, because if it didn't suit him he'd cut it. So there was always a climate of uncertainty. It was the same with records. And whenever things started to go a bit wrong, Django would play louder and louder. Then when he did that he'd break a string. As soon as that happened he'd put his guitar down and take Joseph's off him and continue to play. Joseph would then have to pull a string out of his pocket and reset the broken one. So you can see that things were often pretty fraught. There was no question of him having a second guitar, or any other way of solving the problem. He wasn't interested in things like that.

He'd had several guitars and given them all away. He just had the one Selmer – the rest he'd abandoned or given away.

When Django took long solos Joseph would get very fed up. He was always in the shadow of Django, from whom, after all, he'd learned everything. So he was very jealous of his brother too. There were always problems in the Quintet arising from that. On the job it often happened that they got on each other's nerves.

MADELEINE GAUTHIER   I remember one day the Quintet was playing in this very chic club in the rue Fromentin. The orchestra was crammed into the chimney. And this particular night, Django and his brother Joseph had some sort of an argument and pulled knives on each other. Eventually someone had to go off and find their mother. She was the only person who could separate them.

STEPHANE GRAPPELLY   Ah! What troubles he gave me. I think now I would rather play with lesser musicians and have a peaceable time than with Django and his monkey business. . . . One time he disappeared was when we were playing in a posh place in Biarritz called the Four Seasons. For once we were living like the customers in a good hotel. Django says to me he is going fishing, and I tell him I will go along too, although I don't like to fish. Django loved to fish. He would cut a branch and fasten some incredible string with a worm on the end, and catch a big fish, although people with a modern stick would catch nothing. So I went to his room, but he had gone – clothes and everything. I look and look and finally I find him in an abandoned caravan on the outskirts of town. I say, "What have you done? What pushed you to leave the hotel where you had such good lodging?" He says, "Oh, I don't like all that carpet. It hurts my feet."

LOUIS VOLA There weren't always good feelings between Django and Grappelly because there was so much jealousy between them. Grappelly, when he played in a cabaret, would take five, six, ten choruses, and the others behind him would get really tired and fed up. Sometimes Django would get so mad he'd drop his guitar and go across the street for a drink, and then I'd have to go after him to fetch him back. And so it would go on. There were times when I just felt like leaving them to get on with it.

CHARLES DELAUNAY The atmosphere between its [the Quintet's] two chief protagonists was far from ideal and one evening when the Quintet was due to broadcast to the United States a catastrophe seemed inevitable. It was a dreadful evening with the musicians really on edge. The technicians were fussing around the apparatus of the radio van which was parked outside the Big Apple. The broadcast was to be beamed across the Atlantic, forming part of an exceptional program featuring the most famous American jazz groups. At last the time came. "Five, four, three, two, one, zero. . . ." "And now, from Paris," the announcer said, "you'll hear Stephane Grappelly and his Hot Four!"

Django went white and rose to his feet. The band, not knowing what to do, stayed silent. Signs were made begging the other musicians to start, and while the broadcast was going on they convinced Django in undertones that it was all a mistake and amends would be made later in the program. Django returned to his place in a fury, glaring at Stephane even though it was in no way the latter's fault. He could hardly be held responsible for the American announcer's error, who presumably knew of the Quintet through the records which had come out under Grappelly's name. Following this incident Django addressed not a single word to his colleague for weeks on end, and I am disposed to believe he bore him a grudge about it until his dying day. . . .

Django was interested in nobody. For instance, Jean Cocteau was intrigued by Django, probably because he was a gypsy, and Cocteau liked sending his chauffeur out to look for him. But Django's attitude was typical. He knew that Cocteau meant a lot to people – he was a big name, a celebrity, and he was proud of that. But his attitude was: he's nice, he likes me, he invites me to his room. But I don't think it went further than that. I think Django took musicians seriously – the rest I'm not sure about. Musicians he had a respect for. I know that he once met Segovia. It was not a good experience. Nothing happened. He was invited by some director of a music magazine whose son was one of the members of the Hot Club. The idea was to introduce Django to Segovia and to ask him to play, which he did. And Segovia said, "Well, that's nice." You know, like someone would say, "Well, you must continue to practice. Don't give up." The same thing happened with Louis Armstrong too. I was there too. I introduced Louis to Django. Louis Armstrong was living in a smart flat in the Rue de la Tour d'Auvergne, and Django, who had not yet made the sides with the Quintet, was all agog to meet the "King of Jazz," convinced that Louis would sign him on and take him back to America as soon as he heard him! An interview was carefully arranged. Louis played the only disc then on hand, Jean Sablon's "Le Jour où Je Te Vis," with a guitar solo. Without evincing any marked enthusiasm, Louis agreed to meet Django, who came along all on edge, flanked by his brother. After hasty introductions Louis announced that he had been invited out to dinner and had to get changed in a hurry. The two musicians were waiting for their host to ask them to play; as for Louis, he crossed the room now and again, wearing that well-known silk stocking on his head. At last we persuaded Django to play: we were sure the sound of his guitar would claim the attention of the great trumpeter.

However, it was all in vain that Django, accompanied by his brother, swept through endless choruses; Armstrong, preoccupied by his toilet, kept rushing across the room to fetch a shirt or a tie. Only once did we hear a "Very good, go on!" emerge from the dressing-room. Django was mortified. Beads of sweat stood out on his forehead. And it was an utterly dejected little delegation – the two brothers, Pierre Nourry and I – that made its way down the ill-lit staircase.

PIERRE NOURRY   After the meeting with Louis, Django was very bitter. I consoled him. But it didn't put him off Louis' music. He didn't blame Louis when he was listening to one of his records. The man was completely carried away by music.

STEPHANE GRAPPELLY   One evening when we'd just gone back to our place in Montmartre, Bricktop, the famous cabaret hostess, telephoned to say Louis was at her place. It must have been about five in the morning and she asked Django to come and accompany Armstrong. Naturally Django and I set off at once, and for the only time in my life I heard Louis sing, accompanied only by Django's guitar. There was no discussion as to what key they'd play in or what tunes they'd choose. Louis began and Django followed him in the twinkling of an eye. It was a revelation for me, and all of us were entranced.

ALBERTA HUNTER   The other American musicians thought that Django was wonderful. Right now if you mention Django Reinhardt they have a fit. It was something

about him because first of all he had no fingers. But what he could do with that bad hand!

DOC CHEATHAM   The Quintet knocked me out. It was a different style to what I heard over here. He wasn't playing American jazz, but he was swinging. It was upsetting to hear a man who was a foreigner swing like that. Because they were swinging! I don't think there was a band in America to compare with them.

ALBERTA HUNTER   If there was any jealousy among the American musicians I never heard about it. But I'm going to tell you that they admired that man so much that sometimes you'd stop and wonder: "My Goodness, to think they're saying all this about a French guitarist." They loved Django. They were surprised that a European could come up to an American when it came to playing jazz.

ALIX COMBELLE   Coleman Hawkins thought a lot of Django – they all did. One night Hawk came down to sit in with us. He stopped playing only when the place closed. I remember we did a version of "Sweet Sue" where Hawkins improvised for an hour and a half without stopping.

DOC CHEATHAM   The thing about Django was that first of all he was a foreigner, so where did he learn to play like that? Then as far as I can remember most of the guitar players around America were blues guitarists. So I think he inspired a lot of guys to play. I mean Johnny Mitchell for instance – you couldn't compare them. Johnny was a straight man on strings. He had no chance with Django because Django was a soloist. Johnny Mitchell was not that kind of a soloist. That's the difference between Louis Armstrong and Del Stegers. In Django's music – the chords and harmonies he used – he was very advanced for the time. I think

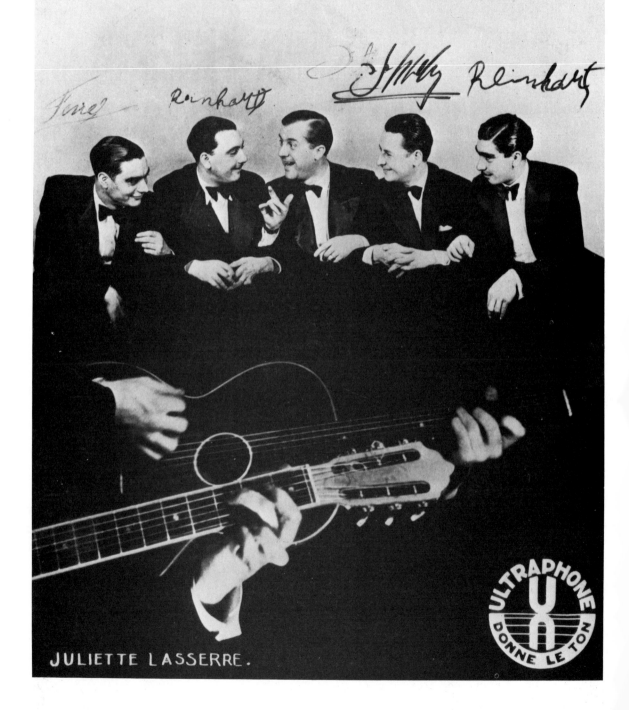

DJANGO REINHARDT
et le QUINTETTE du HOT CLUB de FRANCE
avec STEPHANE GRAPELLY
EXCLUSIVITÉ ULTRAPHONE

JULIETTE LASSERRE.

ULTRAPHONE
U
DONNE LE TON

MON
CHÉR GÉRAR
JE É CRI ÇAIS DEUX MAUX ~~POUR~~
POUR DE DONNÉS DE MES
NOUVÉL NOUSOMME EN TOURNÉ
LA PREMIÉR VILLE BUFALO. 2
ARRISBURG. 3 CLEVELAND. 4 TORONTO
5 TOLEDO OHIO. 6 CINCINNATI. 7
INDIANAPOLIS. 8 CHICAGO. 9 ROCHESTÉR
10 MINNEAPOLIS. 11 LINCOLN. 12 OMAHA. 13.
KANSAS CITI. 14 IOWAS. 15 NEW YORK
DEUX CONCERTS CARNÉGIE HALL.
16 PÉTERSBURG. 17 NORFOLK. 18.
PHILADELPHIA. 19 NEW YORK. 20.
BOSTON. 21 PROVIDENCE

22 DÉTROIT TU TE RENCONTI
DES VOIAGE MAIS AVEC DUKE
TOUS LES MUSICIEN SONS COUEHET
MAGNIFIQUEMENBIENT ET DUKE ET
MOI NOUS AVONS UN PETIT LIIVIG ROOM
SÉS VRAIMENT FORMIDNBLES
SÉS UN PEU MIEA QUE LA PLACE
PIGALLE TIEN TOI BON JE CROI QUE
JE VAIS TEUX FAIR VENIR COMME
A RENGEUR IL A QUE COMINC A QUE
TU PEUX VENIR. ON PARLES BAUCOU
DU QUINTÉTEUA AVEC GRAPPELLI.
MAIS A VEN DE MAITRE CA SUR
PIÉR SA DEMANDE BAUCOU DE TENT-
RAPOR A LUNION MAIS SA VIENDKAS
BIENTO SI TU PEU MAVOIR LA DRESSE
DE MON FRÈRE NIN NIN ANVOIMOILA
TUE MÉSCUSERA DE MON OLTOFRAFI
JE NE VOIS PLUS GRANCHOSE A TEUX DIR
JE TE DI ELLO BONJOUR A TÉ PARENS
Nello Narnd... son ... Lele. DJANGO

ABOVE Django
Reinhardt's damaged
hand – he had the use
of only two fingers and
the thumb on his left
hand.

LEFT A letter from
Django to Gerard
Levecque describing
his tour of the United
States with the Duke
Ellington Orchestra
in 1946

LEFT An Ultraphone
publicity picture for the
Quintet du Hot Club
de France.

ABOVE Roget Chaput,
seated front left and
playing the banjo, in
Bal Musette, *c.* 1927.
Chaput later became
rhythm guitarist with
the Hot Club quintet.

RIGHT The Quintet on
the balcony of Pierre
Nourry's home in
Paris – (from back to
front) Louis Vola,
Django, Stephane
Grapelly, Joseph
Reinhardt, Roget
Chaput, Jerry Mengo,
unknown lady, and
Charles Delauney,
the discographer.

TOP Django's caravan.

ABOVE Django plays for his son.

ABOVE Django's mother.

ABOVE Jam session at
the Hot Club de France,
1934 – (left to right)
Rex Stewart, Django,
Duke Ellington, Louis
Vola, rest unknown
except for Django's
brother Joseph,
standing second from
right.

RIGHT Gerard Leveque
transcribes one of
Django's compositions
in a hotel room.

ABOVE Joseph and
Django Reinhardt with
Gerard Leveque in the
early 1940s.

LEFT Django.

253

Django in a Paris night
club where the Quintet
were playing in the
mid-1930s.

ABOVE Django arrives
in London with André
Ekyan (second from
right) and Jean Sablon
(left).

LEFT Jean Sablon.

255

Django's mass is transcribed for him in the early
1940s.

ABOVE Django with Charles Delauney.

LEFT The Quintet play the Casanova club in the mid-1930s.

LEFT Louis Vola.

TOP Django during a war-time jam session with members of the Glenn Miller Orchestra.

he was sort of ahead of his time. No one in America was playing guitar as well as Django.

EVERETT BARKSDALE The tops in my estimation was to go down to Bricktop's and hear Django play. I'd never heard anybody play guitar like that in my life before. I'd been trying in my small way, but when I heard what he was doing with two fingers and sat up there and watched him, I said. "The heck with it! I think maybe I ought to give up music. I really should think about doing something else with my life."

DOC CHEATHAM Who knows where he got it from? A lot of people say he was a gypsy. Gypsies have a hell of a talent for playing you know. I've heard that all my life. I heard some hell-fire violin players up in Roumania. Now if we trace the evolution of man, we'd learn a lot about all this. Probably it goes right back to the black man. Who knows? You go to Africa – I know that the Africans had a lot to do with jazz because I was in Africa, and I went around and heard some things – I don't say they were jazz – but I really believe they had a lot to do with it. Perhaps if you looked into it you could trace Django back to Africa. Who knows?

HUBERT ROSTAING The gypsies are a very musical people, and Django was their greatest musician. This was why all the gypsies describe themselves as cousins of Django. They all wanted to be Django. It led to some amazing situations. There was one incident which occurred after the war. I was playing with Django in a place on the Champs Elysées, in a club which is now a restaurant. And there was a customer who was making a fuss and was obviously upset about something. And Django wanted me to sort it out because I could do these things

better than he could. So when I asked this guy what was wrong he said, "I was a prisoner in the war and Django was a prisoner with me and I know that that is not Django playing there." And it was a cousin of Django's who had passed himself off as Django. He was quite convinced it was not Django playing there.

ALAIN ROMANS When we used to go down to do a gig anywhere near Toulouse with Stephane and Django, instead of one guitar we had at least fifteen or twenty guitar players because all the gypsies from the surrounding areas of Toulouse came and played with us. There are a lot of gypsies in that region and they all claim to be cousins of Django's, so instead of having maybe ten musicians in the band we had maybe thirty or forty. They liked to play with Django, and they played quite well, but Django was the leader.

LOUIS VOLA When we were in the Perpignan area we'd get loads of cousins who'd come by to play and just be around – there'd be Spaniards, Catalans and all sorts. Everybody wanted to play.

At Cannes, when he and Nin-Nin, his wife and my wife were there, after a couple of weeks there'd be a line of caravans along the front by the Casino. There'd be four, five, ten, fifteen, twenty, forty, fifty gypsies all come to see Django. And the Maire who was director of publicity at the Palm Beach Casino would come to me and say, "Tell Django that his friends can't stay there because otherwise I shall have to get the police to move them on." Because they'd set up camp right there and cook, do their laundry and light fires right there on the Plage. So Django would have to tell them to move.

We had some good times I can tell you. I remember after we made the first disc for Ultraphone, we left at about five in the morning and went down to St. Denis where there were a lot of gypsies. Django's mother lived there at the time. Well, we got there at about six o'clock in the morning. And we just started to play right there in the open. And first one little window in one of the caravans opened and then another. And little by little people started to gather around seeing it was Django and his group. And then people began rushing around organizing provisions so we could eat. So we ate and played and ate some more and kept on playing. Later on in the afternoon we went to a restaurant where you could get a big bowl of mussels and once again we played some more. We finished up in the bar getting more and more drunk. Finally Stephane fell asleep and I took him home, still sleeping, so I had to carry him all the way up to his room five flights up. I put him on the bed and he still kept on snoring. So that's a story of how we used to like to play!

BERTIE KING Django was a pure genuine gypsy. And his best playing was when he was alone in the street on the sidewalk and the right mood was on him. I saw him do it. This was when the true Reinhardt came out. He'd just get that mood and then he'd take his instrument out and put all his emotions into his playing. When he was pulled into a job he'd lose a certain percentage of the feel to the whole thing because money was never his bag. He was just a down to earth gypsy. Any time there was a performance to give they had to stay with him all night to see that he turned up for the job, otherwise he'd stray. But whenever the mood took him that's when he liked to play and then it was that the real true feelings would come out.

☆ EUROPEAN PIONEERS

LEO VAUCHANT

The first jazz band that came to France – the first black one – was Louis Mitchell's. He was a drummer – a very good drummer too. I imitated him. I learned from him. Whatever he did, that was the way I was doing it. I played timpany and snare drums when they first came. I also started playing trombone with that band. The next time I heard them Leon Volters of the Casino de Paris had got them back from England. This time I was playing cello and drums with a tango band. And I listened to those Mitchell guys – I had a trombone back home – and right away I knew I could play all that shit that guy played with them.

Later on things got better because other bands came. Art Hickman was one. There was another orchestra called the Georgians who had a trumpet player called Frank Guarante. There was a drummer called Jimmy Lennon whose brother has some kind of an orchestra now. So there was always something the guys could copy. I was still going on what I had picked up from Mitchell. I never heard the Georgians; I never heard Art Hickman. I was working. I had no way of going to listen and there were no records available to French people. There was only Salabert who published a few stocks and then put his own name on them as arranger so he could collect something. But he hadn't written them or arranged them either.

I learned jazz more or less on my own. I started analyzing a bit what those Mitchell guys were doing – just by hearing them play. I didn't have the records. I knew the tunes they were playing. I could hear the phrases and I was trained. I knew the names of the intervals and the degrees of the scale. If you look at a chord as a question they were giving the answers by playing a certain phrase. I could readily see what they were doing because there are only twelve notes and some are automatically tabooed. In fact in the C chord all the notes are good. The only one which is tricky is the F and nowadays they all use it.

To the blacks, life in Europe was like heaven, I can tell you. One good reason was the white women. But it was also being able to go any place, and live where they wanted. Also they were looked up to as stars. And that must have been pretty pleasant after life in the States. A lot of French guys resented the blacks going off with their women. But every guy I knew found himself a white broad – Montmartre women mostly, not necessarily whores. They met them as hostesses who danced with them and they got a tip as an escort.

I started as a professional musician at the age of eight. Later I went to the Conservatoire in Lyons. I graduated there when I was about sixteen. This would be about 1920 or 1921. I didn't get the first prize that year because I took my sabbatical. I went to study with Weingartner in Berlin. While I was in Germany I played trombone with an Hawaiian band. They had an English trombone player called Bligh who went back to England to die. I replaced him on trombone and got someone else – a Turk – to replace me on drums. I found him working in a furrier. I went there with this woman, and there was this guy with two long sticks beating all hell out of the pelts. He had a fantastic rhythm, rather like those guys here in America who used to shine your shoes. I said, "Let me see you do that while you tap

four to a bar with your foot." So he did, and I asked him, "Could you do that to music?" He said, "Easy." I said, "You want a job as a drummer? I have everything you need." So I showed him what was wanted and I found he could even do a roll. So that afternoon Raged Osman the Turk was dressed as a Hawaiian and played the tea dance with us. The other guy in the band was a fellow named Lewis. I forget his first name. He was English and played very good jazz violin and also soprano sax. I played trombone. We were the only two horns in the orchestra. There was another guy, a Dutchman called Freddy van Root, who played piano. The rest of the outfit were Hawaiian. The Hawaiians had a good feel for American stuff. They were very much like Americans. We played a lot of American tunes. It was easy to get piano copies so our repertoire was way out. Most of our music came from England. Some guy got them from there. I can't remember his first name but his last name was Levy.

Anyway, I was playing with tango bands when that Mitchell band came back to France. I was playing cello mostly. If I played for pit orchestras I'd play timpany and snare drums. I stopped that around 1922. From then on I played jazz trombone whenever I could. I played jazz drums too. At the end of 1917 I was playing with a very small orchestra – about five pieces. I played double drums. You had to play cymbals and snare drums as well as bass drums. Most people used to do it by hitting a cymbal with the left stick and have the drum on the right side. I was doing it with two cymbals and I played the drum with one stick. The conductor was a man named Fred Melly. He became the conductor at the Moulin Rouge later and made some horrible records there. At that time it was a burlesque house, but arty. You know, they have the girls come on bare-breasted with big hats on which they held with their hands because it helps the façade! The sketches usually ended in a blackout. And the girls would be in the wings waiting to go on the stage looking their best. And usually the fireman on duty would be back there – stage right let's say. And before the girls would go on they'd ask this guy, "Would you do my nipples?" And the fellow would oblige and start sucking them until they were ready to go on for the big number. I heard about it. And I see that the girls come from both stage right and stage left. I was stage left in the pit. So I used to go there until the very last moment when I had to come back to play the choral at the end of the sketch. And I was doing what the fellow on the other side was doing. This was at the Gaiété Rochechouart Theater. The shows would be a series of acts. A guy comes on first and he sings or tells a joke, or maybe a dancer would come on. Then there'd be intermission after the finale with the girls. The second act – you're going to laugh – an act of *Faust*. From the opera *Faust*. – with twelve musicians in the pit! It was like a burlesque house, as I say. There was nudity, but it was not prurient. It was just bare-breasted and they held those hats. It was the poor man's Folies Bérgères.

My father yanked me out of that place. I had to quit that job. We made eight francs a show. We only had one matinee, so we made sixty-four francs a week. So I got myself a job at the Restaurant Pigalle, where I was getting fifteen francs to begin with, a meal, and the tips were often fifteen francs or more. I had to wear a smoking-jacket. I was supposed to get one made or find one my size. I was quite small – I was only fourteen years old. My father took me to a place called the Cahut in a district called the Temple, close to Notre Dame, where you bought second-hand things. Smoking-jackets in those days were a big

deal. They were all too big for me. People used to get married and buy one, then they sold it right away. You couldn't rent them like you can today. So we went there and found a suit that fitted me. It had lots of pockets inside, outside, everywhere. So we bought it very cheaply. I just tried it. The guy turned me around in front of my father and said, "You like it?" My father said, "take it off," and they wrapped it in newspaper. It had seven vests with it: all kinds of colors – pearl grey, tan, white, black. We got home and I put the suit on for my step-mother to look at. And she started laughing. This suit belonged to a magician who, unfortunately, was a hunchback. Anyway she fixed it. She made me put it on inside out. She removed the lining from the back, opened it out and made it fit. Then she sewed it up, and put the lining back. I had a tuxedo for maybe ten dollars with seven vests.

So I started working at the Restaurant Pigalle for two hundred francs a week, where before I'd only been getting sixty-four. The World War One air aces used to come in there. Guinmere was the big shot. But they all came. They were gods in those days. They had the Croix de Guerre loaded with palms for each plane they'd shot down. They were allowed to design and determine the color of their own uniforms. One son-of-a bitch shows up in pink! I adored that man. I said, "Man, you're for me!" Anybody that had the guts to assert himself that way.

In 1918 Saint Saens was in Bourbon La Cambeau which is near Vichy for his arthritis. He was there with André Messager, another composer. They were our best customers. My Dad played bass, I played cello, and there were two violins and a piano. We played everything, right up to condensed versions of operas. We played light stuff and heavy stuff but arranged for that kind of combination. And Saint Saens used to come in to have coffee with one or two of his friends and a big St. Bernard dog. He didn't pay much attention to what we played. One day somebody went to him. There was a big hotel converted into a hospital, and they decided they would hold a Mass for all the badly wounded people who would be carried into the church on litters. And they asked Saint Saens if he would do an organ recital. He said no, but if they could find somebody to do the Ave Maria he would accompany. They looked all over and they couldn't find a singer. So the next best thing is a cello. And so they got me. I said, "Fine, but I'll have to get with the organist." They said, "He's right over there in the hotel." So I went to see him in his suite and I said, "Maître, I understand I'm going to play with you next Sunday." He said, "Yes, that's right." I had my cello in its little canvass case. I said, "Would you like me to rehearse with you?" He said, "You know it?" I told him I knew it and that was that. We didn't rehearse. We went to the church on the Sunday morning, and he just dragged his cane up and down the keyboard – the white keys. It worked. And then it came to be time for us to play. You know, you just get a nod from the Abbé and we start. I come in right on time and the accompaniment is going along fine, and suddenly there's a grating noise. The B♭'s not working. There's a B♭ and an F sharp that are not on the white keys, and they're both out of commission. And I can hear Saint Saens muttering, "Now we're buggered. Why don't those assholes fix this thing?" And I can hear this swearing going on and I'm trying to hit the notes. So we went through to the end, and after it was over I asked him if I had played properly, and he tapped me on the cheek and said, "You did very well. But that damned organ – instead of spending all that money on candles, why don't they fix that bloody organ?" In 1970 I went back to France and I stayed in the same place and they still haven't fixed that organ!

About that time I cottoned on to something else. At that time there was another jazz band that came up. Some agent got a bunch of guys together. There was a Belgian drummer who spoke English. It was in a rollerskating place at the Alcazar next to the Ambassadeurs in the Champs Elysées. They had a bowling alley like you have now. They were the first to do that. So we played there – it was a jazz band. And the drummer was making ten times what we were making. And I used to watch what he did. He could play a one-step. He'd learned that much, I don't know, maybe in London. He was making a hundred francs a day. We were working for maybe eight or ten. So I said to myself, I'm going to get into that. So my Dad, he made me a bass drum – he made the whole instrument, and it didn't look at all bad. And I started doing this too. I was a lot better than that crap band was.

Around 1924 I was playing with a tango band again – cello as usual. And there was a band called the Chicago Hot Spots. It was a band that used to play on the riverboats from Chicago to New Orleans on the Mississippi. There was Vic Sells. There was a fellow called Tracy Momma who played clarinet. Real Dixieland, but good. There was a fellow called Webb somebody, a sax player. He left and another guy came. Homer Vance Pybrock his name was. And Freddy Flick was the banjo player. Again no bass. Anyway their trombone player got homesick and left. So they asked me if I knew of a trombone player who could fake. I said, "Yeah, I'll get you one tomorrow." So I got a dep in for me on cello and I went and played trombone with them. They didn't know I played trombone. I knew every note that guy played. And I knew the tunes.

Even if I didn't know the trombone part I could make it up, knowing the tune you know – harmonizing. So I got to learn those tunes anyway. I didn't learn any jazz with them. But I learned those tunes. About three months before joining them I was playing cello, but I was learning all the time through listening to what they were doing. There was a big repertoire of what they call Dixieland. Everything was Dixieland at that time. You didn't have sections, but they were easily harmonized three ways. This Dixieland thing didn't move me too much, but to tell you the truth I didn't have to try too hard. I liked the music OK, but what I really liked was the life it made for me and the money I was making. So I played the music – it was a means to an end. I wasn't a jazz buff in any way. I liked it. It was creative in a way, and to a certain extent, as I started to write stuff for it, it was difficult too.

But the life was the thing. I couldn't get over it. A kid of fifteen years old. I could stay away from home because I was making money. There's no kid in the world who doesn't like to stay up and make money. And there were plenty of girls around too – even when I was fourteen. Oh, yeah. I was an old-timer at fourteen. So making money, I was able to get out of that lousy life. I came from a pigsty. My father and his second wife – she gambled the money. I don't really know what she did with it. We were two men working for one woman, and there was never any money for food. I got one day's pay a week to keep for myself, but I was spending it on food. A kid should be able to buy something he likes for himself. I was spending it on ham sandwiches and beer. At intermission I would run one block the other way. I had just discovered pistachio ice-cream. I would take it in a glass and drink it. The next day I'd return the glass and get another one.

André Ekyan was one of the first to play jazz. Also he played flute before anybody was playing jazz flute. And there was Roger Fishback, a very fine sax player who also played violin. He died quite a while ago. There was another guy who called himself Harry Parsons. His real name was Henri Pruniau. There was a fellow who lives today on Riverside here in Burbank, called Maury Cutter. His name was Maurice Couteau. He was from Nice. I was Leo Vauchant. There's no name more un-American than that. We never got together in jam sessions. We'd play on the job. There were some good piano players. There was a fellow called Colleaubonner, a Swiss. There was a fellow called Bergerer. There was Romans, who is still around. A good band could have been made in France with the people who could play. But there was always one among the rest who couldn't make it. There was no money to get the guys together. To us the money was good because we played with people who all earned much less than we did. They wanted what you would call a star – a guy who could stand up and pump it out. But you couldn't get a band – a decent band even with three brass instruments and four rhythm. You couldn't get anybody that would pay the guys that could play.

There was a band – Ray Ventura's band. I started in his band as a pro with a bunch of college kids. There was a fellow called Bandale who played trumpet. Montaigue also played trumpet. Eddie Foy played sax and there was a baritone sax guy called Jean Gompel. Guy Pacquinet played trombone with him for a time. Also René Weiss. I played with him a little bit at a few recordings and things. So he got together a few elements that could play, but they were mainly college kids who weren't very good.

Hugues Panassié started quite early you know. Serge Gliksen the sax player took me to see him one day. He wanted me to transcribe something for him from a record. He would work the record and keep going back because it takes time to get all those notes. So I would write down the things he heard on records. I wasn't interested to go and listen to this or that record, but he was a nice man you know. I don't remember whose recordings they were. Some could have been black but some were white too. I can't remember their names now. Maybe Roy Matson was one. Sammy Lewis, an American trombone player, maybe was another. I heard maybe four records in all, and not necessarily good ones.

By this time I was playing jazz full-time. I didn't play tangos after I played with those Chicago Hot Spots. The things I learned from those guys! I'd never seen anyone eat bread and butter with soup. They all did it. I also learned about Listerine – it's a disinfectant that Americans can't live without. I also learned about those PVD's they were wearing. It was an underwear that has a little trap-door at the back. The girls that we knew who went with those guys would describe the PVD. How they laughed. In France, you see, we had shorts and shirts made of silk. We couldn't believe that guys would have underwear that goes through the knee – all in one piece with all kinds of things which cross over in the front so you could open it, and at the back there was a trap door that you lower.

Soon after working with those guys I left home and I never went back. I knew a girl who went to Ostende to work. And she wired me to say they were looking for a guy who played all kinds of instruments. So I went there with the trumpet and the trombone. I left home and I was only sixteen. The fellow that had the band had a drum kit so I could play drums as well. I never went home again.

The theater shows had a big effect – *Blackbirds* and those others. However, the first show to come was a white one. It was at the Marigny Theater in 1918 and the only black element in it was the Mitchell band, and they were hardly concerned with the show. They were brought in as an attraction for the bar when the people came in at intermission. They put them on stage but they didn't play by themselves. They played with the pit orchestra. They weren't even featured, they just played the finale like everyone else. The show played for about a month and then closed. I remember we didn't get paid. You know, one night we got there and the place was closed. We couldn't get in. So we got an injunction. I came the next day and I got my bass drum – the one my father had made me – my snare and all my other stuff, and Louis Mitchell said to me, "Hey kid, you're not getting paid?" So I said, "No." I spoke English after a fashion. I had learned it in military school with an English instructor. Mitchell got a big kick out of that because I was a good scholar. Also he liked me because we played the same instrument, and I played the show on timpani and opened his eyes too. We respected one another. I did things he didn't know how to do and he did things I had never heard of. We were friends. I'd go there early when the people came in and they're playing in the bar. I loved those guys. Frank Withers, he was old enough to have been my father and I was like a son to him. We talked music. I was fortunate to be able to speak English – that was the thing. And I told them where they could buy the salami or where to get a slide fixed. I was one of the boys. That's why, when they started that Tempo Club, they invited me in. So anyway, Mitchell says to me, "You want to get your money? Come with me." And there was a fellow either by the name of Hopkins, Hawkins or Perkins – I don't remember which. And Mitchell was a big guy, with a thin waist like you and broad shoulders. So we knocked on the door of the office. And they said, "Who is it?" He says, "Louis Mitchell." He says, "You open that door or I'm going to break it down." So the fellow says, "There's nothing I can do for you here." And Mitchell says, "You open that door or I'm going to shoot the lock off." And he was a very refined gentleman. Anyway the door opened and we got in. And the fellow starts to give him a song and dance you know. So he pulled the gun and said, "You owe me so much for the band and this kid gets his shares." So I got paid.

The cats in the Mitchell band, they saw what was happening in the pit orchestra. They had found out that I was fixing the arrangements more in the manner in which they were playing the same numbers. And they said, "Hey, you got something." Because Cricket Smith couldn't have put down what he played. And they said, "There's a guy that can hear us from the other side of the room, and he can fix it." At that time I was playing drums. Then Mitchell said, "Come on over and visit our club, we'll make you a member. So I went. I had my trombone under my arm. In those days we didn't have cases. They were made out of men's trousers. You put the horn in one leg and the slide in the other, and that's the way it was done. Anyway I went along, and there was Maisie Withers practicing the piano and she had a trombone on the floor underneath. And Frank was there. He used to play with her. So he said, "Hey, we're going to play." So he gave me the notes and I played. So I started to write stuff for the three of us. The Tempo Club! That was the name of it. It was upstairs next door to Zelli's where Tom Waltham had the band. Members could go to the Tempo Club and drink – no licence you understand. There was a big black guy. Where they got him I don't know. He was a good cook, what you call a short order cook. He did all the stuff Americans like: hash and chile con carne. To me it was America. I wanted to come to America so much, you've no idea.

They started a thing – Frank Withers and some other guy. They called it the Synco Symphony. It was kind of an orchestra. About fifty guys. And it laid an egg. They had gotten all the violinists who played in the tango bands who could play rhythm instead of just schmaltzing away – because the real tango is very close to jazz, there's a big Latin influence. And we'd work with this. And Frank had made all these arrangements which were very clever. And I went and played trombone. In that club there would be a lot of sitting in. Other black guys would come by. It was the first time I heard jamming going on. We just sat there and played the tunes that we knew. They were tunes like "Arizona," and I guess "Hindustan" was already in. We didn't play the Dixieland tunes – more sort of ballads and the tunes that were in vogue at the time, but we improvised on them. This would have been around 1920. I remember it was from that club that I got word to go to Ostende and play that job. Then I came back. Then I went to Germany and the money fell down and I came back to Paris and resumed with those fellows.

I can't remember the names of other black guys that were there. There was one man, a clarinet player – Sidney Bechet. I heard him. He played great. But I don't remember him playing in that place. He came by for a beer maybe, but I didn't play with him. I talked to him I think. I heard him play where he was working because you could hear it from the outside. It was on the Rue Caumartin. It was with his own outfit – five musicians maybe. Those clubs couldn't afford a band. He'd got a little contract as well as his job with Sissle.

In those days everything was new to me.

Tom Waltham, who worked in Zelli's underneath the Tempo Club, was a fine musician. He played good dance piano. He would have made you dance just playing the piano alone. He'd pull the time around and anticipate the beat. He would get the chord and with the top note anticipate down to the chord. I hadn't heard any black piano players other than Parrish who played with that band. But he never took any solos. They played the tunes all together. They never stopped for a solo. So Waltham was the first pianist I heard who really played different – American. He composed a lot of tunes. He must have made a lot of money in royalties. He died recently.

When the black theater shows started to come in – I didn't see most of them – I was working, and not always in France either. I was in Germany, I was in Spain, I was in Turkey. So I wasn't aware of them. I do remember one show. That was *Blackbirds*. There were lots of shows that followed it. *Blackbirds* was in 1926. At the same time there was Paul Whiteman, Noble Sissle and Sam Wooding. The following year it was Irving Aaronson and his Commanders with a white show. It was 1927. I remember Cole Porter wrote the music for that Aaronson show. Fred Waring was at the Ambassadeurs in 1928 with a white show. I don't know where they had the *Blackbirds* but it wasn't at the Ambassadeurs. In 1929 I don't know what was happening because I was in England. 1930 I was in England. 1931 I was in South America with Gregor. After that I was in America so I lost track.

As far as the black shows and the dancing in those shows was concerned, the types I saw in them until I came to America were the type you saw in the minstrel shows. They wore baggy pants, although they weren't using that black-face make-up. I never saw Negroes in fabulous suits until I came to New York. The ones in Paris did humorous dancing. They'd raise their foot on the heel and then use the other foot to press it down again. They'd do the same thing with their Adam's apple and the tie that wobbles. They could spin a derby hat on their heads and they did tap dancing. They were very good – not just better than whites, there were no whites doing it.

There was a fellow in France who was famous. His name was Harry Pilcer. He was a dancer and he liked jazz. He used to work with the Dolly Sisters. And he also worked with Gabby Deslys. I knew Harry very well because I used to fix up the orchestra parts for him. One night he'd come and he'd say, "Hey, you did something I liked." It wasn't written down, you see. We used to improvise a lot of stuff for those people. Really he walked around doing very little. He wasn't a tap dancer. So he'd just glide around the floor, put his arms up over his head and fall on his knees on the floor. Then he'd straighten himself up again as he put his arms down. That was his big trick. Girls used to do the same thing. They would do a backwards thing and then stand up. So Harry would slide around the floor doing a one, two, three and slide a little bit looking at the people as if to say, "Here I am – well dressed." He had a pearl worth half a million dollars. I picked him up one day on Sunset Boulevard years later. He told me he was waiting for a cab. He wasn't waiting for a cab, he was waiting for a bus. So I gave him a lift and he talked. They were making a picture about the Dolly Sisters and they wouldn't hire him to do anything. He said, "Can you imagine? They do a picture about the Dolly Sisters and nobody wants to hear from me." Back in Paris he had his own club. He liked jazz. He had some Negro musicians playing for him. There was a fellow called Seth Jones, a drummer, and a fellow called Vance Laurie, a sax player – real great. I never heard of either of those two guys again.

As far as the black shows and the dancing in those shows was concerned, the people who could afford to see those shows didn't learn anything from them because they were dummies. Some of the kids may have been able to get something out of it, but not many. So it was strictly the music that did it. Of course at that time there were no sound pictures. But there were American tourists. They were the ones who brought the charleston, the black bottom and the varsity drag, etc. So the gigolo dancers in those places would look and look and the next day you would see them doing something you wouldn't believe – it was awful. The next day I could do the charleston because I was a dancer. And I would teach the gigolos at the Perroquet the easy way to do the charleston with another person. I don't mean how to do an exhibition by themselves, but the step the way it was, turning the feet.

I didn't know Bricktop personally. You see those clubs were fairly expensive and functioning at the same time as I was working. And they weren't the sort of places you could crash to go jamming for instance. I knew of her. I never saw her to tell you the truth. She had the place. She moved around quite a bit. She had a club that was closed for some reason and then opened another. She was a personality. She knew every American that came in. But she made herself well known and she could bring 'em in. Joe Zelli had a speakeasy in New York. Every American came in – he used to say he gave them the Royal Box – that was his phrase. And he was an Italian American who went back to France and started that place. And it was a jazz place, you know. Except it was limited to just that one band. But anybody could sit in. It was Tommy Waltham. It was a white band, but black guys would come in and sit in. It was Tommy Waltham, Freddy Holt, the drum-

mer, Billy Williams on alto sax, and Emile Christian on trombone. It was really a jumping place and he added another orchestra who played tangos. It was called the Ad Lib and run by Joe Zelli. It wasn't too expensive. It was in Montmartre – Rue Fontaine. And you could go there and four guys could go and have a bottle of champagne. And that wouldn't kill you then you know. And if you were a musician there wouldn't be any cover charge. In the early evening he probably had four girls and four fellows who pretended to be customers. If there was nothing happening nobody came in the place. If they saw somebody come in they'd dance together because nobody wants to be the first. It got things going. The music was basically fox trot. It was pretty formal stuff but it was already very jumpy.

I had a band at a place called the Abbaye Thélème. It's on Place Pigalle. I ran the band there. Roger Fishback was on sax, there was an English drummer whose name I forgot. I tell you how we got that band. I was working for a man called Jimmy Lennon, brother of the Lennon with the society orchestra in New York. He had a brother who played piano – very inexperienced and very bad piano player. And we had trumpet, trombone and saxophone. I forget the name of the trumpet player, piano and drums. We got a job through this Mr. Lennon and his brother the pianist. And collections were made twice a night for the orchestra. We hadn't signed a paper. He kept that. So we said, "We participate in this. It's not for the Lennon brothers that they take up a collection. They make it for the orchestra, and we are the orchestra." And he said, "Well, you should have thought of it before. You work for so much a week and that's it." So I got an idea. I went to see the boss. I said, "How would you like to see the same orchestra with another

269

drummer and another pianist?" He said, "OK with me." He said, "How much do you get now?" I said, "Well we get so much. How much do the other two guys get?" He said, "Same price." But he said, "I have to break the contract with the other two guys." So the next night we got a . . . like a solicitor . . . who makes a stipulation that at the starting time the orchestra is not there. The brothers were there, but no trumpet, no trombone, no saxophone. We didn't show up. So he broke the contract with them. And an hour later we brought the pianist. It was Freddy van Rupp the Dutch guy who was with me, and that English fellow who played drums and sang. He used to sing "Mother McCrea." So I said, "We got two Americans to replace the other." So we used to say, "Where you from in the States, Mr. van Rupp?" He used to say, "Cleveland." He had never been to America in his life. It was a nice clean nightclub. At one time I think it was one of the Voltera brothers, Joseph I think, who owned it. And he had a man, a personality guy who would dance with his partner, Maurice Mouvet. He had been one of those like Fred Astaire guys who did the one-step, the two-step and the waltz, with a girl, I forget her name, an English girl, beautiful. And the tulle dress, you know. So that was the only entertainment apart from the band. It was a place where people went to dance and eat. Sort of supper and champagne.

There was plenty of improvising in that band. The trumpet was strictly a guy that plays with syncopation. We worked it out a little, but it didn't take off. But Fishback and I did. And van Rupp played some stuff.

I was at the Kit Kat with Jack Hylton. And one day I was driving home along Hyde Park to Victoria, where I lived. And I stopped my car and a cab pulls up and stops right at the back of my car and a fellow comes out and he orders fish and chips. I was eating mine right there in a newspaper. And he turned around – he had been at the Kit Kat. He said, "You're the chap who plays trombone with Jack Hylton." I said, "Yes, sir." And I said, "You're the chap who used to sit in on drums with my band at the Abbaye Thélème in Paris." He said, "Rather," or something like that. And it was the Prince of Wales. I didn't take much notice of it. I had worked at the Ambassadeurs, where we had the Prince of Wales, King Alphonso XIII of Spain, King Carol of Roumania. They were customers there. And Elsa Maxwell was there, Chevalier, and the Dolly Sisters. They moved around, you know.

We did one party Elsa Maxwell organized for Rothschild. There were some Americans in Paris more or less stranded and they were friends of Irving Aaronson and his Commanders and they had booked his band to play at the party and they couldn't make it. So she got a band together fronted by a man named Maurice Loupiau. He was a dancer – very tall and thin. And he jumped around in front of the band. He was a very handsome boy. And there was Danny Polo playing clarinet and Dave Tough on drums. He had lost one of the pegs that kept the drum from slipping. So he had put a glass that would just catch one of those metal rods. But while playing, the drum would move and each time he would hit the cymbal, the whole thing would turn around, and everything would spill on the floor.

Elsa Maxwell was a hustler. She got them to spend money and got most of it herself. Gloria Swanson used to come to those affairs. She was married to the Marquis de la Falaise. There was a woman – Pearl White. She had been in pictures and lived in Paris. She was in *The Perils of Pauline* and all that stuff – those serial things that went on forever.

I'm trying to think of those names. I knew Bennett Cerf . . . that might have been a little later. Because I spoke English I knew some guys – Americans that I met. I would live in an hotel in Montmartre when I was away from home – I was about sixteen or seventeen already. And I would meet some guys and they would say they wanted to buy something. I'd say, "I'll help you." They'd say, "Well, would you meet me at Harry's New York Bar at five o'clock tomorrow?" So I would go there at five and I'd meet the guy and they were people that I'd met at the club. I met Fitzgerald, Joyce. They were hanging around there all the time. . . . Bennett Cerf, he was a publisher for Random House. He died recently. But he had his fling. I never met Hemingway. And they were impressed because I knew Maurice Ravel. That's much later. But at the time I had played already at Proust's house. They had a name for themselves. Not the Expatriates – some other name. Gertrude Stein was one of them. I never met her either. I want to tell you, to me it meant very little at the time. I was no more impressed by those people at the time because they were very young and hadn't accomplished anything. It all happened later on – forty years later, fifty years later. But I knew them. You'd just see them at the bar. Actually they weren't that brilliant there in a bar. They'd start, "Did I pull one on last night! Jesus Christ!" It was a long hangover for most of those guys.

From 1924 to 1928 I worked with Ravel, except for a little lapse for a few months when he came back in '27 – he made a tour of the United States. But he came back and took up where he left off. Let me tell you a bit about that Boeuf sur le Toit. It was in the Ruse Boissy d'Anglais. There was a piano team of Wiener and Doucet. They played ricky-ticky piano . . . but they were good pianists and very nice. They played during the cocktail hour and the dinner. Then after that a bass player, a drummer and myself would come around and we'd play for dance music. There are a lot of things written about Les Six. I never saw all the six there. I saw members of Les Six. And others who were not members of them as a little group.

When Ravel and I worked together we developed some rules, loosely speaking. Things that are fashionable, things that one should avoid, playing loose syncopation instead of the jerky kind which was fashionable. So he got that. And then he said, "Look, I want to play some tunes the way you do. And I'm going to see what comes to me not doing arpeggios and not doing scale." We'd already gone through the chromatic, so you had E, E♭, D, D♭, C. I analyzed it after, to see how I could explain that. And I found out that there were some pretty concrete things that almost made a rule.

Ravel was trying to understand what I was doing. That might have been the only club he ever went to, that place. . . . And I never saw him anywhere else. For instance, at the Abbaye Thélème, I used to see Rubinstein. He'd been alone with a bottle of champagne and some nuts. And he probably went to other places – always alone. I don't know for what reason he was there. Not getting drunk or anything. He'd just look around like a bird looks. He'd look right and left. He'd never speak to the musicians. I think he was listening. He was never affected by it in any way that I know of. He enjoyed the atmosphere I guess.

Ravel wrote the rhythmical *Bolero*. The way it's written is more Spanish than jazz, but for that matter "Ain't She Sweet" is not a jazz piece either; "Sweet Sue" is not a jazz piece. They're little songs. People have made them so. Anyway, I tried to make my portion of the *Bolero* a jazz piece.

Milhaud's interest in jazz was to copy everything he could from the Americans. Listen to his *Creation of the World*. If I were going to write a symphonic piece in those days I would have got the idea from the Americans but not the notes. Not note for note. Like that "Royal Garden Blues" he put in that thing of his – written by Spencer Williams who also was in Paris. Ravel was the best. He was the most interested and the most appreciative of what was being done. I learned a lot from him too. I'd study and analyze his scores to see what made them tick. It was the orchestration mostly. What to double, what not to double. Where to find something better to do. He never acted as a teacher, he was like a friend.

In 1927 I was conducting an orchestra at the Bouffes Parisiennes. We did good shows there, you know. Legitimate things. With a legitimate orchestra – no jazz, nothing like that. And then I used to go to the Perroquet and play jazz till five o'clock in the morning. And sometimes you would see me in the church on the Boulevarde St. Michel, St. Germain des Près. And we'd have a string quartet and we'd play with him for something that maybe he had written and so forth. After having conducted the show and playing till five, I am in church there playing the cello. But I would say the most enjoyable thing for me would be nine till five at the Perroquet, playing jazz. It was the freedom. Making a living and feeling that I was a free man. You played the notes you wanted to when you want to. You used the position of the slide that you wanted to.

Of course I had a lot to do with the band. I was the arranger. And I called the tunes you know . . . called the shots. Gluskin had the band and he had a very good band – very good players in it. A lot of American fellows in it from Detroit. There was a fellow called Russ Goudy. Much later, he

played and I played with Zinky Cohn the pianist and Nat King Cole's brother, Eddie Cole. He played bass with us. And he played good jazz piano. He died in Hawaii I understand. I never saw him since. Zinky was with the act that I came with to America, Arlene and Norman Selby. Before he came to Paris Zinky had replaced Earl Hines with Jimmy Noone's orchestra. So I'd ask Eddy Cole, "Hey man, you want to go and jam some place?" And we'd go out in Montmartre and he'd play real great. We'd just play together, you know. By the time we finished the show things were jumping in lots of clubs. We'd find one club where there's nothing much happening and we'd go and we'd play the blues. He'd hit the chords – Bam! And then we'd go. When you get through he hits another. We'd play games that way you know. It was very good.

Gluskin started by joining a French band. He was an American. He was a drummer. He joined a band – the man's name was Paul Gazon. He was a saxophone player – great technique, lousy tone, but great execution. The band was French and the only American was Gluskin. Gluskin worked his way. He got the band away from Gazon. He got some guys from Detroit to come and work. Gluskin did great for himself. He had a brother who was a criminal lawyer who worked things out for him. He was head of CBS music at one time. Now they've faded away. You see he had a bunch of guys who didn't want to make it in music necessarily. One was Ted Gobal, who owned the Brewery. He died. Gene Prendergast came back. He's lost a lung now. He's tuning pianos now to make a living. He played alto before but when we were jamming the other day there was a tenor lying down and he picked this tenor up and wow! He played great.

We had a regular job at the Perroquet.

272

That was the most fashionable place. That's where Louis Mitchell had played years before. We'd be playing for nightclubs – midnight supper and dancing. No show. We played straight jazz. The other band played the waltzes. They played pasadobles, tangos, maybe a waltz every now and then. But we played solid jazz. And we took all the choruses we wanted. Nobody could get in the place to sit in. I'd go and sit in those little clubs where you could afford to have a ham sandwich and beer. I could only see the world through a ham sandwich and a beer in those days.

I got to know Cole Porter. I did his first piano copy of "Begin the Beguine." The thing Eddy Heywood made a hit out of. He was nice. To me he was great. I heard plenty of things about Cole Porter. I met Cole Porter in Paris. He was a rich man, very elegant, very society conscious. Not necessarily a snob. He was a man who enlisted in the French Foreign Legion you know. He was very gifted. He lived at the Waldorf Astoria. That's where I saw him after I met him in Paris, for that "Begin the Beguine." We were to do it with Waring and there wasn't a piano copy of it although they were doing it in the show already. So I made it and then they did a piano copy of it. I did it in a Latin version. Nobody heard of the beguines there in South America. It was Brazilian and it was also Haitian. I had seen the Balle Noir in Paris where they played beguines. When I did the Waring arrangement I did that and I sent him a copy of it. I only spent about two hours with him at the Waldorf. In Paris I spent more time, because he was at the rehearsal of the show. He was a very refined, very gracious person. We weren't that close. It was a question of a very rich man who'd written the show, and I was just a guy who played trombone in the band who did a little arranging for straightening out things. He wasn't what I'd call a

scholar musician. But he was a smart pianist. He had a gift for that. It wasn't like Irving Berlin, who can play in only one key. Irving Berlin had a piano where he could switch the keys around. As far as jazz was concerned, he had the feel that all Americans have who write – the syncopation of it, not the notes necessarily. They just fish for something different. Hoagy Carmichael was much closer to jazz than any other composer except Harold Arlen. Arlen used to do all those Harlem shows. He was a very gifted man. He loved the idiom and he knew the idiom. "Stormy Weather" is an Arlen tune you know. He did a lot of those things. You know the blues at one time – most blues singers were white Jewish women. At one time they were more numerous than black blues singers. Sophie Tucker would have been a blues singer but she couldn't make a living out of it.

I was with Jack Hylton in 1929. While I was in England I used to fly over to Paris to play in jam sessions with Joe Hayman. There was another guy with him called Edwin Swayzee. He later played with Cab Calloway. For a long time I thought Joe Hayman was Benny Carter. I was doing a radio show from Paris every Sunday. At that time there were no commercial shows in England. At the end of 1930 somebody got the idea for a program of dance music – I think it was the Barley Soup people or some cigarette firm, I forget. So I used to fly to Paris with the mail. There was a guy there called Felix Passeron who played tenor sax. Later he became the percussion teacher at the Conservatoire. He was also playing drums at the opera. He sometimes did recordings as an extra drummer with the London Symphony. He contacted the musicians I needed. I would send the music on ahead. Then I would come over to rehearse the band and do the show. That was Sunday afternoon. Afterwards there

273

was nothing to do. So I'd go somewhere to jam. I'd go to the Abbaye Thélème or Zelli's – anywhere. I knew all the musicians so I could go where I wanted. Most of the trombone players were guys that sat there and played from the stocks. So I could go anywhere and be welcome. I wouldn't go to the big places. I'd go to the little clubs and sometimes there'd be black Americans and we'd play till about five o'clock in the morning.

I was always especially glad to play with the black guys. It was always better to play with them. In the first place I liked to speak English. Talking about jazz in French always seemed to me to be ridiculous. It didn't ring true. "Hey, stay in B♭ for the first ending." That meant something. The language has a lot to do with it. In America, even today, musicians dress differently, talk differently, they even shake hands differently. It's another life. In 1934 I was offered the spot as first trombone with the Boston Symphony. I turned it down. What I was doing with Fred Waring wasn't very glamorous, but I was making more money. When Waring heard I was going to leave and go with the Boston Symphony he gave me an extra fifty bucks a week. So I didn't leave because I always watched the money angle. I never had a manager or an agent. I did everything myself. Besides, I liked the jazz. I never let go of illegitimate music.

Before I went to the States I went to South America with Gregor. Stephane Grappelly was with us, but we never saw him. He wasn't exactly a cagey guy but he didn't have any friends in the band that I knew of. Not that they didn't want to be friends with him. While we were there we had Michel Emer and Stephane Mougin as pianists. We enjoyed going to a place where there was a piano and jamming but Grappelly would never come. He had other things to do I guess. He was a dull boy as far as the orchestra was concerned. We had our jokes – he never did. He was very talented. He played piano very well for the jazz stuff.

Eddie South was the best on violin around. Nobody played the violin the way he did. I used to see him in clubs late at night. He'd go there to play or sometimes he worked there. I never played with him. He was incredible. He'd never do the same thing twice. He'd do it the way it hit him. It was so sweet and in such good taste and good jazz. Even in a slow tune. He could play a fast tune but he didn't like it. He liked to expose the real beauty of a tune and whatever notes he added were just gems. Eddie South was like Coleman Hawkins. Grappelly was a guy that liked to play a lot of notes but Coleman Hawkins never played sixteenth notes in his life and if he played eighth notes he wouldn't go on indefinitely. Eddie South concentrated on the beauty of tone and the feeling – never went for the tricky stuff. Now Grappelly has his own style. He's playing great today. In those days I didn't think he had his own style.

After Gregor I went to the States and joined Fred Waring. There I met Jack Purvis. Jack Purvis put his head in the gas oven. He called someone first. They called the police and they came to get him. If they catch you in the act of suicide they take you down to the station and charge you. So they did just that. They said, "Come on, we're taking you down to the station." He said, "Let me put my coat on. Do you want me to die of pneumonia?" You know what he did? When we started at the Roxy Theater he got himself an apartment in an adjacent hotel. And he put it in the newspaper that the first trumpet with Fred Waring had inherited a lot of money. It wasn't true of course. So he goes to the hotel and he says he's Jack Purvis. He always wore a black homburg hat and an English greatcoat with an inverted pleat at the back and a sort of half belt. Like that he always shows up like he's Chamberlain or somebody. He said, "I want the best suite you've got." So they showed it to him and he finally said he'd take it but they had to remove all the furniture. So he went to Ludwig Bowman and he bought himself a bed and everything. He didn't say he was Purvis. He was "Mr. Purvis' valet" and he showed them the piece in the paper saying that he'd inherited 350,000 dollars. So they delivered everything. He even rented a harp. He didn't play the harp but he liked to have one around. And he stayed there – he didn't pay any rent. He didn't bother with trifles like that. We played that engagement for exactly six months. So Purvis leaves a month before we did. First he got about a hundred dollars out of everyone in the band. He didn't get me – I knew the guy. But he got everybody else. Everyone thought he was loaded so it was OK. Then he left town and we never saw him again. Some guy!

We used to go to Adrian Rollini's place. It was in the basement of some hotel around 48th Street. That was the place where Joe Venuti bust the teeth of Johnny Davis for no reason at all. We were having a good time and Joe Venuti resented it. Anyway, we used to go to this place to listen to the group. It was Adrian and his brother and guys used to sit in. Sometimes Purvis would sit in or some of the others would. We also used to go to the Famous Door on 52nd Street. It was speakeasy time you know. I loved New York when I first came there.

I was with Fred Waring but I wasn't playing with the band. I was just arranging. Waring had a fellow called Listock who danced. He didn't play an instrument, he just held a trumpet or something. He had an act with Dan Dailey. He used to teach Judy Garland how to dance. He was a fine actor. We were room-mates. We were in Chicago. We'd finished our part of the engagement so Waring said, "Why don't you two take a couple of days off before we finish here? You can drive my car to New Orleans with Listock and you can see a bit of the country." So we did. I had my trombone with me. And we got someplace – Louisiana somewhere. And there were these black guys and women picking cotton. And this guy Listock played a little guitar – he knew a few chords. So he gets his guitar and I got my trombone and we take off on a blues right there in the field. Nothing! They still go on picking cotton. They must have thought, "What are these idiots doing?"

I was with Roger Wolfe Kahn. His father was a millionaire who at one time was practically supporting the Metropolitan Opera single-handed. Roger was the guy that wrote that tune "Crazy Rhythm." He played several instruments, not well but all the same pretty smart for a rich kid. He knew what was going on in the orchestra. We made a few records. He had good arrangements. It was a very good band. There were three saxophones only: there was Arty Shaw, there was a fellow called Max Farley who played clarinet and oboe and there was Larry Binyon who played tenor sax. We had Chauncey Moorhouse on drums and Charlie Teagarden was one of the trumpeters. I was first trombone and the other guy was Danny or Andy Russo, I never remember which. Perry Brodkin was the guitar player. He was with Russ Colombo later. I think that the pianist was Marlin Skyers. We opened at the Fordham Theater. Then we played the Palace, which is as high as you can get in New York – the best gig in vaudeville. On the bill was Ethel Waters and her pianist Art Tatum. And we had a music room downstairs where the orchestra tunes up and where there was a piano. We used to get together and play. That was the time they discovered the whole tone scale and we'd mess around improvising on that. It fits with practically anything. I would put some bass notes down on the trombone and sustain them to make the scale less crude. If you put it over a pedal it's better. They would play it all ways – in thirds and picking odd notes but just keeping to those six notes of the scale. And Ethel Waters would come down there and sit and knit. She had the most wonderful smile. She was a wonderful singer in that style. She used to sing "Stormy Wetter" – not weather, wetter. It was so natural. Not forced like Yves Montand. She was very southern and very black but very good. She was magnificent in *Cabin in the Sky*.

The quality of the black guys is to be natural. I haven't been that close to them because I spent thirty-six years confined to the studios doing something entirely different. When it came to doing a jazz scene for Hollywood we used the guys from the studio because they were good. Anyway, when I was with Waring we used to go uptown. There was little Frankie Zulo, Purvis, the three trumpet players in the band – they were the swingers – and I used to go with them. We'd get four girls from the show and we'd go to Harlem to see a floor-show. Usually the band was Don Redman or Fletcher Henderson. There were a lot of bands that were very good. Those floor-shows were amazing. I'd always been dreaming about that kind of entertainment. I was a sucker for tap dancing. I used to see two guys going it together in Paris. I don't remember their names but they were great dancers. You very seldom see Sammy Davis doing it now. He jogs along these days. But the Sammy Davis girls are still great. He lent them to a show with Isaac Hayes which I played and I've never seen anything like it.

They broke themselves in two jumping over chairs and then they did a thing where everybody does their own step. That's very exciting. You applaud one number and another one starts. I like it when they have those groups and all the girls take turns dancing with the others clapping and cheering them on.

JEAN WIENER

I'm not at all a specialist in jazz. Nevertheless, I was amazed the first time I heard syncopated music. It was before the First World War at the Casino de Paris. There was an English dancer called Harry Pilcer who was with a very pretty girl called Gabby Deslys. And they did a number – it was something by Handy I think. This was absolutely the first kind of ragtime. It was incredible. I can't remember now if it was a French orchestra or not. The details escape me but it was certainly not black musicians.

Then the war came. And there I met British troops who had records – "St. Louis Blues" and such like. I spent a lot of time with British troops and in addition we began to get American records – Handy, Gershwin and so on. When the war was over I came back and I had a friend called Jean Cocteau who was a kind of genius, although we didn't realize it at the time because he didn't take himself too seriously. He was very charming, very elegant and sophisticated. He went to bed very late and did a lot of crazy things. He was a great writer, couturier, film-maker, decorator and knew a lot about music. I saw a lot of him around 1919. I met him through one of my brothers, who was in class with Cocteau, so he used to come by the house a lot as a boy. And then I ran into him above all because I was a great friend of Darius Milhaud – that was since about 1911.

276

What struck me about jazz were two things. The first was that the trumpets and trombones let themselves go freely – you could almost say "rhapsodically" – while all the while the tempo remained fixed. This was something which classical music has lost. That's why the team of two pianos of Wiener and Doucet used to give concerts of Bach and Mozart and then Handy and Cole Porter. Our point was that there was no such thing as great music and small music – only music which was good or bad.

I never learned to play jazz, perhaps because I had a grandfather who was black, but I never learned. The musician whom I studied the most was Bach because, as my teachers used to say, I had a metronome in my stomach and that's what you need to play jazz also. And that's what I wanted to demonstrate in my concerts also. At that time there were perhaps ten people in Paris who got the point of all that. The rest understood nothing. For me it's the metronome regularity of Negro people and their music – it's very close to Bach.

What interested Stravinsky and the others was above all the syncopated rhythms. But for me the Negroes are naturally expressive. Their traditions are aural, not intellectual like ours. I'm not at all religious but one of the most remarkable experiences of my life was when I was in America in 1931. I was making a big concert tour with my colleague Doucet. And we were invited by the black university at Tuskegee near St. Louis. It was a splendid university with a library of forty thousand books. And they asked us if we'd like to go to the Sunday service. It was one of the greatest memories as a musician I've ever had. The rector was all dressed up in his regalia with a cane with a gold top to greet us at the gates of this huge park. There was a trumpet and trombone fanfare when we arrived – it was extraordinary. Then they led us across the park with the band in front until we got to the church. It was indescribable. It still brings tears to my eyes when I think about it. There were about two hundred choristers – a hundred boys and a hundred girls all wearing the same thing. No cheerleader. There was no orchestra in the church. And for about three-quarters of an hour they sang. If anything was going to make me believe in God that would have done it. It was of such an extraordinary musicality. It began with two hundred people humming with their mouths closed. And it got louder and louder and more and more hypnotic. And after about forty minutes there were two or three women passing out. It was so beautiful it was unforgettable.

Also I was often up in Harlem. And if you knew where to go you'd end up on the fifth floor of some particular building – "First door on the right" – and there would be some huge lady behind the piano who was singing and playing fantastic stuff. It was all a bit wild but fabulous. Then there was the Savoy – big as the Gare St. Lazare. From five in the evening until five in the morning people came to dance. The maids and butlers came early in the evening and then the rich blacks came later on – because there were a lot of rich blacks. And by three o'clock in the morning it was complete hysteria. And all around the edge you had mothers and grandmothers who sat knitting. And when a couple began dancing a bit too violently one of the grandmothers would throw down her knitting and would go on the floor and stop them. The dancing was out of this world – no comparison with Europe at all. You felt you were very close to the roots of music.

ALAIN ROMANS

One of the first to come over here was a banjo player called Vance Laurie. He had been with Louis Mitchell. He was very good on banjo and he also played sax. This would have been about 1918/19. Laurie remained here until the Second World War and then went back to America.

I was working with another banjo player at the time called Tommy Tuck. He too I think had worked with Mitchell. Tommy Tuck was very tall and not very dark. He was also very intelligent and educated – a fine musician and a good singer who could arrange for voices. The band consisted of me, Tommy Tuck, Bobby Jones on sax and Charlie Clark on drums who later went insane. It was a singing group mainly but it was also jazz because we used to take choruses – we would scat them. We did Negro spirituals and also blues. Later we had Valaida Snow, a singer and trumpet player. The band was called the Versatile Four. Before Bobby Jones, the sax player with the band, was a man called Jenkins who played very well. He went back to America and played with Bix Beiderbecke. I heard he committed suicide afterwards. After working with us Bobby Jones worked with Cricket Smith at Zelli's for a while.

I must tell you that at that time there was no racism between musicians. If there was any racism it was our people that used to give preference to the colored musicians. It was quite difficult to get a job as a white musician because they used to prefer to give it to blacks.

At that time the jazz in an orchestra was the drummer. The drummer used to be in the front and he had all these different things for making noises – cow bells and so forth – and he used to throw his sticks about and sometimes even stick his tongue out. We had a drummer called Banks at the Croix du Sud who used to do that. Anyway, the drummer was the big attraction and the musicians used to be behind him on the stand. Little by little they learned they had

to make some music as well.

We had few good musicians in France in the early days. They had no idea about improvising. There were only a few who did. There was Leo Vauchant, Stephane Mougin the piano player, there was Grappelly and Philippe Brun the trumpet player and Pierre Allier who also played trumpet and a little later Alix Combelle on sax. The other musicians needed arrangements before they could play. And there were two Belgians called David Bee and Peter Pacquet who used to publish arrangements imitating Red Nichols, Paul Whiteman and Bix Beiderbecke.

At that time Bricktop started to have a place called the Grand Duc. The fellow that used to have the Music Box left and Bricktop took it over. And little by little Bricktop moved up the street. She took Mabel Mercer the singer with her. We played there with a very small combo. There was Jimmy Boucher, a black fellow who played very beautiful violin. He died a couple of years ago in Switzerland. He was a fine musician and a friend of Grappelly's. Cole Porter used to come in very often. He was very fond of Bricktop and Mabel Mercer. He wrote a lot of his hits in Bricktop's. He was left-handed. He used to play the melody with his left hand and write the lead sheet with his right. Many times I've harmonized for him – things like "Love For Sale" and "Night and Day." He was a very nice fellow – very simple. Frankly, if you hadn't known it was Cole Porter you would think it was Mr. Nobody. He didn't show off. He always asked Bricktop not to say, "Tonight we have Mr. Cole Porter with us." He was very clever, with a good sense of humor. He used to live in the Rue Mademoiselle and there is another street nearby called the Rue Madame. And one day Bricktop was joking about how rich he must be getting with all his big hits, and he said, "Yes, now I will be able to afford Rue Madame."

All the really big shots used to come into Bricktop's. People like Barbara Hutton and Jimmy Donahue. Jimmy Donahue was Barbara Hutton's brother. When he used to sail back to America on the *Normandie* he would phone Bricktop's every night and we used to play for him and Mabel Mercer would sing. When he arrived at New York he would say, "Now it's the last soirée because I'm in New York." Coming back was the same story. He particularly liked the piece from *Showboat* called "My Belle" which Mabel used to sing.

Bricktop also used to manage a place in Le Touquet. The Prince of Wales used to come in there all the time. He had a special set of drums set up there and he used to play. Prince George used to come in too sometimes. They were very polite to each other. Prince George was in love with a girl, one of the most famous singers we ever had in France called Yvonne George. She took that name from him. Unfortunately she used to take dope and she died very young. The band in Le Touquet was that Versatile Four I was telling you about with Tommy Tuck and Charlie Clark.

Bricktop really had something. I started to play for my living at the age of thirteen so I've had some experience of life and I can see what kind of psychology attracts people and what doesn't. I've known a lot of places that were full and then went down-hill. The only place which was always full was Bricktop's. Bricktop had something – a sort of flame as soon as she started to talk. I never met anybody like Bricktop. If Mabel Mercer became a very great artist it's because she was with Bricktop – of that I'm positively sure. She used to just look at a song and just reading it off she'd sing it, improvising all kinds of gags in the middle. She was also the first person in Paris to appreciate Django and Grappelly. She was the first one to promote them. She did it before anybody else knew them. She knew show-business – she knew how to bring out the value of somebody. Through Bricktop the Quintet got a lot of work playing for the rich society people.

Joseph was not as good as Django. Besides, Django had a handicap. His fourth and fifth fingers were fixed together after his accident so he only had three fingers to play with. The funny thing was that he could take a violin and imitate gypsy music very well. He also could do little things on the trumpet. He couldn't play jazz on the violin but he could do gypsy music well.

The relationship between Django and Grappelly wasn't easy, but when it came to making a record Django needed Stephane more than the other way around. They were altogether different characters. Stephane was much more serious. He was very hard-working.

The first job Stephane had was playing in a silent cinema. It was somewhere near St. Michel. And one day he came to me almost crying, saying that they had asked him to take the candy around between the two films. That wasn't Stephane's style at all. He had got the first prize in solfège at the Conservatoire. Because of that he was able to help Django a lot. Django had so many ideas. He tried hard to write music. He started a Mass which was never finished. But Stephane was able to write down a lot of his tunes and he enriched them too because Django had a bad habit of starting things off and then not finishing them.

I met Fats Waller when he first came to Paris. This was in about 1924. I was very friendly with a black chap called Rollins. Rollins had a sort of visual act in the music-hall with his two little daughters. He would throw billiard balls up in the air and catch them on the end of a cue while he danced.

At that time I was playing in a place called the Music Box with another black American piano player and composer called Spencer Williams. And one day this Rollins comes in with a fellow and says to me, "Meet Mr. Thomas Waller." I didn't realize that Thomas Waller was Fats Waller. He and Spencer were very good friends. Unfortunately he was on his way to Germany so he didn't stay with us for long, but on his way back he sat in with us for about a month and sometimes we played together. I was amazed at the simplicity of the man.

Spencer had a big round face like sunshine. He was always smiling and had a little cigar. He and Fats were very funny people. They used to call us white musicians "ofays" and they called themselves "spades." And when they didn't want us to know what they were talking about they would use jive talk. They used to call that "spagingee." A jam session was called a "grand splazz." I used to be invited to their jam sessions sometimes. To be accepted by them you had first of all to speak English. The second thing was not to try to teach them anything. Then they had confidence in you. I suppose after being black in America they had this sort of complex. A lot of the white musicians – Americans – wouldn't play with them. They recognized that they were good musicians but they wouldn't play with them.

In 1930 I wrote the music for a picture with Josephine Baker called *Zoo-Zoo*. Spencer Williams was also involved and came back from the States to do it. He gave me Fats Waller's address and when I was working on Long Island in 1936 I met Fats Waller again. He was playing at the Yacht Club. Through him I met people like W. C. Handy and Andy Razaf.

There is a story about Fats Waller I want to tell you. The violinist Fritz Kreisler used to go around to different places in Paris. And I was playing in a very smart place called the Café de Paris. I had a marvelous violin player with me called Michel Warlop who played classical as well as jazz. So one day Fritz Kreisler came into the Café de Paris and when he heard Warlop play he sent back to his hotel for his Stradivarius so Warlop could play it. And then Fats Waller came in – this was on his second visit to France in '32. Fritz Kreisler had heard of Fats Waller so they were introduced and they all sat down to talk. And Kreisler was asking how Fats could play in clubs with everybody talking. So Fats said, "That's all right, I never listen to them," which Fritz Kreisler thought was very funny. So they talked some more and Fritz Kreisler bet Fats Waller that if he took his violin out into the street and played nobody would pay any attention and he would not get any money. So they went out in the street near the Trinité Church and Fritz Kreisler played some little tune which was quite difficult and the people passed by and looked at him and nobody paid any attention. So when he had finished he put his violin back in its case and took a taxi to his hotel. He'd won his bet.

Fritz Kreisler used to come to the Music Box six or seven times a year. He liked to listen. I wouldn't say he was impressed but he liked it. Jazz was sort of a novelty. It was exciting when you got different musicians sitting in. I remember when we were at the Croix du Sud with Grappelly and André Ekyan around 1931 we used to get all the American musicians coming by to sit in. Sometimes you had a band of fifteen or sixteen musicians. Jimmy Dorsey used to come and Muggsy Spanier. Also Manny Klein when he came to see his brother Dave who was working with Ted Lewis. Sometimes there was very good music in those days.

280

☆ THE AMERICAN VIEW

ARTHUR BRIGGS

The truth is that I did not learn to play jazz. At that time [1918] in the States you had quite a few dance schools that ran two or three times a week. Most of the musicians that played in the dance schools were amateurs or else they were members of the Amsterdam or the Clef Club. Then the Clef Club finally discarded their dance school because they didn't pay enough. The churches helped a lot too. There was a church on almost every street. And most of the churches had a brass band. That gave a certain scope to the youngsters because they could get to learn an instrument without actually having to buy one.

But so far as jazz was concerned, when that was starting we mostly just played what was written. Sometimes people couldn't read and then they'd start taking little liberties to see how this or that will go. And maybe one player – because we always had a violin in the orchestra – the violinist might do something that sounded good to us all and we'd all rave about it. Then someone else would think of doing something else in the same number or in some other number. So there was a kind of competition among the players. We learned the hardest way. The whites had mastered their instruments. They were way ahead. You see, it's a question of organization. When you're supposed to play your part as written it's an organized thing. We weren't organized at all. We just learned the best way we could without any theoretical organization. Also, the Caucasians have possibilities for arranging music – they knew what they wanted. When they arranged something they wanted it played as written. We didn't have that.

That started with Leroy Smith and Ford Dabney. James Reese Europe also could arrange and there was another very interesting man called Fred Simpson. He was first trombone with the Ziegfeld Follies.

Times were hard if you were a black musician with training. Take Will Marion Cook. Cook was originally from Tennessee but I think he studied in Washington. I can't remember where he studied but I do know he was first violinist with the Boston Symphony – not the soloist but the first violin. Anyway, the soloist passed on, so Cook figured that he would automatically replace him. So the orchestra committee had a meeting and they told him, "From tomorrow you will sit in the first chair, the soloist's, but unfortunately we can't allow you to play the solos." This was because he was black – although he wasn't even that. He was an octoroon and he looked white. So he took his fiddle and broke it. He stamped on it and walked out.

So afterwards he taught at the Martin Smith School of Music and that's where he met me. The Martin Smith School organized Sunday concerts of symphony music played by youngsters. And Will Marion Cook was teaching there more or less to help out. So he heard me and he asked my mother if she would allow me to tour the States with him. Naturally I wanted to go because as far as I was concerned it was so amusing to sit down and read something off at first sight. It was a wonderful thing for a kid. I felt as if I'd really learned something.

You see, after he'd left the Boston Symphony, Cook had met a very intelligent and interesting person, a lawyer called George Latimore. Latimore's brother was the only black broker on Wall Street. So Cook explained his position to Latimore.

From then on his attitude was, "If I can't get fame, I'd like to make money." Latimore, who was a businessman, said, "Well, I have contacts. If you make the artistic connections I'll make the business contacts." So Will Marion Cook started his Southern Syncopated Orchestra. He contacted groups from all over the States – quartets, choirs, musicians and everything else. We played the classics – Brahms, Grieg and so on – and also quite a few of Cook's own composition. Also some pieces by Coleridge Taylor, another fine black composer. It was an orchestra to play everything at the time. We didn't play jazz, we played ragtime – numbers like "Russian Rag." The truth is that the only improvising that was done was by Sidney Bechet, although we had a very fine fiddle player by the name of Shrimp Jones, and he improvised too – rather like Eddie South later. They would get featured numbers but the majority of the music would be written out and arranged by Will Marion Cook. Cook had his way of arranging things – slides and glissandos and lip slurs. He'd put those in and after rehearsals he'd tell you if you didn't do it as you should. He'd have you stay and rehearse it as much as necessary.

We didn't have a show as such. We had two or three quartets and a big choir. Quite a few of the numbers in the program were spirituals arranged specially for the choir and orchestra.   . .

Sidney Bechet helped the orchestra a lot. He played "Characteristic Blues" and his way of playing helped to get those kind of effects – glissandos, etc. Even the brass had to do them. He was marvelous at them. There was a curious thing about Sidney. It was said he couldn't read. But I've seen him sit at the piano and play chords and say, "This is so-and-so. This is E♭, this is B♭," and correctly. Now how did he learn? He wrote several compositions. And this piano player was trying to harmonize it and he stopped him and told him, "No, that's wrong. This is it." And he played the right chord. He used to play a little piano and some trumpet too. He wasn't bad.

Cook didn't make money in the States. We did concerts but we weren't a great success, but we did make money with our contract in England. I think they figured on taking the orchestra on tour to England and Europe. So they didn't make money in the States, they even owed us money, but they'd signed this contract with André Charlot in London for a six month engagement at the Philharmonic Hall on Great Portland Street.

I don't think the American part was very well organized. It all comes down to business management and bad publicity. Also, that winter between '18 and '19 was awful. Our tour started around January 15, and kept on until the middle of April. And we'd get into towns by rail – you couldn't travel by bus. And you'd have snow so high. Business was awful, just awful. Anyway, we were getting enough money to live and by the time we left for England we were paid up entirely. They had had an advance on their future contract.

Over in England we had a Royal Command performance at Buckingham Palace. It went very well. In my experience all the aristocrats and so on didn't applaud much in the cabarets and casinos. But in Buckingham Palace they did applaud. They were terrific. I remember when Bechet started playing his blues with his weird tones, I could see the expressions and all the whispering going on. I said, "Oh Lord, what's going to happen now?" Nothing happened, they were very satisfiable. Otherwise I can't remember much about it. It was very well organized. The cars came to collect us and when we got there the service was organized to take us where we should go. And they gave us refreshments before and afterwards. We had a wonderful time. They didn't talk to me. They talked to Cook and to George Latimore, the managing director. Naturally he arranged everything. They didn't talk to Bechet I'm glad to say. At that time he used to drink too much and we used to worry ourselves to death about whether he would make it to the concert on time.

I believe Bechet was older than his papers said, because when he died he was supposed to be sixty-three. To me he was about seventy-five when he died. I remember meeting him in Chicago in '19 while we were on our first tour. He was at the Elite Number One club in Chicago with Freddie Keppard and Tony Jackson the piano player and he was already a man more than three years older than me.

There's a big mistake about Louis in Chicago with Joe Oliver. Certain persons say that Louis left New Orleans in 1921 or '22. Louis was in Chicago with Joe Oliver's orchestra at the Dreamland when we were on tour because I went – I visited the Dreamland and I saw him in 1919. After that I was in Europe. I remember I was with Maisie Mullins the saxophone player and Frank Withers the trombone player and they said to me, "Son, at twelve o'clock you have to leave. We'll take you home and then we'll come back." And Louis was sitting up there playing second cornet to Joe Oliver. Oh, yes. I told them all. I told Jean-Christophe Averti. I said, "You can all say what you want. I saw and heard the orchestra."

At that time Louis wasn't Louis. The wonderful thing was that Louis had more parts. He improvised his second parts with Joe Oliver. But Louis wasn't Louis at that time. He didn't start that until he came east to join Fletcher Henderson's band in 1924. That's when he started to get a break. Bechet on the other hand was always

Bechet. Bechet played very much better than everybody else. There were two other guys – Wilbur Sweatman and a man named Williams who was terrific. But Bechet was ahead.

There were other good players in that orchestra. Bobby Jones for one. He was a trumpet player that played a chorus when a chorus was to be played. He played the solos and I was the straight man. Then there was Maisie Mullins – she played C-melody sax. Then there was Frank Withers, a beautiful trombone player with a lovely tone. He was a schooled musician.

While I was in London I was introduced to this music professor at the Royal Academy. I was introduced by a clarinet player by the name of Edmond Jenkins who was the son of the Jenkins that had the Charleston Orphanage Band. Well, his son was studying at Nether Hall and he introduced me to this John Solomon. So Solomon gave me an appointment. He saw me in Brixton. I tried taking Bobby Jones with me, because in those days we were two youngsters together. We were more like brothers than anything. Anyway, I ended up taking two lessons a week for my technique. He taught me how to study and how to produce my tone without forcing it. I studied with him for two years. The first year I went almost twice a week. Then I went once a week, then once a month. He told me, "You don't have to come back anymore. You can come whenever you want. Just phone me or drop me a line." But I continued to study. I'll never forget it as long as I live because I realize that the facility and all the other things I learned with him and above all not to fight the instrument were invaluable.

After the Syncopated Orchestra broke up we all formed little orchestras and worked different places. I went up to Scandinavia to Norway for about six months. Then I came back to London where I got a cable from a drummer called Pollard. He was from Chicago. A terrific drummer – a musician just like Benny Peyton was, a thorough musician. Anyway, Pollard was at the Alhambra in Brussels with Mistinguett's revue. He wanted me to join the orchestra. Roscoe Burnett was also in the band and there was a trombone player called Patrick, also very good. We called him "Trombonsky." He died. We buried him in Paris, young. You see a lot of the boys that came over, they realized that they were going to have a good time from the first and some of them had too much of a good time. They mix all the good times together, dissipating and drinking as well as doing their work and it finally gets the better of them.

At that time in Paris there was a nice little colony of blacks. We had artists and musicians and boxers. We had certain bars where we met and we all got along nicely. Most of us behaved ourselves pretty well. Others took advantage. Because, you see, there were certain facilities in France that we didn't have in the States. Some of us appreciated that and some took advantage. One person that had a lot of trouble was Gene Bullard. The blacks used to get insulted a lot by white Americans; for instance, if they walked into a restaurant and a colored man was having a meal they would object. And Bullard had French citizenship because he'd been an aviator with the French Air Force as well as a volunteer in the Foreign Legion in 1914. So he'd be in the police station almost every time.

We didn't just come here for the lifestyle. We had wonderful contracts. It was a question of business and pleasure both. There was very little prejudice among musicians. Most of my orchestras were French musicians. It wasn't a question of color. It was a question of talent. Most of the work was cabarets and tea and supper dances. Not like the Hammersmith Palais, more like Ciro's in London or Murray's. You always had two orchestras, one for tangos and one for jazz. And in the evenings you had a couple of acts, like a small floorshow. For the French people the jazz band was the drums. They called that the jazz band. The instruments meant nothing to them until they learned that the drums was just an instrument to accompany the musicians. The drums used to have to make so much noise I wondered how people could dance to it because there was no rhythm. The drummers just played anything until we had men like Pollard and Louis Mitchell. The majority of the drummers were not musicians or even instrumentalists.

After I'd gigged around Europe for a while in Vienna and Belgium and other places, I eventually ended up with Noble Sissle. Sidney Bechet was with that band too for a while. In fact, I went back to the States with Sissle too. It was surprising, the contrast. At Ciro's in London and other smart places we'd have to play quiet. Even if we were swinging we'd have to play quiet. Even Sidney played quietly. He'd be featured on only a few numbers. The rest of the time he'd play whole tones in the low register. He'd a hell of an ear for harmony even though he couldn't read.

Anyway, when we went on tour with Sissle in the South back in the States it was just the contrary. Then we'd have to play loud. That was what the people wanted. They liked to dance and they wanted their music loud. They'd get so excited sometimes that you'd look to see if there was any other reason why they were so excited. But usually there wasn't. There was hardly ever any trouble. Even though they were colored affairs Sissle had a certain reputation and his manager only booked him into what you

284

might call proper places.

The touring was tough. The guys would take long solos if things were going well. In fact, Sissle liked that. He'd call on someone saying, "Brother so-and-so, lead us in prayer." But it was real tough. That's why I decided to stay in France. I reckoned much more of that and my life would be considerably shortened. We'd play sometimes from nine in the evening until five in the morning. Then there'd be eight, ten, sometimes twelve hours in the bus to the next gig. That's why when Sissle came back to France I decided not to go back with him. For instance, in New York all the guys would go to those gin mills after finishing work at two in the morning and stay there drinking until ten the next day. They'd drink and jam and drink some more. Tommy Ladnier was one who liked to do that. I played some of those sessions, but not too many. I wasn't considered a get-off man. A lot of guys in those days reckoned if you had technique you couldn't swing – you could actually have too much technique. I had a good technique and so I played first trumpet and that was that. It was the same with saxophone players at that time. Of course it changed later. Eventually it caught up with Tommy Ladnier. I remember he came to see me in New York – we'd been sitting next to each other in the trumpet section for almost three years by then – and he said, "I'm always getting lip trouble. Maybe you can help me find the cause of it." Because he had a very limited range. He'd have trouble making A above the stave. So I asked him what kind of mouthpiece he was using. He showed me a Bach number seven, a real big deep affair – what we used to call in France a "pot de chambre." So I told him that was the first thing that was wrong. And Tommy got cross. "If you knew I was playing on a Bach seven all this time, why didn't you tell me?"

I said, "Well, I knew you were playing on some kind of Bach but I didn't know it was a seven. Anyway," I said to him, "I've just had a silver mouthpiece made for me. If you like it, take it. But it's costly." So he said, "How much?" And I told him thirty dollars. "Well," he said, "never mind. If it blows I'll take it anyway." So I told him, "You get to the gig a little before time every day and blow a bit on it to see if you like it." And he did, he liked it. He said, "Art, this is like day and night." A few years later I heard some records he made with Mezz Mezzrow and he played better on those records than I'd ever heard him in the whole time I knew him. He made a D above high C several times and he'd hardly made A below that before. He died soon after that. He drank a lot and I think he'd had it very hard when he was young. Like Louis Armstrong, he was playing those sporting houses when he was a kid. Once one of those prostitutes get a hold of you, you can catch a whole lot of diseases. I think that had something to do with his lip trouble too. I think so. Also Noble was tough on trumpet players. He wasn't a musician. He'd keep us swinging without ever knowing that your lip couldn't always take it. He would have been better if he'd played an instrument.

Back in Paris, the booking office Lartigue and Fisher, knowing that I'd left Sissle, made me a proposition to re-form my orchestra that I'd had before I joined him. They got us a job in Monte Carlo at the Casino. I had a wonderful sax player, a Puerto Rican whose name was Ralph du Chesne. I also had a very, very old friend of mine who was more like a father to me in the Syncopated Orchestra, Benny Peyton. I used him on drums. In the end Benny Peyton took on the band. I had a little difficulty with some of the boys in the group so I turned the band over to Benny Peyton after Monte Carlo. After that Freddy Johnson and I got together and we went to Bricktop's. What happened with the Monte Carlo band was that I was ill for about fifteen days and I left Benny, who was the oldest man in the band, in charge. That was the mistake I made because he was an ex-orchestra leader. When I came back I realized some of the guys were acting funny. So I asked Benny what was the matter. He said, "Oh, some of the boys are dissatisfied. I don't rightly know what the trouble is but we've had a lot of difficulty. Some of them want to quit." Anyway, what was the trouble was that Benny Peyton had got hold of some young guy that had come over to work in the agent's office from New York – just a young guy that didn't know anything about the business – and used his influence on him, telling him he was a band leader and that this fellow Briggs was just a young kid from the Syncopated Orchestra and saying, "Here, I can show you pictures of my orchestra at the Casino in Deauville," and different things like that. So this young guy figured that Briggs could get along by himself and booked Peyton and the others into the Florida Cabaret in Paris. And someone told me that they overheard Benny mention the name of Teddy Brock, a trumpet player. So he went with them and I said to the orchestra, "Well, you're free. I'm not your father. You're free to go with Benny or to go to hell if you want." And that's what happened. Benny went to the Florida and didn't last a month. The band was OK and Benny was a fine musician, even though he was a drummer, but times had changed. In order to hold a band together you had to be a horn player. But from the drums he couldn't direct the attractions. He couldn't make it from the drums. He didn't have his men in hand.

Anyway, I came to Paris to Bricktop's with Freddy Johnson. Freddy had just come to Paris. He'd just left Sam Wooding in Brussels. That was where Willy Lewis had taken over Sam's band and Freddy said he'd rather try it in Paris. Sam really lost his band on account of trying to take all the money. So he went to work one night and he found he hadn't got a band. Before the war salaries were so good that a leader didn't have to rob his men to make a living. He got a good price for himself and the guys. A real orchestra leader, when he gets a good job, should make his men benefit by it and pay them accordingly in case he then gets a bad job. That's what I used to do. If I got a bad job I'd say to the men that I'd show them the contract or even take a delegation with me when I signed it. So they always believed me.

Freddy Johnson was a very very good piano player – a really fine accompanist. He played for the audience and not for himself. When he backed you he backed you. He wasn't taking a chorus of his own like Herman Chittison. We worked together like clockwork. We just felt it – we didn't have to say a word. In that band at Brick's we had Big Boy Goudie on sax, Peter DuConge on clarinet, Billy Taylor on drums, Herb Flemming on trombone and Juan Fernandez on bass. It was a very good band.

To some extent our work at Bricktop's was hard. She had a very select clientele. We had to play all the musical comedy numbers. We played them our way, with swing, but never noisily. It was just society music you know. We'd take solos but with a mute – softly, so as not to disturb the guests. Even so, we could sometimes play some reasonable jazz like that. But certainly Brick's was not a noisy place because of the select clientele. We worked from about 11.30 until three or four o'clock in the morning. We all had little breaks, except for Freddy Johnson, who didn't get any at all.

The society people liked our music so

long as it wasn't noisy. They appreciated things like "Some of These Days." I think we were the first orchestra to play "Night and Day." Cole Porter played the piano with us for that. He made out a lead sheet and played it with us. The Prince of Wales used to come in all the time. There was one tune he asked for all the time. It was "Don't Put All Your Eggs in One Basket." That was his favorite tune. He would sometimes play drums late in the morning after everyone else had left. But when we played private parties he would play drums all night sometimes. He was OK. He didn't worry us. His tempo was reasonable. We didn't pay much attention to his left hand as long as he kept what you might call the "oom-cha" going. We didn't have much conversation with him. If he wanted a tune he'd ask either Bricktop or Mabel Mercer or Louis Cole. He didn't suggest numbers to sit in on because when he did we always played "Don't Put All Your Eggs in One Basket."

Bricktop was very intelligent and a natural hostess. There was something different about her carriage from everyone else which appealed. If someone got out of line she could straighten them out with just one or two words.

As a musician I managed to keep up with what was going on in the States because I made arrangements with recording stores in all the countries I worked, and I would go by at least once a week to listen to the new things. I'd get stuff from all over the world because they had good things in England too. You could sometimes get the race records from America. We used to get Okehs and stuff like that. And I'd listen to these and buy the stuff that was good. I had most of Fletcher Henderson's and also the Wolverines and Frankie Trumbauer. My motto is that jazz comes from the heart and that every human being has a heart. Perhaps the blacks have a little more natural facility but I don't think color has much to do with it. You either have a heart that's in place for rhythm or you have one that's for the classical.

Of course the work we did was very commercial. We had a pretty hard time trying to slip the jazz stuff in. Especially in Germany, because the Germans were way behind where jazz was concerned. Most of their stuff was in march time – "Ein, zwei, ein, zwei." We had to play commercial things for them except occasionally we were able to slip in "Bugle Call Rag" or something a bit like that. This would have been around 1928.

Some of the blacks fell behind in their music but it was because they did not have a very good foundation in the first place. Probably music wasn't really their calling. A lot of black musicians were hustling other things. A lot of them were not really musicians. Also there were not that many black musicians around in Paris. It was a chic thing to use them whether they were any good or not. It was the style to have a black orchestra like an ornament. By 1935 all the bad musicians had faded out of the picture.

When Louis Armstrong came to Paris he didn't play at all because he was having lip trouble. That was immediately after the Palladium. I think they worked him to death there. When he came to Paris his lips were as hard as a piece of wood and he was bleeding and everything else. We thought he had – well, we didn't say cancer because in those days we wouldn't have thought of it – but we thought he had some very sad disease. While he was there Louis stayed with Bricktop and Pete DuConge, but he didn't come to the club because it was closed for the season. I know because at that time I was living only two hundred yards from Bricktop's villa and I used to be with them all day.

Coleman Hawkins came to Paris a couple of years later. We got along together nicely. He was such a wonderful person. I couldn't believe that anyone could drink so much alcohol and that it would have so little effect on him. When we were working together in Belgium at that Casino he would drink a bottle of brandy a day between his room and our restaurant. He would be featured at the tea dance. He did three numbers so most of the time he was free in the baccarat room. He didn't gamble. He'd just be at the bar. And when I sent someone to fetch him to play he'd come on as straight as ever. I never knew him to practice. I think he did all his practice before he came over here. He didn't talk much. But he had wonderful taste. I remember him paying twenty dollars for a pair of socks. He was crazy about beautiful shirts in silk and things like that. He would dress like a prince. I think Europe was a rest cure for him. Think of the work he'd done in America with Fletcher Henderson. In Europe he was playing an hour a day maximum. He never played jam sessions as far as I knew. In Paris we all used to go to the Cabin Cubain. I never saw Hawk there. The guys in Paris that liked to jam were Fletcher Allen, the sax player, and the trumpet player Charlie Johnson. Charlie came over with Leon Abbey's band. He died a few years after that. He was a wonderful man. He was much older than I was. Such a fine trumpet player. You see, America will kill you. Charlie was such a wonderful trumpet player who blew so easily. But he had too much bad liquor in the States and his kidneys just gave out. He had the first operation in Paris to take them out. He swore he'd never have another drink but apparently the other kidney was affected and he died.

You see, that was the original surroundings. It all started in the cabarets in America. Those were low-down places where musicians were just considered as objects and the clients, instead of giving you a tip, would just fill your jug with whiskey which rotted your guts. I remember places like Baron Wilkins' where musicians would get liquor for their salary. And they worked you so hard too. It killed a lot of the boys. I remember when I met Bill Coleman for the first time in a gin mill in New York, he was with another trumpet player called Joe Keyes. He was from Kansas City with an orchestra called Jap Alman. Poor Joe. He had a pretty rough life. He hadn't got on at all well with Sissle. He left the orchestra and a couple of years later I heard they pulled his body out of the East River. Apparently Joe had started drinking. And his mother sent him two or three hundred dollars for his fare back to Kansas City. And he was drinking and boasting about all this money he'd got for his journey home and someone did him for the money. New York's a bad place. That's why I stayed here in Europe all these years and that's why I'm alive today.

CLAUDE HOPKINS

I got the offer to go to Europe because the lady that had the show was . . . her husband was at the French Embassy. And he was responsible for the show being able to come into Paris. She searched around the country to find a band that would fit her scheme of things. Caroline Dudley Reagan was the woman that owned the show. We didn't work the show here in America. It rehearsed here and then went right on over to Paris.

It was a musical comedy. We had chorus girls and a comedian and a dance team and a band. No story, just a series of acts. I was the musical director of the band. On drums was Percy Johnson, and alto sax was Joe

Hayman. And then there was Henry Goodwin on trumpet and Daniel Doy, trombone, and a fellow named "Bass" Hill on bass. And then when we got over there we added Sidney Bechet. It was a nice little band. They were very good readers – except Sidney. This lady's husband did all the permits and everything because there was a little trouble about getting outfits of that size into the country and he made it very easy. The show opened at the Théatre des Champs Elysées and was an all-black show. Josephine Baker was in the show – they were grooming her for the lead. There was another girl who was a favorite – I can't think of her name. You could call her the star when we started out but Josephine had so much natural talent that it just blossomed. This other girl was a comedienne. She had a good singing voice too – Maude de Forest. That was her name. The show stayed on the Champs Elysées nine months – a big success. And then from there it went to Brussels and played the Circle Royale there for two or three weeks. And then from there into Berlin and stayed at the theater in Berlin – it was the Nelson Theater, a very small house. Stayed there about thirteen months. The show disbanded eventually. Josephine went to the Folies. I had a job in Dresden but I didn't make it because the drummer, the trumpet and the trombone left me in Berlin when the show disbanded. So I had to go to Paris to get some more musicians. And I played around the various countries for a while and I got homesick and I came on back.

When I went back to Paris to get musicians I got the trumpet replaced and the trombone and the drums – the trumpet player was an Italian boy. Sidney went back to Paris when the show broke up. You know, he'd been living over there for quite a number of years so he was kind of familiar with everything. He did some things in

Sweden. I had an offer to go to Japan but I didn't take it because it didn't look interesting. I enjoyed Paris. I met a Frenchman and he and I became very close and that enabled me to get around Paris with the language barrier because then there wasn't too much English spoken.

The band we had there was really a show band. We had a lot of things that we did that were really show numbers. It was a good dance band because the drummer had exceptionally fine rhythm. There was some jazz in Europe at the time. Buddy Gilmore, who was a great drummer, lived there and he had four or five jobs a night. He used to do fifteen minutes here on the drums and then ten minutes somewhere else. He really made a lot of money. He was an American but he'd lived in Paris for years. He was good at that type of drumming – throwing his sticks up and acting like a showman. I would say European people got along with jazz pretty well because the theater where we were in Berlin was converted for dancing afterwards and the floor was always full of dancers. And then when we were in Paris we worked a casino for the two brothers – Oscar Mouvet. They were very very popular. And Gloria Swanson was on the bill. Josephine and my band and Gloria Swanson. We did maybe an hour or an hour and a half after the theater.

But I enjoyed Paris – I enjoyed the night-life. By comparison with New York it was really something else. The red-light district was very prominent there and that made a big difference. There were quite a number of clubs that had four and five musicians. They'd be a mixture of French and Americans. A lot of them were French musicians and some were very good. Well, you know, they would buy the records and copy them. Then they had a lot of what they call in the States dance halls where you'd pay ten or fifteen cents a dance. They had a lot of those in Paris and that gave a lot of work to musicians.

There often used to be a lot of high society people around – particularly in Germany. The Krupp family, they were there almost every night. They really liked the music and they really liked Josephine. She had the ear-marks of a star. She knew how to act, she knew how to carry herself. It was just a natural occurrence with her. She was a big hit. She began to get marriage proposals and this and that. Automobiles were given to her. She lived a star's life – she wasn't always making the money to do it. And then she had good public relations. Her singing wasn't a thing. It was her dancing and her body. She had a beautiful body.

The thing about Europe was that the people were more receptive to the music than the Americans. They are today. And yet the musicians are better here in America. I guess it's because the beginning was here and it just developed.

As far as the dancing was concerned in those dance halls, trucking was a favorite dance here and they were doing that in Europe. And the charleston. But of all of them the lindy hop was the most popular because they're still doing it now. It wasn't done with the same grace that it was done in this country. But they had the idea. I enjoy playing for dancing the most. It's like I'd watch the faces and enjoy their enjoyment.

Josephine and I were sweethearts for a while. She always wanted to be a star. She was in the chorus of a black play called *Shuffle Along*. And in those days the end girl in the chorus – when the chorus would exit off the stage – she would do maybe eight bars of her own and go off. And that's how she got noticed. Ethel Waters was supposed to have gone with the show Revue Negre but she wanted too much money. The lady couldn't afford her so she took Josephine. And this was Josephine's big break. We

started to be sweethearts after we got to Paris. She was invited around in society a lot but I only went occasionally. In some instances I did but not too often.

She had a nice disposition – always smiling. A very happy person. She was always happy to have you in her company you know. The Folies offered her something like 1,500 dollars a week and she got out of her contract by saying that she was sick and had to take a rest.

There was a prejudice thing in Paris. Yeah, a couple of the bars refused to serve the blacks. But there were so many other things going on that it didn't matter. You wouldn't walk over to Broadway to get a drink if you could get a drink next door. But on the whole things were better there than here I'd say.

It was really a novelty, the night-life, because you didn't have it here in America and some of them overdid it, but they survived. Here it was all undercover and again it wasn't supervised, medically I mean. That was very important. It was fairly cheap too, as I remember. They had some inexpensive houses to fit the modern-day worker. I imagine this country would be better if they had the same thing. As far as the drink was concerned we had Prohibition here but the guys were drinking here anyway. But some of them went a bit wild. Joe Hayman was a wild type of guy. It was very enjoyable you know. We went over on the *Berengaria* – delightful trip. Take you four or five, six days. That part of it was very enjoyable. It's true that musically you would get a little behind in the general flow of things. Musically, New York was where it was at with all the guys coming up. It was sort of a working vacation to go to Europe.

The Europeans were listening to all the records. I was there when all the Hot Five records were made with Louis. And they were coming out over there. Some of the

European bands were so like Louis' band you could hardly tell the difference. They'd probably get the record and go to a rehearsal and just play it until they got it down perfect. The tone and the range weren't as good but the overall picture was pretty similar.

A lot of musicians go from door to door just to sit in. Personally I never liked it. I guess it's a good exchange of ideas but I never enjoyed it. I think it made a lot of difference to the way jazz developed – sort of modernized the music if you like, with the new guys coming up trying to cut the older ones. I think that the jamming in Paris was mainly for the music – not the chicks and all that.

The French musicians were very impressed by the American musicians. I don't know if they thought they were better or not but they were impressed. The thing we had was the easiness in the playing. You know what I mean? The relaxation and the feeling. At that time the guys weren't as well schooled to analyze the music as now. But they knew seventh chords and diminished chords. But today it's overdone. I mean these modern bands – I don't even know what the hell they're doing. I think that you should study to be a good musician. Even then different schools were opening if a fellow wanted to advance himself as an arranger or a composer or just for his own satisfaction. And then the scene became more demanding – difficult scores that had to be read. Of course, you had to have training for that. The blacks didn't seem too interested in that to start with. Where they picked up a lot of knowledge was at these jam sessions from club to club. You might hear Coleman Hawkins playing and you'd say I like that little riff he did and they would try to get it. Guys often came to me and said, "Hey man, what you got," with this or that little thing I was doing.

I started out at the Conservatory in Howard. And there were some clubs opening up in Washington and somebody asked me did I want to try a job in one. And I said no – I can't play that type of music. But anyway I tried it and liked it and it went on from there. Duke used to be one of the guys around there then. We were friends all our lives. At first he wasn't too good – he was a very bad reader. But as time went on he developed of course.

DOC CHEATHAM

Well, I had just arrived in New York from Philadelphia, where I'd been working with Bobby Lee's Cotton Pickers. And I came to New York to work for Lou Henry, the trombone player, who was doing theaters. And I stayed there a few weeks and then I worked for Lieutenant Tim Brymn, who had just come back from Europe with Jim Europe. And he had a little act on the Keith circuit with a band and I joined him. And then from there I went to Chick Webb's band, which he was just organizing – that was in '27. And Sam Wooding came back from Europe and someone sent for me and asked could I join Sam Wooding's band – I was with Chick Webb then – and I said, "Yes." I went from Chick's band to Sam Wooding's band. I wanted to go to Europe. It was a European thing and the band was organized and so on – I just wanted to go. I'd never been. You know, when you're young . . . in those days it was a heck of a thing to get an opportunity to go to Europe with a band. You'd never heard of a thing like that. That was something grand and I jumped at it. Anybody would have jumped at it. I knew nothing about the conditions of work – I didn't even think about it. I had nothing to worry about. I had no ties back here, so to me it was just going to Europe with a great band. And he had a great band.

On trumpets he had Bobby Martin, Tommy Ladnier and myself. I think we had one trombone which was Billy Burns. Freddy Johnson played piano. And the saxophones were Willie Lewis, Gene Sedric and Jerry Blake. King Edwards on bass and Johnny Mitchell on guitar.

We went from New York to Berlin – that was our first engagement. That was a great engagement. We had a good band and a good act. We had girls and dancers and singers and Slow Kid Thompson was the comedian, and we had I think three or four girls dancing. We must have stayed in Berlin about five or six weeks. We were three years in Europe. And in 1930 we went to France. He wouldn't take the band to France because he thought there was so much going on in France that he was afraid he'd lose the musicians. That's why he didn't want to go there. So he waited until he couldn't help it, before he took the band there. And he was right. That's where I left. Two of us left there.

I came back to the States. I thought that after three years I'd had enough. I felt myself getting sort of stale, because we played the same thing every night you know. And I wanted to do a little more than that. I wanted to progress. So the only way to do it was to come back home because there was nothing going on over in Europe at that time that would have helped me. So I was in Paris only about two weeks. You see, you couldn't stay out of New York too long if you were going to progress. Everything that was happening was here.

That was only true after about 1927, because New York was the worst place in the world for jazz in those days. Chicago was the greatest town for jazz in the twenties because of all the Creole and New Orleans musicians that settled in Chicago. So Chicago was loaded with good musicians and good bands from New Orleans. I tell you, coming out east from Chicago I saw the difference. There was no good jazz here at all. Everything was written down and played by music. In Chicago they didn't care too much about playing from music – it was all free playing. Here in New York everything was stocks. That's all you did. The pioneers of New York jazz were Duke Ellington and Cab Calloway, because the Cotton Club was the biggest thing in New York in those days. Then you had the Mills' Blue Rhythm Band which sprang up at the same time. You had Lucky Millinder, Chick Webb and Teddy Hill; they all sprang up at the same time. Benny Carter's band came in there too. Dance halls and nightclubs opening up all the time. Of course there was the Savoy, which was jumping at that time. There wasn't a lot of money to be made but there were a lot of bands.

While I was away I didn't get any news of what was happening in New York. All I got was records that were done while I was away – Louis Armstrong, Ethel Waters and so on. "I Can't Give You Anything but Love" – that was one of the most beautiful recordings I heard in those days. Also I heard McKinney's Cotton Pickers. I was interested in joining McKinney's band and I did. When I left Sam I came over and joined McKinney. They were looking for a trumpet player at that time and Benny Carter knew me and he told me about it.

There were some guys in Europe and I never heard anybody play so bad in all my life as those guys. Just playing with no feeling, like they were trying to copy it off somebody – like Johnny Dunn: no ideas! Because Johnny Dunn was a very popular man on trumpet in those days. So a lot of those trumpet players were copying Johnny Dunn's style over there in Europe. And then when Louis came in they all got so confused. You hear those guys and you want to give up the trumpet. Man, they were terrible. You take Sam's band. There's a record with one side of the band he had before I joined, and on the other is the band after I joined. Sounds like two different bands. You never heard anything so bad in all your life. You can turn on *Mickey Mouse* and you can hear all that stuff. If I had heard that before I joined them I'd never have joined them. I never heard them at all. But he picked up some good musicians. He picked up Jerry Blake. You couldn't get a better alto sax player than Jerry Blake. He got Tommy Ladnier. He was the best jazz player around at that time. So he replaced all the cornier type players out there. So we rehearsed and opened in Berlin and everybody said they couldn't believe the damn sound – it was more modern. Clean and it wasn't that corny stuff. Freddy Johnson was in the band. He was playing piano. Before that Sam had played piano. So he took a lot of young cats with him, you know, that knew what it was all about. We'd all been playing around here. We weren't playing that Mickey Mouse stuff they had over there. So that's why I went.

All the European musicians would come around – Jack Hylton's band and every other band. Of course, at the time, I didn't know all those European musicians. But you bet that if they were over there they came to hear that band. I heard Nat Gonella play and I heard Jack Hylton's band. They didn't impress me too much. You see, my problem was that if I had been to New York at that time I would have listened to them in a different perspective. But I was fresh from Chicago. I was from Freddie Keppard, Louis Armstrong and Shirley Clay and all those guys. And Bob Schaffner and all those guys. Jimmy Noone. I was practically raised in that field. When I came out this way they sounded to me like they were clean but they were copy-cats from Paul Whiteman. That's what they sounded like

to me. Not that they weren't good players and good musicians. Don't misunderstand me. And what they played was good. But when you get mixed up with New Orleans music and you hear something else it sounds terrible to you. In fact, that's why I continued playing after I got to Chicago, because I was playing saxophone and I ditched that right away after I heard the trumpet. So I had absorbed all that type of Creole music and when I got to Europe and heard all that Paul Whiteman type of music – I don't say it was bad, but I didn't like it. I never liked it. But Jack Hylton had a great band. Nat Gonella was the only one over there that impressed me as trying to play a New Orleans type of music. In fact, I liked him better than I liked Muggsy Spanier.

When I first came back I first joined Marion Harding's Alabamians. They were at the Savoy and he offered me a job and I accepted traveling out of Chicago. And I stayed there maybe a year of less and then after that I went to McKinney.

I was back in Europe in '34 with Cab. He didn't stay long – just about three days. We just did one concert I think. I left Cab's band in '39. I was teaching here. I wasn't playing because I was sick. I had a breakdown. Then I went back to Paris in '49. In '39 I joined Teddy Wilson's big band.

When I was in Paris on vacation in '39 things had changed so much from when I was there with Sam in '27. In '39 everything seemed to have closed down and people seemed to be having a hard time – I could tell that. When I was there in '27 there were a million places like Chez Florence and lots of others. Arthur Briggs impressed me more than the other trumpet players I heard there. He had originality and style. He was a stylist. He had a lot of technique – very clean and a good jazz swing man. He was one of the best over there at that time.

Alix Combelle was a very good player – very close to the standard of good American players – very close. Although you can only play so much over there because you had no one to listen to. Over here you had so much to listen to that it inspired you to play. So Alix Combelle was a great saxophone player but he didn't have the competition he needed. Over here you had to go around listening to everyone because you wanted to to outdo this guy and he wanted to outdo somebody else. If you want to go on playing jazz and creating in jazz you can't do it in a place like Europe. Even today I don't think you can. Because what have you got? You got guys in Denmark and a few more in Holland and of course a few in London or Paris. So who you going to listen to? Because jam sessions were what jazz was all about, because without that you can't learn, you can't improve. You have to have jam sessions. And they're beginning to have them here now because nobody's paying the union any attention now. The union can't stop you taking your horn out and playing somewhere.

I think it's great that you get guys like Panassié and those critic people because it's too bad that the black guys never did that. You take someone like Sam Price. Now he can tell you more about jazz than anybody around, writer or not. Those are the guys that should write books. Sam Wooding and Willie the Lion. But it's a great help to get all these theories about jazz because the last year I was at Nice and I had some kids come up to me while I was walking in the place where I was playing and they would quote things from Panassié's book which were true. And these kids – they sort of make you feel good. Otherwise they would never know about it. "You played with so and so," etc. That makes you feel good. How else would they ever learn? Certainly it's a great help.

If it wasn't for Panassié they wouldn't know anything. I hear a lot of people didn't like him. But I only knew him the way I knew him and I liked him. I don't know what was going on when I wasn't around. But as I knew him I liked him. He really cared about the music. Of course, about Mezzrow – they were great friends. That has a lot to do with it you know. I don't believe that he really meant that Mezzrow was the greatest – I mean to the extent that he was going to put Mezzrow above Jimmy Noone. I don't think he would do that even though Mezzrow was a great clarinetist. I have friends that tell me, "Doc, you're the greatest trumpet player in the world." I know damn well they're lying.

Paris was the greatest place in the world – not for playing, because I just liked Paris period. I don't know why. I don't even get a kick out of playing there particularly. But Paris is the greatest place in the world as far as the city is concerned. I think a lot of the guys had family problems. They wanted to get away from them – alimony and so forth. Then there was the racial thing. You know, years ago when I first came to New York there were black bands playing in the city in the hotels. You had Leroy Smith. He had a band for years in a white hotel in Philadelphia. But during that time something happened and they started freezing those guys out of there – out of hotels and out of clubs. You had to go to Harlem. You had Connie's Inn you, had Small's, you had the Nest Club, you had this and that club, the Cotton Club. They couldn't support all the musicians. There were a lot of small places that had bands. You had so many of them. And of course at that time there was starting to be a lot of opportunities for bands in Europe, and since they couldn't support all the musicians in New York people started going over there. So there were too many musicians in

Harlem, and so they went to Europe when the opportunity came up. So there were musicians going to Cannes, musicians going to Spain, to India – Teddy Weatherford had a band there. Chicago was having the same problem. They were freezing them out of the Loop. They wouldn't let them work there in the Loop and when things got bad musicians were going everywhere, wherever they could get an opportunity to go. You see, the thing about it was that we knew what was happening. We knew we were being frozen out of those places. We couldn't play in those places. Why? Because we had a separate union. Whites had a white union and we had a black union. And the white union would tell you that you couldn't work. They were looking out for the white musicians. The white union controlled everything downtown. And we knew that and there was nothing we could do about it. Damn right there was a lot of bitterness, because they'd come up to Harlem and steal everything you're doing. They'd sit up in your club listening to you playing but you couldn't even go into the clubs downtown. But then nobody wanted to. Nobody wanted to go down and listen to those guys playing but every night they'd be up in Harlem. All of them – Harry James, he was always up in Harlem. Benny Goodman – all of them. All Paul Whiteman's musicians, all Ted Lewis's musicians.

At the beginning you couldn't "goof up a song" as we used to call it. If you started to mess around with it you were nothing. The blacks started to improvise because they couldn't read. So they just made up things on their instruments. At first they didn't have no idea that they were creating anything. It was compulsory for them to outdo one another. This man would outdo that man, and that was the thing that was going around. And those big bands of ten pieces or so would create things right there on the

job. A lot of their stuff was not written down. They just had that creative mind. And the white musicians didn't. They only played what they saw written on the paper. What we call the stocks. But you take Benny Moten's band – things like "Moten Swing." That was all created on the bandstand. Chick Webb did the same thing. Chick Webb's theme song was created on the bandstand.

You see, with the racial prejudice over here at that time, a black man and a white woman – that was not being done. The mixing of races just wasn't being done. The black man just wasn't free. I mean, you can't stop people from loving each other, whatever color they are. But it was being stopped here. They stopped it here. You couldn't go downtown with a white girl. Your life was at stake. So a lot of the musicians got fed up and said, "What the hell." And since you could go to Paris and go around any way you wanted they wanted to go. I mean if you meet a white girl over there and she likes you nobody's turning around and looking at you all the time on the street, or making remarks. Over here you couldn't do that. You weren't allowed to. And then a lot of the restaurants, you couldn't go and sit down, and a lot of the shows you couldn't go into.

So a few guys go over to Europe and then when they come back and say, "Man, you have no problems over there." So that word gets around and before you know it all the musicians are starting to go to Europe, to all the different countries. I met musicians who've been all over Roumania – you know, American musicians who've been up there for years. These were old men when I was over there. Because they said, "Man, nobody's bothering you." They married Roumanian girls and got kids and everybody liked them and treated them like human beings. The neighbors like the family. But you couldn't do that over here in those days. That's why a lot of them left, because they wanted to be free. And that's good from every point of view except the music. But they didn't care about that. Their freedom meant more than that. Of course, when they went to Europe they were playing great and then people over there hadn't heard any jazz like that before when they first went over. So they had all kinds of big jobs and money. They were making more money over there than they were making here. A lot of places like Turkey, people would come into the place just to see a black musician sitting up there because it was such a novelty. A lot of the time they didn't think they were musicians. When I was with Sam Wooding in Germany we couldn't go out in the street because we'd have a crowd of people following us all down the street. And if we went into a store or something you couldn't get out of the store for the people looking in the windows. We played in a lot of places and the place would be packed because they never saw a black man or saw a black hand before in their life. That's why Sam was so great over there, because he had a black band and a good band. And we had novelties and singing – he had everything in that band. And he was an attraction everywhere he played and everywhere he made money.

The qualities you need to be a good jazz player? Well, first of all I'd say you need a sober mind. Because otherwise you're going to be careless – not only with playing but with everything else. Because otherwise I'm going to go to pick up that drink and then one day I'm going to knock it over. I'm not going to knock that glass over so long as I'm sober. I'll pick that glass up. . . . Not everybody can play jazz. A lot of us try. If everybody could play good jazz it wouldn't be a novelty. Now you have to have a sober mind because you have to know what's going on during the time you're playing something. If there's a melody it's got to be in your mind all the time and you have got to know the foundation of the harmonic structure of the damn tune if you are going to play it according to the way it's written. And then you have to know the counterpoint – the timing. Otherwise, how can you take a song and play it fifty thousand different ways. Emotionally it's difficult to say because some guys play better when they're happy than when they're sad and some guys are just the opposite. Some guys play better when they drink – a lot don't.

ELLIOT CARPENTER

This guy Johnstone, who was later with Turner Layton – he was studying to be a chiropodist – we used to get together on account of the fact that he used to play a little drums. So I suggested that we get together to do a few private parties. And he says, "I can't sing." So I said, "You don't have to sing" – he's a handsome guy – "You can just talk 'em through. What I need you for is to learn some songs and stand up and talk 'em through." So we got together and we went out on an engagement. And he was such a success! So he said, "Well, maybe this might turn out to be something." So we began to build up a clientele. This would be about 1915 in New York City.

We never played Negro engagements at all. Because at that time my people weren't solvent – economically they were insolvent. They didn't have no money to do that sort of thing. And at that time they employed a lot of black bands in hotels. James Reese Europe, he was the first to start doing private gigs and parties for the rich. Later he joined the army and became conductor of the army band.

I could get engagements in hotels and nightclubs by myself, but I preferred working with somebody. So when I found out how much effect Johnstone's personality was having we kept on together. Then, after a while I decided I was going out on my own. I had got married you see, and I needed a steady job. So Sammy said OK, and he met up with Layton and they started doing the same thing. Layton was a composer you see – he wrote "After You've Gone" and a lot of big hits. And they tried working down in Florida at the Panama Hotel. And they were lucky. They got so successful they started getting work at all kinds of private parties with the millionaires, just like in New York.

Anyway, Layton and Johnstone decided to go over to Europe. And I knew Peter Bernard over in London, and so Johnstone said to me, "Give me an introduction to Peter Bernard." But Peter Bernard couldn't get them any gigs when they got over there. Finally he got them into the Café de Paris. So when they went to the Café de Paris, Elsie Janis was there at that time, and she saw them and put them in her show. The show itself was a flop, but the Prince of Wales came to see the show – sounds like a funny tale – but he saw Layton and Johnstone and went off raving about them. Elsie's show folded and the agents picked up Layton and Johnstone on the prestige that the Prince of Wales gave them and put them in a cabaret downtown. And overnight they were a riotous success, and within a week all Britain wanted to see Layton and Johnstone because the Prince of Wales had endorsed them. So they put them in vaudeville and all the aristocracy came to see them.

In those days we were all playing the popular songs of the day. Cole Porter was just getting started and Jerome Kern was around. We used nothing but musical comedy stuff. When we were in New York jazz was just beginning to break – Fletcher Henderson and Duke Ellington and all that stuff wasn't known. But what most of us were doing had nothing to do with jazz at all. We just sang the musical comedy numbers of the day. We were singers. We didn't do anything like jazz at all. What we called jazz then was where you took the tune and you improvised around the compositions. You played the tune and then you cut the men loose and they played their own thing on it. You'd have the trumpet take a chorus and then the sax, then the bass – all do their thing – and then we'd all come in at the end after six or seven choruses of this. And we'd keep a little rhythm so people could dance to it. And that's how we started with that jazz stuff. I didn't do that until I went into vaudeville with a boy named Hatch – Hatch and Carpenter.

Hatch had a beautiful tenor voice, and he'd had some schooling. And I said to him, "Why don't you sing the 'Prologue' from *Pagliacci* in Italian. I think that would be a great success." And he said, "Oh, they don't want that from me." And I said, "Listen, you being a black man, it would be sensational." So I used to go on stage and open up with a jazz number – some kind of a jump number. Then he went off stage and I used to do my piano solo. I did a potpourri of the classics. I used to play "Lieberstraum" and such like. At that time I could play a whole lot of piano. And I used to play these classics and improvise things in between. Well, I used to be a tremendous success. And I'd end up playing "Tea for Two," and I'd be clowning like Fats Waller. That was the climax. Then I'd stand up and say, "And now, ladies and gentlemen, from the ridiculous to the sublime. My partner will now sing the aria from *Pagliacci*." And of course the moment I announced that the audience quieted down. And when we finished they used to stand up and we'd take bow after bow. Well of course I went over to Europe originally for three weeks and stayed fifteen years. Because I only went over there in the first place to get some reputation so I could come back here.

Vaudeville acts were the first to go over to Europe. When we first went over, the Four Harmony Kings came over. And the funny thing was that Mabel Mercer was working with the John Payne and Roseman trio. She was part of that and nobody knew her at all. They were doing the same sort of thing we were except that they did a lot of Negro spirituals – that was the basis. Williams and Taylor were another one. They were a comedy dancing act. And Mabel used to go with Williams. He was a fine dancer, and Taylor was the comedian. They used to do an act like Miller and Lisle, because one was tall and the other was short.

Most of the success of these black acts was comedy. Dancing and comedy was the thing because we had singers and dancers that were really outstanding but it was the comedy which got across. The type of comedy they did was very funny to the British people. It was very much a racial thing because it was more or less a burlesque of incidents they see in everyday life. But at the same time it was different to what they'd been used to. Some of it was slap-stick and it wasn't until Layton and Johnstone hit the top that singers tried to get over there. Before that, apart from the harmony quartets, it was mainly comedy.

The type of dancing they were doing was all step stuff – buck and wing, soft-shoe and charleston. Nowadays it's all ballet and acrobatic, but then it was step stuff. The black acts would finish off an act with something acrobatic like a hand spring or something like that, but they mainly did tap. The white acts didn't go for that so much. In the end the white acts got the rhythm, but it

took time. The whole thing originated from the cakewalk. That's where all those things like the charleston and the black bottom all came from. The Negro always had that capacity for improvising. They had it in the music, they had it in the dancing, they had it in everything. As far as the dancing was concerned, it was a matter of perfect timing between the drummers and the dancers. I don't know who was inspiring whom, but there's many a time I've noticed that the dancers would borrow some of those rhythmical beats the drummers were doing and vice versa. When the boys would put in some of those little things they were doing, the drums would pick it up and right away too. So it was a question of improvising between the two of them. It was the same thing in Philadelphia where I was born. There'd be about four, five or six piano players, and we'd go around the cafes and buy beer. And then each one of us would play and try to cut the other. We had one boy called Fats Jenkins – he was marvelous. The others were Sam Gordon, Lonnie Hicks and Eubie Blake. They were all famous around Philly. We used to get in those back rooms and play things to cut each other in jam sessions.

In those Philadelphia joints I'd play anything that came to me. Played all the popular music – I'd improvise that. I'd play the blues too. You couldn't get away without playing the blues. People would come in and buy something to eat or drink and you'd entertain them. There wasn't much dancing because those places were usually small rooms. The room I worked in was very small and it had tables all around it. It sat about twenty-five or thirty people. And then there'd be another room off that where they had about nine or ten booths where you could be private. If you wanted to take a girl in there, well that was up to you. You could go in there. But in the other room you came in to eat.

I got in touch with Opal Cooper, Burnett, Creighton Thompson and Sammy Richardson about going to Europe and off we went. We didn't know nothing. I had some spatterings of French in school. But spatterings was all it was. And we get there and we can't even read the signs. Anyway, I met a couple of Englishmen on the train, and I was asking them about the language and how to get along. According to them it would take me about two years to be able to speak the language. And Cooper, he was listening. He said, "Didn't take me that long. I could speak to those mademoiselles in two minutes. What the hell. They speak my language." So I said, "You're crazy."

So when we get to the Gare St. Lazare the man we're going to work for is Mr. Morgan. And what popped into my head was J.P. the millionaire! I thought everything's going to be OK. So when we got off the train, there's this big, fine-looking brown-skin man. Great big handsome guy. So I said to Cooper, "Here comes the man's valet." So Cooper says, "Yeah man," and he's looking around and he says, "Man, the first place I wanna go is a whorehouse." And I said, "Oh Cooper, for God's sake! Will you get down to business." And he says, "Well, you're doing the business ain't you? Well, I'm going to the whorehouse." So I said, "You ain't going no place until I find out who this man is." So the guy comes up to us and says, "Are you the boys that came from America?" So I said we were. And he says, "Well, my name is Morgan. You'll be working for me." So I looked at him and the others looked at me, and then we all exchanged glances. And I said, "Shit, did we come all the way over here to be gypped by a black man?"

So he got us into a cab and we heard him speaking French and of course he was a wonder to us. So he takes us uptown, and Cooper says that he's hungry. So I ask Morgan if we can find a place to eat. And Cooper didn't even get through eating before he's asking Morgan where the nearest sporting house is. And Morgan says, "You boys really are in a hurry." So on the way over to the hotel he drops Cooper off. Boy, when we saw it, that guy Morgan had a nice place.

In our second week at the cabaret people are starting to come in. We're doing pretty fair. So a man comes in – his name was Rack Coover. He was an agent from England, I learned afterwards. And he was sitting there listening to us. And when we'd finished the first set he asked us to come over to his table. So I went over and said, "Yes sir, what can I play for you?" And he told me to sit down. So I sat down. And he said, "Do you have a contract with these people?" "Contract?" I said. "We don't have no contract. Mr. Wickes over in New York, he's probably got the contract. But we don't have a copy." So he says, "He didn't give you a contract? Well, that makes things different. How would you like to come and work for me?" I said, "Where?" He said, "England." "England," I said. "I don't know about England. We're doing all right here." He said, "Well, I'm going to get you some money. I could get you around 350 dollars a week." I said, "Do we get a contract for this?"

Anyway, I went back for the second set and told the boys. And they went crazy. "Listen, if you let that man get away we're going to kill you. Why didn't you sign right away?" So I told Mr. Morgan and he said, "Don't worry. Take it. You ain't going to get that kind of money thrown at your feet. Don't be a fool. Take it." He said, "You'll make it anywhere with that band." Because, you see, we entertained while we were playing. Cooper was playing banjo, I was playing piano, Creighton was on drums and Burnett on sax. We played everything. We did a lot of popular songs – Opal Cooper had a tremendous voice. So we told Mr. Coover it was OK and so we went to England. We worked a place called Rector's.

Anyway, when we went over there we wore black clothes. So I said to the boys, "I got an idea. We should get some costumes and become a real band." So the King's color is red – I didn't know that at the time – but anyway, I got red coats and black trousers and red-topped shoes and I called us the Red Devils. I got that name from the French air aces. And Rack Coover got us an engagement at the Coliseum, which was the biggest music hall in Britain at the time. And when we got this engagement I suggested we get a red papier maché model of a devil and put it on the piano as a mascot. At first Mr. Coover was doubtful, saying he didn't want us to make a monkey out of ourselves. But finally I persuaded him and we opened with this red devil on the piano. And before we could get started they applauded for about two minutes. And I thought, "What the hell are they applauding for?" So anyway, we got through and we were a riot. And it turns out we're wearing the King's colors.

These boys were making money like they'd never seen before because you see we were doing nightclub work. Anyway, you know that money will tell on you. I called rehearsals. I said we're going to rehearse Mondays. And someone said, "I can't make it Mondays because I've got to go to my tailor's on Monday." So I said Tuesday. "Oh, I can't make that because Tuesdays is the day I go to the masseur." So I says, "Anybody got anything on on Wednesday?" And Burnett says, "That's my day for going to the race track. And you know I ain't going to lay that one down." Thursday? So Cooper says, "That's when I meet my chicks. I like to meet the chicks on Thursdays. I can't put that off. So I says, "What in the hell do you want with them tramps anyway? Let's do it Friday." "Oh, that's a bad day because I've got this that and the other." So we don't learn new songs. No new music. So I don't get any rehearsals out of the boys. Within three weeks I ain't had a rehearsal of any description. I said, "Men, you're deteriorating you know. We gotta work. We gotta rehearse." "Oh," they said, "You worry too much." So I said to myself, "They don't want to do it so I'd better leave them alone."

One day up comes André Charlot. He sent for me to go and see him. He says. "I want to use your band in a show with Jack Hulbert called *Down on the Strand*." And he told me the terms of the contract and I said, OK. And I went back to the boys. This was about a year after we'd come over. So we came in to rehearse this show. And they had us down in the pit, and then we'd go up on stage to do our number. So I'm sitting there waiting for those guys to show up and there's nobody there but me. He says, "Where's your band?" I told him, "Oh, they'll be here any minute." And I kept going downstairs to look in the yard to see if I could see them coming. So I came upstairs and said, "They'll be here in a minute. They're all underneath."

So here comes my sax player. I said, "Sammy, where the hell have you been?" He says, "Ain't they here?" I say, "No. You're twenty minutes late." "Oh, I didn't wake up in time." So Cooper comes about five minutes later. And I said, "Come on up here." And he says, "I ain't coming to work." So I asked him what was the matter and he said, "I'm going to Paris." I said, "You can't go to Paris just like that." You know what was the matter? Tax! Two weeks ahead of this, they'd given me the bill for the entire tax on all this money. And

I told them that was wrong – we were going to split that up. And Cooper said, "I can't pay that. I've got no money." I said, "Well, you can still stay here and earn it." He said, "I ain't going to pay it. I'm getting out of here. I'm going to Paris. I gotta job there." Just then the other boy Creighton turns up. He says, "I gotta get out." I says, "What's the matter with you?" He says, "I can't pay that tax." "Well," I says, "you can stay here and work." "Not me," he says, "I'm gone." "You gotta job?" I asked him. "Yeah, I gotta job in Paris with Cooper." So I said, "What the hell am I going to do?" The only person I got left was Richardson. So André Charlot comes to the edge of the stage and says, "Mr. Carpenter, where is your band?" I said, "Well, I gotta talk to you." So I told him everything that had happened. He said, "I expected that." He said, "You had the most undisciplined band I ever saw in my life. It's a good thing. I'm glad you got rid of them." I said, "Will you give me a chance? Maybe I can get some boys together." "Well," he said, "the show opens in two weeks. See if you can drum up a band to fill this job." So I'm having a hell of a time trying to find some guys to fill this job. I wanted black guys because that was the essence of the whole thing. So I found a guy that played violin named Boucher. And then I got two West Indian boys that couldn't play nothing. I couldn't train them to do what we were doing. So I had to let them go. So I got myself a job in cabaret. And I hadn't been there a week when I got a letter from Seth Jones out in Cairo, Egypt.

In the meantime there's an agent in Paris looking for me to put me in a show with the Dolly Sisters and Clifton Webb. Elsa Maxwell was putting on the show. So when I landed back there he carried me up to see Mrs. Maxwell. She says, "Well, Carpenter, we looked all over the world for you. At last we found you. Now here's what's happening. We're opening with the Dolly Sisters and Clifton Webb and the Red Devils. You still have the Red Devils, haven't you?" "Oh yes," I said. "Sure." I didn't have no Red Devils. So she said, "Well, get 'em together and we'll have a rehearsal." So I asked her, "When are you going to have a rehearsal?" She says, "Well, I'd like to have a rehearsal tomorrow." So I said, "Well, I can do it for you the next day because I've gotta run these guys to earth. They're out of town and I've gotta get 'em back." So I go around trying to find some musicians. I got nobody but Sammy and Opal. So I go out and I find a couple more men. I find Jim Shaw who plays saxophone, and I got another boy who played drums. So we go on and rehearse this thing. And we had a hell of a time because Jim Shaw couldn't play much saxophone and the drummer couldn't play either. Anyway, we go on and do the rehearsal. It seemed to be going down all right but I thought, "God, if we don't play better than this, our opening night is going to be awful." And so when the opening night came we went on and played for the dancing first. Then the show came on. And oh boy! That show was terrifically awful because those boys couldn't play. I mean Cooper didn't play much banjo, so the whole thing rested on me. So Mrs. Maxwell is looking down on me and I was scared to even look up at her. So when we finished the show, which was such a lousy mess-up, she called me. "Carpenter. Come here. I want to talk to you." And I thought, "Oh boy. Here it comes." Well, I had made a contract for three months. And she said, "Where in the world did you get that band? That is the worst thing I ever heard in my life. You get them out of here by tomorrow. I don't care what kind of contract you got. You get them out of here." And I said, "Well, Mrs. Maxwell, I don't see how I can do that because I've got to go and get some more men to replace them." She said, "I don't care how you do it, but you get them out." So I told the boys and they said, "What the hell. We don't want to play the show anyway." So I said, "Well, we go back in tonight and maybe we can play the thing a bit better." So I carried them right back in the next night and we played the show. And it wasn't a damn bit better than the night before. But over in the box seat was Ina Clare – one of the biggest actresses there ever was. And I saw her and I called out, "Miss Clare!" She said, "Hello Carpenter." I jumped up and down at the piano. I had a hell of a time. So she called Mrs. Maxwell and said, "Where on earth did you get that band? They're wonderful."

At the end of the show Mrs. Maxwell called me and said, "Carpenter, what did you do? Miss Clare thinks that you're wonderful!" So I said, "Well, she should know." Do you know I took that lousy band and played the whole two months on Miss Clare's recommendation? When I got through that contract I went with Dooley Wilson at a real run-down joint called the Last Roundup. A real broken down cafe.

The French were peculiar. They didn't care too much for Americans. They were too braggadocio. "Why don't you do this? Why don't you do that? Why don't you get some decent bathrooms?" etc. This was the way they were carrying on. "Why you got bidets?" and criticizing everything. So they got so they didn't like Americans at all. And I guess they figured the black ones were just as bad. After all, they were the same race. Then after the musicians got to fussing and fighting among themselves and making trouble, they didn't want nothing to do with them.

Negroes had a way of isolating themselves. Louis Mitchell opened a cafe – it was an eating place more than anything else. They used to crowd up there and so they'd all be together. Then a Frenchman opened a poolhall across the street from Mitchell and they all flocked over there. And Mitchell started picking up white American trade that wanted to eat fried chicken. And all the blacks would be over in the poolhall with those eighteen-carat tramps they'd collect. That used to be a meeting place. He'd let 'em come in there. And at that time some of the boys were into marijuana. And they'd go in the back room and he never stopped them. In Mitchell's place they couldn't do that.

The Negroes would go into them cafes up in Montmartre and they'd throw their money away as soon as they got it. Drinking wine and spending it on those whores they had up there. But they never got out of Montmartre. I'd never go up there with them. I'll never forget I took Opal Cooper and the rest to a restaurant where they had a very delicious smorgasbord. And do you know, Cooper and Burnett and the other two ate so much it was awful. They had a freedom you didn't get here. Over there you didn't have to hide away. So they were just out for fun. In a way they wasted themselves. They didn't pick out the best women. They all had wives back in the States so they just went for the whores. And the whores took 'em for everything they could get when they saw they were in demand. One of my best friends, Usher Watts, he was working with the International Five. It killed him. He just died from dissipation. He had a brain tumor. That's what brought me back to America. I didn't want to kill myself like Usher. I thought maybe I'd go the same way. I said, "I'm going to get out of here." I'd had all the best there was. I'd worked at the Folies Bergères. I'd played a lot of private parties. I did nothing else for a while. I used to play all Elsa Maxwell's parties. I worked for her. I'd hire bands for her. They were great parties. They'd have a band and a show. And I'd play piano in a little room where people would go off and drink. I played for Maurice Chevalier before he ever decided to come to America. I worked with him at the Dominion Theater in London where he was so popular the people tore his vest. But anyway, I decided to go home. That's another story.

☆ NOTES

I JAZZ REACHES EUROPE

1 For an excellent and comprehensive account of Europe's career see *Jazz: A History of the New York Scene*, S. B. Charters and L. Kunstadt (Doubleday & Co.), New York, 1962.

2 Ibid, p. 66.

3 *From Harlem to the Rhine*, Arthur W. Little (Covice Friede), 1936, p. 141.

4 Letter quoted in *Reminiscing with Sissle and Blake*, R. Kimball and W. Balcom (Viking Press), New York, 1972.

5 English translation by Rollo H. Myers (Faber & Gwyer Ltd.), London, 1926, p. 13.

6 Vauchant's real name is Arnaud, the name under which he has worked as an arranger in Hollywood since 1935. He used the name Vauchant throughout the twenties, and it is therefore this surname that will be used throughout this book.

7 *Early Jazz*, Gunther Schuller (Oxford University Press), New York, 1968, chpt. 1.

8 Quoted in *Black Swallow of Death*, P. J. Carisella and James W. Ryan (Marlborough House), Boston, 1972, p. 202.

9 See *The Story of the Original Dixieland Jazz Band*, H. O. Brunn (Louisiana State University Press), Baton Rouge, 1960.

10 Quoted in *Hear Me Talkin' To Ya'*, ed. Nat Shapiro and Nat Hentoff (Dorrance & Co.), Philadelphia, 1966, p. 42.

11 *Hot News* magazine, April 1935.

12 Interview with Doc Cheatham, New York, June 1976.

13 *Jazz: A History of the New York Scene*, see note 1 (Part One), p. 74.

14 *The Book of Jazz: From Then Till Now*, Leonard Feather (Horizon Press Pubs.), New York, 1965, pp. 23–5.

15 "New York Jazz in the Twenties," Nat Hentoff (article in *Jazz Review* magazine), New York, 1959.

16 *Early Jazz*, see note 7 (Part One), p. 69.

17 Clarinetist Alphonse Picou, most famous exponent of the clarinet trio on "High Society."

18 *Mr. Jellyroll: The Fortunes of Jellyroll Morton, New Orleans Creole and "Inventor of Jazz,"* Alan Lomax (Grove Press), New York, 1956, p. 93. Further edition (University of California Press), Berkeley, 1973.

19 *A Jazzman from New Orleans*, George Lewis (University of California Press), Berkeley, 1977, p. 6.

20 Interview with Joe Garland by Ralph Gulliver, Storyville, October, 1977.

21 Some jazz writers question the pioneering influences of Will Marion Cook's orchestra. They point out that Negro newspapers such as the *Chicago Defender* and the *New York Age* mention the presence in Europe of black performers such as Joe Jordan, Hugh

Pollard, Dan Kildare, Louis Mitchell and Alex Williams as early as 1915. However, it is clear from the same references that such performers played ragtime and novelty music. With the possible exception of Louis Mitchell and Hugh Pollard, these men would have been unable to play jazz even if asked to.

22 *Listen to My Music*, Ted Heath (Frederick Muller Ltd.), London, 1957, pp. 29–31.

23 Interview with Sidney Bechet by Charles Delauney quoted on sleeve notes of double album of Bechet recordings on Vogue label.

24 *Histoire du Jazz*, Robert Goffin (Lucien Parizeau & Co.), Montreal, 1945.

25 *Jazz : From Congo to Swing*, Robert Goffin (Musicians Press Ltd.), London, 1946, pp. 74–5.
Further edition: *Jazz : From the Congo to the Metropolitan*, Robert Goffin, trans. Walter Schaap & Leonard Feather (Da Capo Press Inc.), New York, 1975.

26 One of the very first of the recordings (six sides in all) made by Oliver's Creole Jazz Band for Gennet in Richmond, Indiana, April 5–6, 1923.

27 Interview with Fess Williams, Storyville, October–November 1976.

28 *Early Jazz*, see note 7 (Part One).

29 Brian Rust's Discography (Arlington House), New Rochelle, 1977.

30 Personnel unknown.

31 A good example is the final chorus of "Chicago," recorded December 1, 1922 in New York.

32 Robert Goffin was an amateur trumpet player.

33 Ironically, perhaps, while the classical training given to many black musicians inhibited them from playing jazz, most of the early white jazzmen were untrained and therefore more open to experiment.

34 *Jazz*, Paul Whiteman and Margaret McBride, New York, 1926, pp. 154–5.

2 THEATER AND DANCE

1 *Opening Bars*, Spike Hughes (Pilot Press), London, 1946, pp. 305–314.

2 Quoted in *Constant Lambert*, Richard Shead (Sumon Publications), London, 1973, pp. 38–9.

3 Quoted in *Jazz Dance*, Marshall Stearns and Jean Stearns (Macmillan Publishing Co. Inc.), New York, 1968, p. 143.

4 Ibid. p. 217.

5 *Studies in African Music*, A. M. Jones (Oxford University Press), London, 1959, pp. 200–1 and 202.

6 Concert version recorded at Carnegie Hall with Red Rodney, December 24, 1949.

7 Interview with Henry Goodwin, *Jazz Record* magazine, number 43, 1946.

3 THE SERIOUS COMPOSERS MEET JAZZ

1 *Death of A Music,* Henry Pleasants (Victor Gollancz Ltd.), London, 1963, p. 69.

2 Cacodyl is an evil-smelling liquid that ignites on contact with air.

3 *Le Coq et L'Arlequin*, Jean Cocteau, trans. Rollo H. Meyers (Faber and Gwyer), London, 1926, p. 15.

4 *Chronicle of My Life*, Igor Stravinsky (Victor Gollancz Ltd.), London, 1936, pp. 130–1.

5 *Ma Vie Henreuse*, Darius Milhaud (Editions Belford), Paris, p. 100.

6 Ibid. pp. 115–16.

7 Apart from a short piece entitled "Music for the Theater," written in 1925, Copland's most important "jazz" work was the 1920 "Piano Concerto." The main theme is very obviously derived from the opening of "St. Louis Blues" and the work is very syncopated throughout with sections for piano written in Harlem stride style.

4 JAZZ INTERPRETED

1 *Twelve Years of Jazz*, Hugues Parnassié (Editions Corrêa), Paris, 1946, p. 46.

2 *Jazz Panorama*, Hugues Parnassié (Editions des Deux-Rives), Paris, 1950.

3 Publisher given for *Hot Jazz* is Editions Corrêa, Paris, but no date.

4 *Hot Jazz*, Hugues Parnassié (Editions Corrêa), Paris, p. 5.

5 *Jazz Panorama*, see note 2 (Part Four), p. 38.

6 *The Real Jazz*, Hugues Parnassié (Smith & Durrell Inc.), New York, 1942, p. 53.

7 Ibid. pp. 6–7.

8 *Jazz : Its Evolution and Essence*, Andre Hodeir, trans. David Noakes (Grove Press), New York, 1957, p. 237.

9 Panassié's reference to intervals here is not at all clear. Presumably he is referring to the tendency of jazz and blues to flatten the third and seventh intervals of the scale.

10 *Jazz Panorama*, see note 2 (Part Four), p. 73.

11 *The Real Jazz*, see note 6 (Part Four), p. 21.

12 Bulletin of the Hot Club of France, Number 3, p. 5.

13 *The Real Jazz*, see note 6 (Part Four), p. 36

14 *Aux Frontières du Jazz*, Hugues Parnassié (Editions du Sagittaire), Paris, pp. 95–6.

15 Ibid. p. 88.

16 *Jazz : From Congo to Swing*, see note 25 (Part One), pp. 96–7.

17 *Aux Frontières du Jazz*, see note 14 (Part Four), p. 97.

18 *Aux Frontieres du Jazz*, see note 14 (Part Four), p. 176.

19 *Twelve Years of Jazz*, see note 1 (Part Four), p. 12.

20 Ibid. p. 16.

21 *Really the Blues*, Mezz Mezzrow and Bernard Wolfe (Secker and Warburg Ltd.), 1946, p. 195.

22 Ibid. pp. 196–7.

23 Panassié was always vitriolic in his comments about Jacques Canetti, who had displayed not only an interest in jazz at this time, but was also able to publicize the music on French radio. The suspicion that Panassié was in fact merely jealous of his rival's organizational ability and access to the media is strengthened by the fact that John Hammond described Canetti to me as having "impeccable taste in music."

24 The key role played by New Orleans musicians in the development of swing seems to be beyond dispute. Swing by definition is generated by the rhythm section, and the fact that an amazingly high proportion of the first great drummers and bass players were from New Orleans must therefore be significant. Apart from the three already mentioned, it is important to remember that great second generation players like John Kirby also studied Foster and Braud. Steve Brown, the first great white string bassist, whose driving four-beat rhythm

created such a sensation with Jean Goldkettle and Paul Whiteman in 1926 and 1927, was also a New Orleans man. The list of drummers is also impressive. Zutty Singleton, Baby Dodds and Paul Barbarin were all from New Orleans, and Dave Tough, who was probably the first modern drummer, almost certainly developed his ideas from listening to Baby Dodds in Chicago.

25 Note the earlier reference, note 8 (Part Four), to Andre Hodeir's *Jazz : Its Evolution and Essence*, published fifteen years later, which carefully separated these two ideas and suggested that in fact swing suffers all too often from over-enthusiastic attempts to play hot.

26 *John Hammond on Record* (Summit Books), New York, 1978, p. 72.

27 "The Best Negro Jazz Orchestras" article in *Negro Anthology*, ed. Nancy Cunard (Wishart and Co.), London, 1934, p. 292.

28 *Louis,* Max Jones and John Chilton (November Books Ltd.), London, 1971, p. 134.

5 HIGH SOCIETY

1 Virgil Thomson arrived in Paris in 1923 to study orchestration and composition with Nadia Boulanger.

2 Interview with Hon. David Herbert by Jeanne La Chard, Tangiers, July 1977.

3 *You Don't Look Like a Musician*, Bud Freeman (Balamp Publishing), Detroit, 1974.

☆ LIST OF INTERVIEWS

Any quotes within this book from the people listed below are taken from the interviews I had with them in 1976, 1977 and 1978:

MAE BARNES New York, May 1977
ARTHUR BRIGGS Paris, September 1976
JOHN BUBBLES Chicago, May 1977
ROY BUTLER Chicago, May 1977
ELLIOT CARPENTER Los Angeles, June 1976
DOC CHEATHAM New York, June 1976
NOEL CHILBOUST St. Jean de l'Estorel, July 1977
SPENCER CLARK April 1978 (by telephone)
AARON COPLAND New York, June 1976
BRUNO COQUATRIX Paris, September 1976
WILLIE COVAN Los Angeles, July 1976
JIMMY DANIELS New York, June 1976
LEW DAVIS London, May 1978
BILL DILLARD New York, June 1976
BUD FREEMAN London, July 1978
HERB FLEMMING New York, June 1976

RUSS GOUDY April 1978 (by telephone)
HORST New York, June 1976
FATHER A. M. JONES St. Albans, England, July 1978
CLAUDE HOPKINS New York, May 1976
BERT MARSHALL Manchester, England, April 1977
MABEL MERCER New York, June 1976
OLIVER MESSELL New York, June 1976
JACK O'BRIEN April, 1978 (by telephone)
GENE PRENDERGAST April, 1978 (by telephone)
ALAIN ROMANS Paris, November 1976
JACK RUSIN April 1978 (by telephone)
ADA SMITH (BRICKTOP) New York, June 1976
U.S. THOMPSON New York, May 1978
VIRGIL THOMSON New York, June 1978
LEO VAUCHANT Los Angeles, April 1978
RAY VENTURA Paris, September 1976
JEAN WEINER Paris, November 1976
ELIZABETH WELCH London, September 1976
EDITH WILSON Chicago, June 1976
SAM WOODING New York, June 1976

☆ INDEX